Oct 78
KK

Father
Very best wishes (belated) £3—

Jeannie Rodney Oliver William

AF573639

Master of One

An Autobiography

Dorian Williams

Master of One

An Autobiography

J. M. Dent & Sons Ltd

London, Melbourne and Toronto

First published 1978
© Dorian Williams 1978

All rights reserved. No part of this publication may be reproduced, stored in a retrieval system, or transmitted, in any form or by any means, electronic, mechanical, photocopying, recording or otherwise, without the prior permission of J. M. Dent & Sons Ltd.

Printed in Great Britain by Biddles Ltd, Guildford, Surrey
and bound at the Aldine Press, Letchworth, Herts.
for J. M. Dent & Sons Ltd
Aldine House, Albemarle Street, London

This book is set in 11/12pt VIP Bembo

British Library Cataloguing in Publication Data

Williams, Dorian
Master of one.
1. Williams, Dorian
2. Horse Sports – Great Britain – Biography
I. Title
798′.092′4 SF294.27.G7

ISBN 0-460-04323-4

Contents

Photographs

Between pages 80 and 81

Between pages 160 and 161

For Jennifer

Foreword

It has been said that no autobiography should extend beyond the author's childhood. The trouble is that, except in the case of infant prodigies, it is only what happens after childhood that merits a person writing about himself at all. It is true, of course, that it is easier to write about one's distant childhood, with little likelihood of contradiction, than it is to write about the present or immediate past when the probability is that one will either say too little or too much. If one says too little readers may feel that they have been cheated of all that they would have found most interesting. If one says too much one runs the risk of losing friends and alienating colleagues.

So why attempt to write an autobiography at all? The only justification, so far as I am concerned, for what is not so much an autobiography as a series of episodic reminiscences recorded in a more or less chronological order, is that my diversity of interests has resulted in a life that could perhaps be described as unconventional. It is unusual for a Master of Foxhounds to run a Centre of Adult Education, for a television Sports Commentator to produce Shakespeare, for someone on the Hunters Improvement Society's panel of judges also to be on the Foyles Lecture Agency panel of speakers. In other words, my life has never exactly fitted into an accepted pattern.

It is even possible for me to be involved in most or even all of my varying activities in one day as, for instance, towards the end of November 1977. Having exercised one of my hunters early I drove to Pendley, the Centre of Adult Education I founded at my old family home near Tring in 1945, to discuss the opening of the new Arts Centre. Catching a train to London I recorded the commentary for a film on the Thoroughbred in Kentucky. Later that afternoon, as Chairman of the British Horse Society, I presided at a meeting of the Finance Committee. On the way home I gave a talk entitled *Behind the Scenes in Television*, at a Diners' Club in St Albans. That morning I had had the honour to receive a letter from No. 10 Downing Street informing me that the Prime Minister had it in mind to recommend me for an award. I could not help wondering which of my various activities was considered worthy of recognition: my work in education, my involvement with the horse world, my television job, or even my efforts to bring Shakespeare to the people. I could only be sure that it was not for being, for nearly thirty years, a Master of Foxhounds; nor, I guessed, for my alleged versatility, for in a specialist world versatility is still somewhat suspect. Yet it is such versatility as I have been fortunate enough to be endowed with that has given me, as I am hoping my readers will agree, such an interesting and enjoyable life.

Chapter 1

From a faded album

Looking back on one's early childhood is like browsing through a faded photograph album. Some of the pictures are clear enough, recalling vividly the occasions on which they were taken; others are almost indecipherable, meaning little or nothing. Blessed with a good memory I can find plenty of pictures in my faded album. They are clear enough to evoke not only the occasions and events concerned but even my own childish feelings and reactions, reminding me that, however much one may change physically, there is something of oneself that is permanent, unchanging, the inner 'you'.

No picture is clearer to me than that of Armistice Day, 1918. Recalling it I can still feel almost stifled with the excitement that it created within me at the time. To admit to remembering Armistice Day must necessarily date one; yet I am glad that I was old enough to be part of that famous day, for surely it is one of the most memorable of our century – 11 November 1918. It is as vivid to me as though it were only a few years ago, not more than sixty. 'Visions of boyhood shall float then before you, twenty, and thirty and forty years on'; yes, and sixty.

'Leggy' Whiteman, my father's soldier groom, had somehow had the honour of being selected as one of the 'pall bearers' accompanying the effigy of the Kaiser in the procession through Aldershot, presumably to Rushmoor Arena, where it was to be burned on a huge bonfire. As a special treat I was to be allowed to join in the procession when it passed the end of our road; but being at night it would be long past my bedtime and so I had to rest all the afternoon. Not that this really achieved its object, so hysterical and excited was the atmosphere. All day everyone seemed to be rushing hither and thither, greeting each other, talking in an animated fashion, laughing hilariously, or bursting into tears of emotion, the climax being reached with the sounding of the 'maroons' at eleven o'clock. The War was over! Far from fully understanding, I yet found it all infectious and was as excited as everyone else, even if it was only in anticipation of the great victory procession. Whether it was officially a fancy dress parade or not I do not know; probably not, but always loving dressing up, I had persuaded my mother to allow me to wear my cowboy's costume with its bushranger's hat – a treat in itself. It was the fireworks, however, to which I most looked forward. Obviously I had never seen fireworks, for though the blackout in the First World War was not, I imagine, as strict as in the Second, yet fireworks would hardly have been tolerated, even on Guy Fawkes' day. For a small boy, therefore, they conjured up something completely magical.

Eventually the long day came to an end. We watched 'Leggy' Whiteman set off first, bearing a massive club, the sort that giants carry in fairy-tales, presumably to beat out the bonfire flames if they got out of hand or, as I preferred to imagine, bash the Kaiser, which I half believed to be the real Kaiser who for so long had been held up to me as a bogey. An hour later the rest of our little party set off; Barbara, my sister – two years older than I – Nanny, Elizabeth the housemaid whom at that time 'Leggy' was courting and was later to marry; and, of course, myself. We took up our position in the main street to await the arrival of the procession, behind which we would all fall in, accompanying it to the bonfire. Before many minutes it arrived, preceded by a military band, the bearer party carrying great flaring torches, the most exciting sight that I had ever seen in my life. Unbelievably as 'Leggy' passed he actually spotted us in the crowd, and despite the protestations of Nanny and Elizabeth insisted on seizing me by the hand and marching me along with him. I was actually part of the procession, right at the front. I was almost bursting with pride. Later, when he thought I was getting tired, he hoisted me on to his shoulders, which not only enabled me to see everything much more easily, but enabled everyone to see me! I almost persuaded myself that it was I whom everyone was cheering. Little show-off!

Even now I can see the great flames of that bonfire and feel the intense heat as Nanny held me back. Vividly I can recall watching with fascinated horror as the grotesque, crumpling figure of the Kaiser gradually collapsed into the flames, the cheers rising to a mighty crescendo. Then the fireworks. They were more spectacular than anything I could ever have imagined – entrancing, perfection, a fairyland that I wanted to last for ever. I could not bear to think of it ever ending. That the war that was going to make Britain a place fit for heroes to live in was now over meant nothing, of course, to a little boy. I was only aware of the heady, intoxicating enthusiasm and happiness which seemed to pervade everyone and everything, and which was sufficiently infectious to make me remember it for the rest of my life.

We lived at that time in a house called Warren Corner. My father, who had twice been wounded at the front, was in charge of the Cavalry School at nearby Netheravon. The house itself I can scarcely remember, but I recall clearly two incidents that took place there shortly after the Armistice. The first was the more dramatic, the second the more frightening.

We were playing in the garden one afternoon when, to our amazement, there suddenly appeared a huge stag. Seeing us it hesitated for a moment, then galloping across the lawn it made an incredible leap over a seven-foot high wire fence which separated the garden from the wood, into which it disappeared. A few moments later the garden was full of hounds, unable, of course, to escape until a huntsman came galloping up the drive and called them off. A thrilling experience for us and, an entirely new one, as up to that time we had never lived in a hunting country. It was, I imagine, the old Berks and Bucks Staghounds, which in those days hunted the carted stag.

The other incident concerned a snake. We were going out into the garden through the conservatory one day when my brother, Maurice, who was a year younger than I, suddenly pointed to something on the floor. 'Look!' he shouted, 'there's a huge worm', and, bending down, he tried to pick it up. At once it uncoiled itself, raised its head and spat out a vicious fang. Luckily my sister, sensing danger, let out a shriek which brought my mother hurrying from the hall. To her horror she saw her three-year-old son trying to play with a dangerous adder. Having just come in from riding, she was, fortunately, carrying a stick with which she set about battering it to death – an operation which seemed to take all of five minutes. Satisfied that it was dead she hung it up on a hook by the conservatory door, where it remained until a few months later when we left Warren Corner. Its shrivelled skin against the wall was, in fact, my very last memory of Warren Corner, and I have had a dislike of snakes ever since; of wasps, too. I have a dim, but very real memory of eating a piece of bread and raspberry jam with a wasp in it. I was stung so badly in the mouth that for days I was unable to swallow, or even speak – doubtless to everyone's relief.

Another memory from Warren Corner, an earlier one, should perhaps be recorded, being of a certain significance: my first ride. My sister had a little Shetland pony called Midge. One summer afternoon I was allowed to ride it on the lawn in the middle of which there was a shallow bank where the ground had been levelled off to make a tennis court. I was poised at the top of this bank, or, more accurately, posed, for my mother was about to take a photograph with her old box Brownie, while my father was trying to attract Midge's attention by waving a large coloured handkerchief. Unfortunately my sister was more attracted by all this activity than by Midge which she was supposed to be holding, with the result that she let the pony go. Immediately Midge lowered her head to graze from the bottom of the bank. Gently, with increasing momentum, I tobogganned down Midge's neck over her ears and on to the lawn. Fortunately I thought it hilariously funny, being blessedly unaware, at the age of two, of the indignity of falling off!

Other early prints from my memory album, but now very dim, include seeing a Zeppelin gliding across the sky, picked out in searchlights, and a German aeroplane crashing in flames into the sea off Westgate where, rather surprisingly, we had been taken for a holiday towards the end of 1916, staying at a boarding house called Holmbury. It was here that my father, returning from the front, found me sick and ailing, apparently fading away, for no reason that anyone could diagnose. Having taken one look at me, he ordered 'Give him porridge', after which I never looked back, though the cause of the cure was as obscure as the cause of the original illness.

It was when we were at Westgate-on-Sea that we were taken to see a captured German submarine at Ramsgate. I can remember only the incredibly cramped quarters and the nasty, dank smell. During another seaside holiday, at Littlehampton, I was lost for about four hours. I was three years old. I cannot imagine how it can ever have happened, but suddenly I found myself entirely alone by one of the breakwaters, everyone else having completely disappeared. I can quite clearly remember the fact that I was lost gradually dawning on me and wondering what on earth I should do about it. Wandering along the shore I was near to tears when two ladies, obviously sensing that I was lost, approached me, and asked me who I was. This was most frustrating as although I knew my name perfectly well, I just could not at that particular moment, recall it; other, of course, than my christian name, which I realized would mean nothing to them. I can feel now my shame and embarrassment; shame which was increased enormously when one of the ladies insisted to the other that I was bound to have my name on my combinations and, starting to undress me, proceeded there and then to carry out a search. Mercifully at this moment a distraught Nanny appeared on the promenade and hurried to rescue me, carrying me off in floods of tears to our boarding house further along the front. An alarming and, I have no doubt, a psychologically damaging experience for an impressionable three year old!

I can clearly remember something that happened when I was even younger. I was lying in my cot in the nursery while my sister played to me a musical doll. This was in the form of a punchinello's head and shoulders on a stick. The cap and collar were blue and yellow, with little bells on the points of the collar. When the doll was rotated it played a tune – a tune that I was later to know as 'Oh! oh! Antonio!'. My sister stood at the end of the cot making the doll play the tune, attempting to lull me to sleep. Somehow, infant that I was, I knew that as long as I continued to cry or whimper she would continue to play. This she did, for what seemed to me to be the whole afternoon, in a selfless effort to soothe her fractious brother – little horror! When I was grown up I surprised my mother by telling her of this early memory, but she confirmed that the musical doll was a present on my first birthday, and that a popular tune of that time was 'Oh! oh! Antonio!'. All my life I have loved things colourful, and when young, as already suggested, enjoyed dressing up. Hence the cowboy gear on Armistice Day, and a year later a marvellous Pearly King costume, which had over three hundred pearl buttons sewn on. Many years later my own son wore this same costume at a fancy dress party. Such parties were very popular in that carefree era immediately after the First World War, and one of them led, I remember, to another embarrassing moment. I was dressed up as a dashing St George, attired in shining silver armour made of painted calico, which was uncomfortable, but tolerable as it was so impressive, with a great red cross on the surcoat and a magnificent helmet; a massive sword completed the splendid effect. The maid who looked after my mother in those days, Florence, the daughter of a retired head-lad at Newmarket, being a very clever dressmaker and seamstress, was entirely responsible for this magnificent creation. I was literally sewn into it, which, inevitably, led to a crisis. Overcome by the excitement when were were all lined up before the judges I suddenly wanted desperately to spend a penny, ultimately having no option but to break ranks and flee to the cloakroom, only to find when I got there that there was no 'exit' in my shining armour. By the time I had found someone to come to my rescue it was, to my bitter chagrin, too late. The crude aperture cut down the front of my armour in any event precluded me from winning a prize – another psychologically disastrous experience?

The following year my fancy dress garb was Harlequin, with Barbara as Columbine and Maurice as a Clown. The costumes, all home-made, were superb, winning us many prizes; nor, thanks to the lesson from the previous year, were there any embarrassing moments, except when the child whose bottom I walloped with my Harlequin's clapper-stick, thinking it to be my sister, turned out to be the daughter of our hostess. Bursting into tears, she ran and sneaked to her mother, which resulted in our having to leave early!

So clever was Florence at making these costumes that my father persuaded her to make our riding jodhpurs. They may not have been all that could be desired in sartorial elegance, but they were more than adequate and certainly saved my father a lot of money.

No memories from the faded album period are more vivid than our move to Greens Norton in 1920. My father bought Greens Norton Court when he retired from the Army in 1919 with the intention of farming on a small scale and starting a stud. He chose Greens Norton, a mile from Towcester in Northamptonshire, partly because it was only an hour's drive from the family home, Pendley Manor at Tring, where the old people still lived; partly – even more, I suspect – because it was ideal hunting country: the Grafton – less fashionable and less expensive than the famous 'Shires' which, of course, comprise the Leicestershire packs, the Quorn, the Belvoir, the Cottesmore and probably the Pytchley at the northern end of Northamptonshire. It was not, one has to admit, a particularly imposing house. The front door opened straight on to the road at the top of the hill which led from the village towards Bradden, but across the small, well-proportioned hall there was a small, but characterful dining-room and a pleasant, elegant drawing-room opening on to a verandah which looked out across some six acres of garden. There was a spacious stable yard, beyond which there were another six acres of kitchen garden. Later my father built an additional yard and a cinders *manège*, one of the first in the country.

Greens Norton Court, essentially a homely house and not in the least pretentious, was easy to run, with just one spare room once the whole family were accommodated, together with our Nanny, a cook and two maids. Living in one of the cottages was a butler – a somewhat grandiose title for the big, bluff, boozy William Smith who had earlier been my father's batman and, though a most amiable, happy-go-lucky person, could hardly be described as polished. 'Leggy' Whiteman lived in the other cottage, the other grooms being local lads. *Girl* grooms were, of course, unheard of. There was also a boy from the village who came up and helped, on important occasions putting on a white coat and masquerading as a footman. A certain amount of work had to be done on the house before we moved in; two small rooms were made into the drawing-room and a study or office was built on for my father. I remember very little about it except that it was filled with bureaux, tables, maps, cabinets and had a large notice hung above his desk saying 'DO IT NOW' – advice that I have tried to adhere to all my adult life, as he did.

During the decorations and alterations we stayed with my grandparents at a beautiful little village, Aldbury, about a mile from Pendley. My grandfather was rector there – he and his father were rectors of the parish for eighty-three years between them – and lived in a delightful very old rectory at the foot of Toms Hill, which led up to Ashridge and the famous Bridgewater monument. To stay at Aldbury was always a great treat for us; far more so than to stay at Pendley, which was much more formal and for small children – indeed, not only for small children – a little awe inspiring. There we had to be on our best behaviour and look tidy. At Aldbury we always felt completely relaxed. We were adored and spoilt by all the staff, and seemed for ever to be doing exciting things such as going for picnics at the monument, climbing Toms Hill trees, riding old Princess as she pulled the mower up and down the lawns, or visiting the old mad village nurse, Nurse Fanny; even pretending to be criminals sitting in the village stocks by the pond. We loved, too, the Pears soap always used at the rectory, and being allowed to help old Bessie Croswell in the kitchen. That was a halcyon summer for us in 1920 and, as I remember it, a summer of perfect weather. But then, in one's memory the summers of one's childhood are always perfect.

At last the day came for us to leave for Greens Norton. We were conveyed to Tring Station in the barouche, as the closed carriage was called, with its strange, musty smell, with which there always seemed to mingle a hint of eau de cologne. Edwin, much happier with the carriage than with the new-fangled Daimler, was on the box with Princess between the shafts. The luggage was taken by the station waggon, loaned for the occasion from Pendley and driven by Bowley who, too, to his dying day forty years later, infinitely preferred horses to cars, though like so many grooms after the First World War, had had to learn to drive and become a chauffeur. We changed trains at Blisworth which, with such a party – two grown-ups, three children, all their luggage and one dog, Grock (named after the clown) – must have been quite an operation, finally arriving at Towcester on the little side line that ran to Banbury. There we were met to our delight, on a blazing hot afternoon, by an open pony trap driven by my father's stud groom, Glaire. He had been the regimental barber, but although apparently a nervous rider, always expecting the worst, he was an exceptionally able stud groom. The luggage was collected by a farm waggon, only Nanny's wicker trunk or hamper being allowed with us in the trap. This was her most precious possession. When years later I visited her at her little cottage in Devon I was delighted to notice that she still had this ancient wicker hamper, the top of which fitted snugly like a lid. It was then filled to bursting with papers, photographs, mementos of her long career as a Nanny.

Greens Norton was little more than a mile from the station but on that first journey in the pony and trap, which in any case made only slow progress with its heavy load, it being uphill most of the way – at one point some of us had to get out and walk – it seemed to take the whole afternoon. I recall clearly the sprays of pink dog roses in the hedgerows, the eerie, derelict lodge at the entrance to the Bairstows on the right, our first view of the magnificent church spire which dominated the village – and, indeed, the surrounding countryside – at the top of the hill that led down to the village green, flanked by an attractive black and white timbered house, rather excitingly called The Chantry, on the left, and on the right the magnificent entrance to Falcon Manor, which for a moment I hoped was to be our home. But we jogged down the hill, past the village green, turning right at 'The Gate', one of the two pubs in Greens Norton, and up the short rise to our new home – the 'Court'.

To a small child it was impressive, poised there at the top of the hill – white stucco, gabled, with a large, solid oak front door and a great wrought-iron knocker. But within minutes it was, for all of us, home: the happiest home that any children could wish to have. So it remained for the next twelve years, the most formative of my life. That eventually it was all to end so sadly and so suddenly one had, of course, no inkling. A six year old is only interested in the present, and the present at Greens Norton in 1920 was serene and secure.

It was from Greens Norton that I set out to ride the one mile to Towcester on that, for me, memorable Boxing Day, 1925. It was the first day I had ever been allowed to go hunting unattended; a day to which I had been eagerly looking forward for two or three years. Always before I had been accompanied either by Whiteman, the groom, my mother, or very occasionally by my father, though he, being the Hunt Secretary, was usually too occupied with his more important Hunt duties to be looking after small children. I was riding our pony, Freckles, whose odd colouring is suggested by his name: just under 14 h.h., he became known far and wide, partly because of his appearance, but partly, too, because of his remarkable cleverness, adaptability and courage. He was a unique character.

I cannot remember why I was completely on my own on this occasion. I know that my father had broken his arm and could not hunt, my brother was probably considered too young, but I do not know why my mother and sister were absent. It may be that we were going through a measles or chicken-pox phase. At any rate I arrived on my own at Towcester in plenty of time, one of the first, but already there was what seemed to me a huge crowd. For the most part at this time they were foot people, cyclists and cars, funny old-fashioned vehicles that to me always symbolize the twenties: bull-nosed

Morrises with dickies, open tourers, cramped saloons, all with starting handles jutting out at the front, even of such aristocrats as Daimlers and Buicks.

As the church clock struck 11 am the hounds turned into the square in front of the town hall with the huntsman, Will Freeman, in their midst. Will, though overshadowed by his famous brother Frank of the Pytchley, was a good, probably an under-rated, huntsman and a great friend to us. Because my father was Hunt Secretary we used to spend hours at the Kennels, then at Wakefield Lawn, the home of Lord Hillingdon, the Master, who a few minutes later arrived himself in a posh limousine. Wearing a long coat, and what today would be considered a voluminous cloth cap, he was accompanied by an immaculately habited and veiled Lady Hillingdon, with one or two other smart companions. Their horses were immediately produced and, divested of their coats, they all mounted. At the same moment the whole of the centre of Towcester was suddenly filled with mounted riders – a huge, splendid throng, all top hats and scarlet, somewhat overwhelming to a small boy on his own for the first time. Several people spoke to me and when the occasion demanded I managed to doff my outsize bowler hat.

I particularly remember one elderly gentleman speaking to me. He was lean and withered, but had a fine presence and told me that he was George Beers, whose father, Frank, had been huntsman to the Grafton at the end of the nineteenth century. This was indeed a link with the past, which, with my natural interest in history and tradition, even at that early age, much impressed me. In fact, Frank Beers had been appointed huntsman to the 6th Duke of Grafton in 1862, succeeding his father who had been on the Duke's hunt staff since 1830, nearly a hundred years before – a truly fascinating link.

At about 11.15 am we moved off, going straight to Easton Neston, the magnificent home of Lord Hesketh, already the venue of Towcester Races, which in those days were run the opposite way round, anti-clockwise. It was very wet that year and much of the park was flooded, but we found in one of the coverts, and for an hour or so galloped about to everyone's enjoyment, at the same time being provided with some much needed after Christmas exercise. Many of the field went home when hounds were taken across to Stoke Bruerne, another fine palladian mansion, designed by Inigo Jones, in the midst of a beautiful park, now, sadly, but for one wing, razed to the ground. I have no recollection of what happened at Stoke Bruerne, nor can I honestly remember whether it was a fresh fox that we found in Plain Woods or whether it was all part of one hunt. All I knew at the time was that hounds seemed always to be running and that the farther we went the fewer people there were with them. I knew too, before long, that I ought to be going home but, having no idea where we were, thought it better to keep with hounds, blissfully unaware that we were going in exactly the opposite direction to Greens Norton. It cannot have been a very fast hunt, nor can we have crossed very difficult country, or I would not have kept up, though I remember Freckles carrying me safely over some quite big fences, at one of which one of the whippers-in had a fall. I remember too at some stage Lady Hillingdon, who was always very kind to children, asking me if I would be all right as they were going home, 'We have to go up to a party in London'.

Dusk was descending when eventually we checked by the side of a main road, cars already having their lights on. Those still out were grateful for the breather, and none more than Freckles and his young rider. Suddenly, Will Freeman, pointing to his right, set spurs to his horse, calling out, 'Come on! Come on! We'll have him yet'. Off we galloped and, sure enough, after five minutes or so hounds caught their fox at Far Cotton on the outskirts of Northampton – now near its centre. It was almost dark. There was but a dozen of the vast original Boxing Day field still there, including one small boy in an outsize bowler hat on a speckled grey pony, determined to let no one realize how exhausted he was.

Will kept repeating to everyone within ear-shot that 'it was the crows what killed 'im', at the same time making much of his beloved hounds. 'That's what it was,' he insisted, 'them crows; it was the crows what killed 'im.' He was obviously ecstatic. When finally we set off for home down the main road, Will assured me that I would be all right if I stayed with them, as I was only too ready to, still having no notion where I was. We had not gone very far before we stopped outside a pub, at Milton I suspect, which although it was not yet opening time readily welcomed Will who was no stranger, I learned later, to any public house in the Grafton country. While we were standing there a car which had presumably been following all day – though few did in those days, except perhaps on Boxing Day – drew up at the pub, two men got out, one of them asking me what my name was and where I lived; I told him. 'Greens Norton! That's all of ten miles from here,' he said. 'You'll not be home till midnight! You'd better let us give you a lift. I'm sure someone'll take your pony for you.' But I would not hear of it. In the first place I had no idea who the gentlemen were – 'Never talk to strangers!'. Secondly, I felt that it would be 'infra dig' to be taken home by car instead of riding my pony. Nevertheless, I was very relieved when half an hour later, as we jogged through Blisworth, there pulled up another car which I recognized as our own two-seater Morris. My mother was driving with a young groom by her side. Apparently one of the gentlemen having learned my identity had decided that it was his duty to telephone my parents. In fact, my mother had already been out in the car for some time touring the countryside looking for me, understandably becoming increasingly anxious as it grew later and later, then darker and darker, and there was still no sign of me. She had telephoned home a few minutes after the call from the stranger.

Relieved at my safe return my family treated me as something of a hero after such an adventure, while over a scrumptious tea of boiled eggs, crumpets and Christmas cake, in front of the drawing-room fire, I related my experiences, doubtless adding considerable embellishments and finishing with the remarkable statement that at the end, on the outskirts of Northampton, 'it was the crows what killed 'im'.

This was too much for my father, who could neither understand nor believe it, but had to wait until he knew that Freeman would be back at the Kennels – which with so many possible hospitable calls on the way might be as late as ten o'clock – before he could telephone him to learn the facts for himself, as eventually he did. On a fading scent hounds had checked about a mile short of Northampton, somewhere near the Queen Eleanor statue. Freeman was just about to give up, darkness descending, when he noticed that two or three fields away to the right crows were circling low. At once he realized that they might well be circling over a sinking fox – an accepted part of hunting lore – so, lifting his hounds, he took them to where he had seen the crows. Immediately they hit off the line, catching their fox within a few fields. I was teased about this episode for many years, 'It was the crows what killed 'im', becoming a family catch phrase. According to my old hunting diary this hunt lasted four-and-a-half hours, hounds having made a ten-and-a-half mile point, covering in all eighteen miles – a remarkable performance for my very first day's hunting entirely on my own.

It was at about this time that I developed my two great boyhood ambitions. The first was to become a Master of Foxhounds, and the second to ride in the Grand National. It was hunting that now became something of an obsession with me, the whole pageantry of it appealing to me almost as much as 'riding to hounds', though understandably at that age it was the latter that was the priority. On non-hunting days we would go for long walks, drawing imaginary coverts, holloa-ing foxes away, picking our lines across country, even enjoying simulated falls. My brother, Maurice, was equally enthusiastic and we would be prepared to run for miles. The hound puppies which we 'walked' were naturally expected to join in, and on more than one occasion put up a real fox, not always with my father's approval.

In the evenings I used to draw and paint hunting scenes, attention to detail making up for the lack of talent. Everything had to be correct, in its proper place or position; the huntsman with the hounds, the whipper-in ranging on or turning hounds, the Master at the head of his field, the skirters, the stragglers, those who preferred going through the gates to jumping the fences, the fallers, on the road the second horsemen. They were all there in my crude pictures, those in the background little more than matchstick figures, but all *correct.*

It was old Sergeant Murphy's popular victory that first inspired my enthusiasm for the Grand National. This legendary horse had been fourth both in 1920 and 1922, and was thirteen when eventually he won in 1923. He was ridden by the leading amateur, 'Tuppy' Bennet, a marvellous all-rounder – he even swam the Channel – who at that time was hero to everyone in the horse world, as was, for instance, Lord Mildmay a quarter of a century later. Shortly after winning the National he was killed in a bad fall, as a result of not wearing a crash helmet. After Bennet's death crash helmets, which were then a rarity, became compulsory. In the between-the-wars years amateurs played a great role in the Grand National which made it natural for a boy to wish to emulate them. Jack Anthony won in 1920 and Harry Brown was second in 1921. In 1923 amateurs were first and third, in 1925 Jack Wilson rode Double Chance to victory, while in 1927 Bobby Pennington, now Sir William Pennington-Ramsden, was only pipped on the post by Ted Leader on the favourite, Sprig. This latter's performance was a great thrill for us as Bobby Pennington hunted with the Grafton, was well known to us all, and though we were so much younger was always very friendly. His horse, Bovril III, was a rank outsider, being blind in one eye and 'fired', it was alleged, on three legs. I vividly remember hearing the running commentary (probably the first time the race was ever broadcast) on an old cat's-whisker wireless belonging to my prep school headmaster's wife and feeling possessively proud. Many years later Bobby Pennington became a Joint-Master of the Grafton.

Nor was this the only connection between the Grafton Hunt and the Grand National. In 1908 Colonel Frank Douglas-Pennant, later Lord Penrhyn, a close friend of my father, won with Rubio. He had bought this American-bred horse as a hunter for £15. Having won a few races it broke down and was then sent to the Saracen's Head at Towcester, to pull the carriage that plied between the Hotel and the Station, in the hope that this would make its legs stronger, which it certainly did. Rubio was ridden by another well-known local, Bernard Bletsoe, being trained by Fred Withington, yet another local, who also trained the second, Mattie Macgreggor. To have two Grand National heroes from within a few miles of our home was, inevitably, an inspiration, making the Grand National more real to us than to most children. I always loved talking to Lord Penrhyn, although he was a somewhat irascible old man, about Rubio and the Grand National. I even did so when he was over a hundred, and not a lot less irascible. I have enjoyed, too, dining at Bobby Pennington's, surrounded by pictures, both paintings and photographs, depicting Bobby on Bovril in his well-remembered blue and yellow.

Just as we 'hunted' on foot in the countryside round Greens Norton, so we 'steeplechased' over a course of various obstacles round our garden, wearing colours and jockey caps, all made by the skilful Florence. We did it all at the 'canter', until my mother firmly forbade it, convinced that it would result in our finishing up with one leg shorter than the other. Years later, as an adult, when staying with a friend who was as keen on National Hunt racing as I then was, I discovered that his garden with clipped yew hedges and little walls made an ideal 'course', so once again we started 'steeplechasing' – and always at the 'canter'!

As will be seen in due course circumstances conspired to prevent my taking up race riding, just at the moment when I normally should have done. My father had even had the foresight to buy me a two year old which he reckoned would be just about ready at the same time as I was. But it did not work out like that, and so my ambition to ride in the Grand National was never fulfilled – now the very thought of it terrifies me! But I did achieve my other ambition, to be a Master of Foxhounds, some twenty-five years later.

Chapter 2

Towards the scarlet thread

My childhood was extraordinarily happy. Looking back to Greens Norton it is difficult to recall a single experience that clouded our endlessly contented existence. Obviously there were the odd illnesses. Both my brother and I contracted glandular fever, which was unpleasant, and there was an anxious time when my parents were involved in a serious motor accident; my father in particular being critically ill for many months, and prayed for each Sunday in church, which was both exciting and embarrassing.

Greens Norton was such a relaxed home. By today's standards the staff was sizeable, yet there was little formality. The staff were friends rather than servants, and they were always referred to as staff, never as servants. The majority of them remained with us most of the twelve years we were at Greens Norton, though shortly before we left my father felt obliged to get rid of William, our butler, as he had a habit of running up large bills, in my father's name, at the local pub. His departure was a great relief to my mother who found his habit of bellowing out popular hymns in the pantry at the top of his voice all through her dinner parties rather tiresome. Alice, too, left to marry my father's part-time secretary, Arthur Hornsby. When years later I became Joint-Master of the Grafton, I found to my delight that Arthur still did all the Hunt accounts.

Our great favourite was Florence. In 1921 my beloved old Nanny left. I say mine, because I was always her favourite and with everyone else it was Maurice. She left partly because my parents felt that we were getting too old for a Nanny, and partly because she used to insist on singing a song with a refrain 'I like boys the best', which, not surprisingly, upset my sister. I can remember to this day Nanny coming up to the room I shared with my brother, sitting on the bed and bursting into tears. At once we sat, one either side of her, and joined in her tears, crying even louder, more heartbroken, than her. After some time my sister came in and said, 'You don't even know what you're crying about', which of course was true, and when we did we cried louder than ever. She had been given her notice, but she kept in touch with me until the end of her long life. She never forgot me at Christmas or on my birthday, and after she had retired and I had been to see her in her little cottage in Devon, she wrote to me every month until a few weeks before she died at the age of ninety-five.

Florence, who succeeded her, cannot have been more than twenty-two. She was a plump, jolly person, always full of fun, never in the least put out, however much we teased her or however tiresome we were. Much of our great happiness at that time was due to her. She did everything with us, and for us. The best holiday that we could have was to stay at her father's farm near Newmarket, then to be taken to the races. Picnics, sunshine, farm butter, brown eggs, home-cured hams, the cock crowing early in the morning, hay-making, watching the milking, and a warm, lovely, loving family. We could not ask for more anywhere. Indeed, we never went away for holidays in the accepted sense because we were always so happy and had so much to occupy us at home.

We were a very close, very 'family' family. Although we had many friends, both as a family and as individuals, we were always content and self-sufficient amongst ourselves, preferring to do things together, whether it was hunting, exercising the horses, going to shows or point-to-points; or to a theatre, only very rarely in London, but almost every week to the Northampton Rep, or just being at home. We seemed always to find so much to laugh at, probably in a rather 'in' way, my father having such a wonderful sense of humour which, of course, was infectious and which, I think, all his children inherited. My brother Maurice certainly had a brilliant wit and, more than that, he had the extraordinary warmth of personality which made both him and my father so greatly loved by all manner of people.

My father and mother were very devoted, for the most part sharing identical interests. My father was heir to his uncle at Pendley, my mother was the daughter of the local rector. They had become engaged when they were in their early twenties, but it had been agreed that they should not be married until my father had got his commission. Already horses dominated his life, which meant that he spent far more time racing and hunting than working, but also finding time to play hockey in an England trial and shooting at some of the best shoots in the country. All these things came easily to him. He was later invited to captain Northamptonshire at cricket and although he seldom played he managed to achieve a single figure handicap at golf. As a young man he was, by all accounts, fairly wild, as were other members of his family. His elder brother was disinherited, a real scoundrel; his youngest brother, possessed of great charm and wit, never settled to any job until, late in life, he married someone who had the character to help him succeed in running a very successful pub. The fourth brother, very easy-going, did well in the R.A.F. and had a happy family life. The only sister still alive, well into her nineties, is a remarkable character, one of her grandsons being Robin Knox-Johnson, the lone sailor. Their mother had deserted their father who died shortly afterwards as a result, indirectly, of a hunting accident. As teenagers, they were adopted by their childless uncle and aunt at Pendley, where they were never really made to feel welcome or completely at home. Certainly they must have been a handful, which nevertheless did not stop 'Uncle Joe' and 'Aunt Katy' doing all they could for them.

After being engaged for two or three years my mother finally told my father that unless he succeeded in getting his commission at the next attempt she would break off the engagement. Immediately he passed his exam with flying colours, enabling them to get married in 1911. My mother was to be a great influence on him, the transparent goodness of her nature affecting all with whom she came in contact, not least her husband. After his marriage, while never losing his high spirits and sense of fun, he became a person of great honesty, integrity and responsibility, directing all his energy to things worthwhile. Fortunately my mother appreciated that his real genius lay with horses. She even agreed to spend their honeymoon hunting in Ireland, although she had then ridden very little; certainly had never been hunting. In a short while she became not only an exquisite horse-woman, riding side-saddle, but also an extremely good judge of a horse. Thus was developed the foundation for a wonderfully happy marriage which in turn provided the background for an equally happy family life. I remember a master at my preparatory school once saying that our family and the Russells were the two happiest families in the school. The Russells were to be closely associated with me for the whole of my life. Dick, the second son, went to prep school on the same day as I did, and later we went to Harrow together. Each of us is godfather to one of the other's sons. His elder sister, Gwendy, married Laurie Stoddart who, as Chairman of the Whaddon Chase Hunt, was responsible for my appointment as Master in 1954, and their elder son, Peter, became my Joint-Master in 1969.

Although my home life was so idyllic, I did not in any way dislike school – far from it. I was extremely happy, despite the fact that the conditions at school in those days would today be considered unendurable. Hawtreys was one of the first preparatory schools in the country, the Reverend John Hawtrey, a house master at Eton, having been given permission by the Provost and Headmaster to start a new school for all the younger boys in his house, convinced that boys of eight and eighteen should not be together in one residential school. He bought Aldin House at Slough, now a Convent School, and at once had more boys than he could accept. A few years later, convalescing at Westgate-on-Sea after an illness, he decided that Thanet was the ideal place for a school. He therefore purchased four unfurnished boarding houses, less than a hundred yards from the station, two on one side of a road and two the other, all four separated from the playing-field by the road that connected the main London road with the front. Not the perfect environment for a school, one might say, but it became one of the most successful private schools in Britain. It was at that time called St Michael's, having been founded on St Michael's Day, 29 September. When Edward Hawtrey, who had succeeded his father soon after the move to Westgate, died during the First World War, it became known at Hawtreys. His widow, my own grandmother's sister, continued to run the school, making her son-in-law, Frank Cautley, Headmaster. When I went there in the twenties it was at the height of its fame, completely dominated by this remarkable old lady, already in her seventies.

Perhaps the most extraordinary feature of the school was the fact that every boy, as at Eton, had a single room, with double rooms for brothers. There is no doubt that sharing a room with Maurice for so many years, both at home and at school, was instrumental in making us so exceptionally close. We were as much friends as brothers, which is not always so.

The standard of teaching was extremely high, and the standard as far as games were concerned even higher. Cautley was a double blue and an outstanding coach, and while I was there the school teams were unbeaten at any game for three consecutive years. Life could certainly be spartan and the discipline was strict, but in no way brutal. One of my lasting memories of Hawtreys will always be trying to do up my starched Eton collar with fingers completely numb with the cold in the twenty minutes between the end of football – compulsory, of course – and 'absence' which really meant 'presence', a roll call of the whole school in the 'dancing room' as the Assembly Hall was called. It used to be said that there was nothing between Westgate-on-Sea and the North Pole. It frequently felt like it.

Each day's routine was full and seldom differed, any change there might be, therefore, being all the more welcome. For instance, there were only two whole-holidays in the school year, one on St Michael's Day and one on Ascension Day. We looked forward to them with keen anticipation, nor were we ever disappointed. In the morning there were the Swallow and Crusaders matches – on arrival at school one became either a Swallow (mauve and white stripes) or a Crusader (black with a Maltese Cross), the origin of the two bodies being lost in the past: presumably a substitute for Eton's Oppidans and Collegers. After lunch, there arrived three great coaches, always referred to by the Headmaster as the Red Leviathans. At a given signal and in a most orderly manner we all climbed aboard, receiving sixpence as we did so. We were then driven to Canterbury Cathedral, Reculver or some castle ruins where we spent the afternoon, and where we could spend our sixpences. In the evening there was a film show or a conjuror. Audience participation was not encouraged and I remember on one occasion an entertainer inviting us to join in a chorus 'Now, all together', he said. 'No!' the Headmaster firmly replied, 'that's just what we don't want!' Seen, but not heard! A half-holiday that was always appreciated was the one awarded each autumn for those who did Voluntary Work. It was, in fact, anything but voluntary, and everyone in the Upper and Middle Schools had to opt for one of the selected subjects – mythology or a classic book such as *Ivanhoe* or *Quentin Durward*. Only those whose efforts in the exam towards the end of the term were disastrous were denied the half-holiday, usually a visit to the Powell Cotton museum at Quex Park, Birchington.

Apart from the occasional misery of the cold, and my own problems with mathematics which I disliked intensely and which frequently landed me in trouble, my years at Hawtreys were happy and straightforward. My worst experience, without any doubt, was the death of one of my best friends from jaundice. I was in the sick bay at the time with chicken pox. I shall never forget the Headmaster, who seemed as out of place in a sick-room as a bishop in a brothel, standing by the side of my bed and breaking the news to me; nor, much more traumatic, the sound of the undertakers removing the coffin from the next room. It had, for a long time, a profound effect on my attitude to death.

I loved Chapel, always leading in the choir with my brother, looking no doubt like two little shining cherubs! It was always thought that we achieved this honour because we were great-nephews of old Mrs Hawtrey, but I doubt it. I was convinced that the old lady, her daughter and her son-in-law leant over backwards to make sure that there was no favouritism. I know for a fact that I was denied the Dancing Prize for this reason, as Beryl Cautley told me so! It went to Dick Russell instead, but it is just possible that my attempt to reverse while waltzing with Dick's mother – a very large lady – resulting in a crashing fall, might have had something to do with the decision going against me!

A normal, in no way outstanding boy of average ability both in work and games, as my school report might have said, I enjoyed my time at Hawtreys, recalling few unhappy moments, certainly none of real misery. Nevertheless, I always looked forward to the end of term, especially the autumn term, with four weeks' hunting ahead of me. I was fortunate in that even if I had not ridden for three or four months I could immediately go off for a day's hunting, knowing that I would suffer neither stiffness nor soreness. This used to annoy my father as, long before he was crippled with arthritis, he suffered from stiffness, even when he was hunting regularly four days a week.

Inevitably, with my father Hunt Secretary of a four-day-a-week pack, and with a stableful of horses, hunting very much dominated our life at Greens Norton, although as far as we children were concerned it was only in the Christmas holidays. For anyone never involved it is impossible to imagine the importance, or the splendour in those days of foxhunting in one of the more fashionable countries.

The Grafton was never quite as smart as the famous 'Shires', but it was smart enough and could claim to be one of the longest established hunts in the country, having been founded by the 2nd Duke of Grafton in the early part of the eighteenth century. Just as the Dukes of Beaufort hunted country which stretched from Bath to Oxford, the Earls of Berkeley country which stretched from Bristol to Marble Arch, so the Dukes of Grafton hunted in Surrey, Suffolk and Northamptonshire. In fact, the 2nd Duke was responsible for introducing a special Act of Parliament which resulted, in 1748, in the building of Westminster Bridge. Apparently his Grace found the ferry which he used to bring his hounds from their Kennels at Croydon to the Kennels at Whittlebury and Euston, his Northamptonshire and Suffolk estates, too unreliable.

Although it was not one of the 'Shires' the Grafton could certainly claim, with the Warwickshire, the Bicester and the Whaddon Chase, to be one of the leading 'Provinces'. Geographically well placed, about sixty miles north-west of London, it was then almost entirely grass, except for the considerable areas of useful woodlands. It also had Weedon, the famous Cavalry Equitation School established just south-west of Daventry. The officers attending the course, justifiably described as the cream of the best cavalry regiments, were encouraged to hunt as much as they could as, indeed, both they and their instructors did, three or four days a week either with the Pytchley or the Grafton. This undoubtedly gave both these hunts a certain 'cachet', earning them reputations for magnificent hard riding – an enviable reputation, for the Pytchley and the Grafton were generally acknowledged to be two of the biggest countries to cross in England.

The majority of those who lived and hunted in the Grafton country were people who could afford to do it in considerable style; few, if any, worked regularly in London, though there were a certain number of company directors who occasionally had to miss a Monday or a Friday because of a board meeting. Obviously, too, there were a few of the younger generation who could only hunt on Saturdays and at holiday times as they were working during the week. Indeed Saturday was one of the unfashionable days. It was the Grafton Friday that was the big day, similar to the Quorn Monday, the Cottesmore Tuesday, or the Pytchley Wednesday. Nobody wanted to miss a Friday, those living at the opposite end of the country riding enormous distances to get to the Friday meets, and, of course, home at the end of the day. I cannot remember a single horse-box being used in those days, though one of the first inventors of them, Toby Curtis, hunted with the Grafton. Those coming from outside the country invariably brought their horses by train – horses at that time being welcomed by the railways.

A field of three hundred, which was not in the least unusual, was a magnificent sight as hounds moved off from the village or a private house where they had met. Even more splendid, and indeed thrilling, was the sight of hounds, followed by this huge field, racing in full cry across acres of grass; 'the scarlet thread woven through the tapestry of the English countryside', as, many years later, Lord Exeter once described it in a talk on foxhunting at Pendley. In the famous Cecil Aldin picture 'Away from Weedon Bushes', it is possible to count upwards of a hundred and thirty riders, of which no less than fifty are in scarlet. In the companion picture of the Whaddon Chase there appear to be some forty scarlet-coated riders in a field of a hundred and twenty-five, which means that there could be at least fifty riders in scarlet in any one day. Every lady depicted is riding side-saddle, and there are some ten in the front rank in the Grafton picture. The figures at the back are mere dots on the horizon. Nor was this all, for at any big meet there were at least sixty or eighty second horsemen. Those of the Master and the Hunt staff were all in scarlet, with a spare stirrup-leather across the shoulder as a badge of office. All second horsemen were, or were supposed to be, under the control of the Master's second horseman, who had an extremely responsible job. He was expected to keep in touch with the Hunt, yet seldom leave the road, and when around two o'clock the order was given to change horses, they were all expected to be clean, steady, and with no trace of sweat or blowing. It is not easy, even today, for the second horses to keep contact with the hunt, though brought up in horse-boxes. In those days it must have demanded great skill and exceptional knowledge of the country. Not altogether surprisingly the second horsemen tended at times to get out of hand. The following notice appeared in one hunt's subscription book in 1931:

> There have been so many complaints lately of the behaviour of the second horsemen that the Master is obliged to bring the matter to the notice of the Ladies and Gentlemen who hunt with these hounds and to ask them to caution their servants, giving them instructions to remain with the Hunt second horsemen on the roads wherever possible: on no account to jump fences: to shut gates after them and under all circumstances to avoid giving cause for complaint to the Farmers.

The horses themselves, of course, were almost invariably of high quality and beautifully turned out, the tack superbly produced, double bridles then being *de rigueur*. No one would dream of coming out without their horses' manes being plaited and their tails pulled, thus emphasizing their quality. In those days there was no eventing or show jumping to cream off so many of the highest class horses. All the best horses in Britain were to be found in the hunting field. The splendour, the panoply of it all, was breathtaking; to be part of it, although brought up in the midst of it, was an experience that never diminished. Nor was this reaction limited to those who rode to hounds. People today may be surprised to know that wherever hounds met the village school invariably allowed children time off – sometimes a whole morning off – to see the hounds. The entire village turned out. Farmers and their families came down from their outlying farms, the great majority always extending a warm welcome to the Hunt, though comparatively few, more the pity, actually rode to hounds. One of the original ideas of the Pony Club was to encourage the children of farmers to come out hunting. Obviously it was a difficult time for farmers in the twenties and thirties, most of them being dependent upon the Hunt for their living. It was members of the Hunt to whom they sold their home-bred horses and their forage, whose young horses they took in for their sons to break-in or nag. Without the local Hunt many farmers would have gone under altogether. It must be remembered that after the First World War many large estates were broken up. Although some tenant farmers managed to find the money to buy their land, they could then scarcely afford to farm it. Others who had been managers or subsidized tenants became tenants in their own right, often at unrealistic rents, yet even then they found it almost impossible to earn a living off their land. Nevertheless, if the farmers depended on the Hunt, the Hunt more than ever depended on the farmers, as they had replaced the few great landlords, all of whom almost automatically had in the old days backed the Hunt. An article in *The Times*, in 1929, underlines the problems resulting from the breaking up of these large estates: 'A much larger number of interests has to be consulted, and as the laws of foxhunting are unwritten and a great deal depends on the goodwill of the occupiers of land, the exercise of tact and diplomacy is more important than ever.' The article continues: 'This break-up of large estates has increased the difficulties of earth-stopping which is not so efficient and systematic as it was when estate keepers looked after it, and with a multiplicity of occupiers the question of poultry damage – real and imaginary – is less easy of amicable arrangement.'

In other words the vital qualities in a Master or a Hunt Secretary in those days were tact and an ability to establish good relations between the Hunt and the farmers – as it is today. Before the war Hunts had been run in a somewhat feudal manner, and gradually it was being appreciated that a different approach was required. It surely says much for the way Hunts adapted themselves to the new conditions that they were able to carry on in such magnificence and on such a scale. The cynics might well dispute it, but it is a fact that even in the twenties foxhunting was supported by all sections of the countryside community. Though their attitude might today be considered condescending, the 'gentry' went out of their way to be on the most friendly possible terms with farmers and farm workers. Though their attitude today might be labelled servile, farmers and farm workers had the greatest respect for the majority of the 'gentry', and bad feeling of any sort was a rarity.

As a small boy one was, of course, blissfully unaware of the social and political implications surrounding hunting, tending to take it all for granted. It was just a way of life, and yet for a child, however much involved in it one might be, it must have been something of an ordeal to be a part of this mighty concourse. There were certain people on whom one could rely to be kind and helpful, while one avoided others as invariably, due to their own nerves, they shouted at and cursed one, cut in front of one at fences, and criticized whatever one did. Fortunately such people were few and far between, the majority being very friendly, and none more than the Master, Lord Hillingdon, whose kindness to children in the hunting field I have never forgotten, always attempting to emulate it myself. When he retired in 1928 he presented every child in the hunt with a signed print of a very fine picture by Cecil Aldin of himself on a horse called The Sower, which he had bought from my father. To this day it hangs in my dressing-room. His courtesy was legendary. He would never hesitate to stop in the middle of a hunt to shake a farmer by the hand. He loved his hunting, though it cost him a fortune, and he particularly enjoyed hunting hounds himself on Saturdays, with Humphrey de Trafford and Guy

Shaw Stuart whipping-in to him. It was a very amateurish performance, very light-hearted, but everyone enjoyed those days.

The Prince of Wales, later the Duke of Windsor, was a fairly regular visitor, sufficiently regular for me not always to record the fact in my hunting diary. On two occasions he actually came to Greens Norton. The first time was when hounds met in the village, his horses being brought to our house where he left his car. On the second occasion he came unexpectedly. He and my father collided in mid-air jumping the Langford brook, both going to the bottom. Neither realized who the other was at the time of the collision – my father was then Hunt Secretary – and as they surfaced cursed each other roundly. The result was that my father brought the Prince home to change, by which time he was very genial and, while enjoying his tea of eggs and toast in front of the drawing-room fire, was delightful with us children, who had not been out hunting that day. On another occasion, I remember the Duke of Gloucester falling down the stairs, as he came down from changing in the spare room. My sister was so surprised that she dropped a tray of drinks.

But perhaps the most memorable occasion was when three of the Princes were all out together: the Prince of Wales, the Duke of Gloucester and the Duke of York, later to become King George VI. We had met at Dadford, a not particularly exciting meet, sport in the morning being moderate. In the afternoon, however, hounds ran well, achieving a useful hunt, finishing up in Stowe Ridings, close to the school. My pony beginning to tire I was jogging along a track by the side of the Ridings, when I was overtaken by the three Princes riding together. The Prince of Wales came up on my left, the other two on my right. As they passed me my pony broke into a canter to keep pace with them. For a couple of hundred yards or so we cantered along together. I did not know which way to look, being so embarrassed and excited. Eventually as we reached the end of the track the Duke of York, on my right, turned to me and said, 'You won't forget this in a hurry' and then he asked me my name. I told him. The Prince of Wales asked if I was 'Pudding' Williams' son. When I replied that I was he said, 'Oh, really! Jolly good!' in that individual voice with its slight drawl, almost accent, which was so popular. After which, 'Oh, really! Jolly good!' became a stock phrase with the Williams children.

On one other occasion there were three Princes out together, but on that occasion it was Prince George, the Duke of Kent, instead of the Duke of York. Having broken my collar-bone in a fall the previous week I was not riding, but following in the car. Mike Ansell was also suffering from a broken collar-bone and was with me. Fortunately each of us had one good arm so between us were able to manage, one steering, the other changing gear. Car followers were not encouraged, and few risked the wrath of the Master by systematically following all day. But when the Prince of Wales was out there was always a large crowd, and, like his great-nephew, the present Prince of Wales, he always gave value for money, having a word with many and a smile for all. He was quite fearless and always beautifully mounted, usually on a rather racy type of horse which he probably point-to-pointed at the end of the season.

At the end of the 1926–27 season my father retired as Hunt Secretary. I do not think it is disputed that he was as good a Hunt Secretary as one could find. He was extremely popular, immensely conscientious, treating everyone, farmers, subscribers, foot-followers, exactly the same. On the last day of the season he was presented by the farmers with a very handsome clock, which now stands in our front hall. The following year the country was shocked to hear that Lord Hillingdon himself was resigning. Apparently his generosity and extravagance had caught up with him, and it was alleged that he had spent a quarter of a million during his eight years' Mastership. Obviously this could be an exaggeration, but it is a fact that he kept forty-two horses, sixty-five couple of hounds and a staff of twenty-five at the Hunt Kennels, which he had had built at his home, Wakefield Lawn, near Towcester. Something approaching panic ran through the country. Times were becoming increasingly difficult as the thirties loomed up, and no one could imagine who would ever be able to afford to take over the hounds, which, it was alleged, meant a personal commitment of at least £10,000 a year. Nor had a solution been found when the season came to an end.

Ignorant of the real implication of it all, I began to wonder whether I would ever hunt again as, presumably, if no one took over the hounds the Hunt would close down. This worried me very much, particularly as during the previous holidays my father had bought me a new pony, Freckles having finally been outgrown. We had been over to see it, a quality 15 h.h. grey mare, near Bicester where it proceeded to run away with me three times round a big field. To my astonishment, my father decided that it was exactly what he was looking for, and bought it there and then. He knew what he was about. Within a fortnight I had achieved the never easy transition from pony to horse, the first real hurdle in a rider's life. As a result I now rather fancied myself on this lively, elegant, six-year-old mare, named Tinker after the wife of Oliver Gilbey from whom my father had bought her. I could not wait for the opportunity to display my new self in the hunting field, but would there, for us, be any more hunting?

One morning that spring my sister, brother and I went for a ride with my father. We jogged through the village, trotted up the hill by the church, then turned into the windmill field behind Falcon Manor. We continued at a trot up the track, then half way across, as much at Tinker's behest as my own, I broke into a canter, but immediately my father stopped me.

'Wait a moment,' he said. 'Let's walk to the top; I have something to tell you.'

He seemed to have difficulty in bringing himself to speak, and then suddenly he blurted out, stammering as he always did when he was nervous or excited:

'What would you say if I told you that I was going to become Master?'

We literally halted in our tracks, but for a moment could not bring ourselves to speak.

'Master?'

'Yes.'

'Of the Grafton?'

'Yes, Master of the Grafton with Arthur Guinness. I have not told your mother yet, so say nothing until I let you.'

He then told us, as we rode slowly on across the Grimscote road, how a complete impasse had been reached, with everyone at their wits' end to find a solution. A number of people had approached him, begging him to take on the hounds himself, but he had always refused, knowing that he could not possibly afford it. He had then thought of Arthur Guinness, a friend and neighbour who lived at Greens Norton Hall, and who was a member of the famous brewery family, and therefore well endowed. After much thought he had decided to approach him. Arthur Guinness being a very modest, self-effacing person, and not a very good horseman, though he loved his hunting, was hesitant, but my father, as everyone who knew him well will testify, could be very persuasive. Eventually Arthur agreed to go in as Joint-Master with my father, but would not put up a penny more than £5000, and would only do it for a year or two until they could find someone else. My father knew well enough that he would be hard pressed to meet his own commitments as Master, and would find it difficult to produce the money that Arthur Guinness could not provide. He believed, nevertheless, that with proper management and organization it could all be done much more cheaply, while no less efficiently. He decided, therefore, to take the gamble and try to make a go of it. He informed the Hunt Committee that he and Arthur Guinness were prepared to become Joint-Masters of the Grafton Hunt, initially for one season, if it would help solve their problems. They were delighted as, of course, was I. It was the most wonderful news that I had ever heard. From 1 May, now only a few weeks away, I would be the son of a Master of Foxhounds and, what is more, son of the Master of Grafton. It seemed almost as good as being a Master of Hounds myself. I would now be a part of the scarlet thread.

It was a characteristic of my father to throw himself wholeheartedly into whatever it was that was absorbing his interest at the time, almost to the exclusion of everything else. When he was young it had been race-riding; for a short time it was show jumping – he was one of the founders of the British Show Jumping Association; in the twenties and thirties it was showing; towards the end of his life it was bridge and gardening. Now, in 1928, when he became Master it was hunting that wholly obsessed him. He threw himself into it with an almost fanatical zeal and enthusiasm. In retrospect it could be that his drive and determination to succeed was a little too much for the somewhat staid conservative society that made up the hunting community in those days, though it has to be remembered that he was taking on hounds at a critical time. Not only had the Hunt lost an extremely popular and enormously wealthy Master, but with the thirties only just round the corner my father, alway a realist, was convinced that if hunting were to survive – in particular if the Grafton were to survive – there had to be a radical change in the whole economic approach to the sport.

It is, I believe, true to say that my father was one of the first Masters of Foxhounds to run a hunt with the same meticulous organization that tycoons devote to their businesses. Everything, as his diaries, note-books and accounts testify, was organized to the last detail. It was no surprise to him when I used to tell him in his old age of the dictum always preached by Captain Ronnie Wallace, greatly respected Chairman of the Master of Foxhounds Association today, that good organization is the basis for good sport. It was an opinion that he had held so many years earlier when it was not fashionable. On each day that hounds met my father religiously entered in his Hunt book the number of hounds out, the horses ridden by the Hunt staff, himself and members of his family, the coverts drawn, and the number of foxes found and accounted for. He noted, too, any farmer upset or farm where there had been extensive damage, the importance of which he had learned as Hunt Secretary. It was all strictly factual – for instance in his report on a certain day in January 1932, he makes no mention of the fact that his son had a very bad fall, necessitating twelve stitches in his head! I remember the occasion clearly because in that particular Christmas holidays we were losing a lot of days through frost. At breakfast that morning my father announced in a most matter of fact way that there was little hope of hunting, at which I was moved to remark, somewhat acidly, that as he hunted four days a week the whole season it did not much matter to him whether we hunted or not, but when one had as little hunting as we did, being away at school most of the time, then it was a different matter. I thought we ought to give it a try. 'Very well,' said my father to my surprise, 'we will'; and he forthwith telephoned the Kennels and the Hunt Secretary to tell them that we would hunt at twelve o'clock.

To say that the going was treacherous is an understatement. We slithered about trying to find a fox, then when we did hounds ran much too fast for the horses' safety. At the very first fence my pony slipped, failed to take off and turned head over heels. I not only cracked my head open, but broke my collar-bone. My father's laconic comment merely reports that scent was poor and that hounds killed their fox. His approach to foxhunting was essentially practical. A mishap to a member of his family was, unless very serious, as when my mother broke her back, comparatively irrelevant, while he would record in detail an injury to a horse. To be fair, this was not only because a lame horse could affect his organization, but because horses at that time were his whole life, his obsession.

His Hunt books of half a century ago reveal some interesting statistics. When he became Hunt Secretary in 1923 there were a hundred and fifteen subscribers who contributed a total of £4345. The full subscription was £50 p.a. (£60 for those living outside the country). Ten years later, my father's last season as Master, there were a hundred and fifty subscribers producing £7682, the subscription having gone up to £60 (£70 for those living outside the country). A visitor paid a £3 'cap', a member of the Services £1. In 1923 the Point-to-Point made £120, in 1932 it made £500, the sit-down lunch for about a hundred and fifty farmers cost £124. The guarantee to the Masters was increased from £3000 to £4000 in 1928, my father's first season, but the Masters, of course, were responsible for paying all the wages, providing all the horses, their keep and their tack. In my father's last season there were no less than thirty horses in the Hunt stables which did not include his own. When Lord Cadogan retired as Master in 1940 there were forty-two. When one realizes that in the majority of Hunts in Britain fifty years later members are still subscribing £100 or less, it cannot be denied that the increase in subscriptions over the years has in no way kept pace with the increase in costs. For example, the total postage for the Grafton, a four-day-a-week pack, in 1931, was £17, whereas today it is more likely to be £500. Printing cost £24, rent, rate and taxes for Kennels and Stables £110, repairs £70. All these items have multiplied at least ten times today.

The cost of it all was, naturally, of no great interest to the teenage son of the Master, yet one could not help being caught up in all the Hunt administration that absorbed so much of my father's time. Inevitably, too, one was involved with his various innovations, as they were such an endless topic of conversation in the family circle and amongst my father's closest friends. As children we had been devoted to Will Freeman, but we were delighted when my father announced that he was appointing Will Pope as his Huntsman. Not only had he married the young Nanny of David Satow who, because of the close relationship between our mother and his (who had died at the time of his birth), spent a great deal of time at Greens Norton, but we had all loved Will when he was second whipper-in. In fact, the appointment was controversial as, never having carried the horn before, he was considered an unknown quantity. He had, however, as my father had had the perspicacity to appreciate, been part of a wonderful partnership with the famous Bicester Huntsman Clarence Johnston in an historic era. Even more controversial was his decision to 'dock' the two best horses that he bought for Pope. Docking, of course, in those days was legal, but it was the thoroughbred that was then *de rigueur* in the shires and provinces; docking as a rule was confined to cobs and carriage horses. My father, however, with his remarkable eye for a horse, knew that these two horses, both of which he was satisfied were brilliant performers, could never really be made to look quality, however well plaited their manes, well pulled their tails, however smartly clipped and turned out. They were deep, short-legged horses and, as he saw it, would look real 'sorts', with hogged manes and docked tails, the type of horse so often depicted in a Snaffles picture.

He was certainly taking a risk, for had they failed to measure up to expectations my father would have been a laughing stock. But his judgement proved more than justified. Somehow they suited the chunky figure of Will Pope to perfection, so much so that it is scarcely an exaggeration to say that it was on Cocktail in particular, then only a five year old, that Will Pope completely established his reputation in one season. The other horse on which he could so easily have attracted derogatory remarks, but which indeed increased his fame, was a pale dun, with an exaggerated eel stripe, called The Drummer. Horses such as these were bound to cause raised eyebrows in an era when the shires and provinces prided themselves on the quality of their horses, the majority of them thoroughbreds.

With his reputation in the horse world it was not surprising that my father was always superbly mounted himself. Most of his horses were good enough to win in the show ring, as well as to go in front across a really big country, yet not one that he rode that first season cost him more than £100. I remember well the excitement when he sold to Lord Hillingdon for £300 a horse on which he had made a great reputation himself called The Sower, featured, as already recorded, in the Cecil Aldin picture. It was too big an offer to turn down, despite the fact that it was his favourite horse. The other outstanding horse that my father had at this time was a big bay horse called The Prophet. He sold it together with another good horse, for 1000 gns after it had won at Olympia to America, if I remember rightly. It was considered a fantastic price. His only failure, or perhaps one should say disappointment, was a skewbald horse called Silhouette. When he was a boy his father had had a famous skewbald on which he made a tremendous reputation, particularly in Leicestershire. He can be seen on it in the famous G. D. Giles Leicestershire prints, in which my father can also be seen on a pony. It was my father's life-long ambition to find a skewbald as good, but he never did. Curiously enough, when first I was invited to become Master of the Whaddon Chase I was taken to meet Lord Rosebery who had been Master in the between the wars years and, indeed, had dominated the Whaddon Chase scene for nearly twenty years. When he heard that I was the grandson of Captain Stanley Williams he told me that one of his earliest and most vivid memories was of seeing my grandfather, out with the Rothschild Staghounds, on his famous skewbald jumping a fence which he had thought was quite unjumpable. 'If you're anything like him, you'll do,' he added gruffly.

Looking back, I suppose that our yard at Greens Norton was just about all that a stable yard should be, presided over by Glaire with some six or seven grooms, all of whom were equipped in identical livery of breeches, coats to match and leggings, with highly polished boots. Best of all I remember the Sunday morning routine when after church we went round each box, the horses all in special head collars in my father's racing colours of brown and yellow – or chocolate and orange as they were officially registered – Glaire following with a sieve of sliced carrots which each horse was allowed to take from our palms; occasionally, as with my own pony, from our lips. On Sunday all was serene and orderly in the yard, in contrast to the weekday bustle with the string going out or returning from exercise, being tacked up for hunting or groomed, to the accompaniment of the 'sss-ing' that grooms practised in those days to keep the hairs out of their mouths, their breeches supported by a belt – usually a regimental one – while their braces hung down by their thighs. Routine was paramount as, inevitably, it still is in the best-run and therefore the most successful yards.

In the twenties and thirties no less than a hundred horses went out to exercise every morning in the village of Greens Norton: population six hundred! Hunting in those days was indeed an industry.

Had I no recourse to my father's Hunt books I would have said, looking back through memory's usual rose-coloured spectacles, that my father's first season with Arthur Guinness, his selfless, helpful and generous Joint-Master, and Will Pope, his sensational new Huntsman, was a red letter one. My father sums it up as a 'fair season up to Christmas, then bad. Twenty-seven days lost by frost, nine by Foot and Mouth restrictions'. An article in *The Times* (can one imagine such a thing today?) says, 'Every season cannot be a brilliant one, but the season just concluded was a decidedly bad one. In one country eight consecutive Fridays were lost [probably the Grafton]. The north sides of fences have been treacherous in the extreme and to gallop down hillsides has been most hazardous' – not to say foolish!

It was, perhaps, the following season that really made my father's reputation as a Master of Foxhounds, despite the shortness of his régime. His organization and management were now firmly established, thus enabling the Grafton to benefit from one of the most open seasons ever, precisely one day being lost from frost and one from fog. Sport was consistently good, often brilliant. Even when I returned to the Grafton twenty years later people still talked of that memorable season, the exceptional pack of hounds, the superb sport, the panache of the magnificently turned out field. To be part of it all, even more to be the Master's son, was an experience that could not fail to make an indelible impression on a teenager, to such an extent, in fact, that from time to time I found myself resorting to verse! – partially inspired at least by the delightful volumes that appeared each Christmas by Will Ogilvie, with illustrations by Lionel Edwards: *Scattered Scarlet*, *Over the Grass*, *Galloping Shoes*. I was reading a great deal at this time and developing a considerable taste for poetry, my taste being very much for the romantics, as it was later with music. One of my own verses was fortunate enough actually to see the light of day. A great friend of my parents, Major Harry Faudel-Phillips, published a book called *The Child's Guide to Horse Knowledge* which was the first book of its kind ever to be published. It was dedicated to my sister and brother and myself and had a picture of the three of us, all on Freckles, on the jacket. Knowing that I occasionally attempted to write poetry he invited me to submit a poem, as a kind of preface. It was accepted and duly published. I was just thirteen, but I do not recall any great surprise or satisfaction in having a poem printed in what was soon to become a best-seller. I was much prouder a year or two later in getting a poem published in the school magazine. It was nothing to do with horses and, as I remember it, was written almost at a sitting. It is perhaps, worth quoting:

Tranquillity

The room was quaintly lit, the firelight flicking
  The gloom with lash of flame.
Over the hearth, the clock was slowly ticking
  A song without a name.

An old man lay, in seas of slumber drifting,
  Remote and free from care;
On softened face the glow, forever shifting,
  Trembled, and on his hair.

A cat dozed, purring, by the tranquil sleeper,
  Lay, purring, dimly seen,
While shadows mingled deeper yet and deeper;
  Her half-closed eyes shone green.

And now, in drowsy peace, the cat crept nearer
  Her master's slippered feet,
And stilled her crooning, for her far-off hearer
  Lay lost in failing heat.

The embers, dying, dropped, their death was creeping;
  The last red spark had leapt;
Yet still those placid dreamers went on sleeping,
  And slept and slept and slept.

When Harry Faudel-Phillips was staying with us at Greens Norton in about 1927, he came down to breakfast one morning and found us with our heads buried in the *Daily Graphic*. Being a stickler for good manners, correct etiquette, proper behaviour and so on, he was far from pleased. 'Don't you know that it is very rude for children to read the papers before the grown-ups?' he asked. 'Anyway, I've never seen you read a paper before; what is it that you find so absorbing?' We explained that it was Tuesday and that on Tuesdays there was a 'Tailwaggers' ' page.

'Tailwaggers? What on earth's that?'

'A club for children who have dogs and puppies. We are all members of the Tailwaggers' Club.'

'What rubbish!' he expostulated, continuing to grumble when my parents came into the room. Then quite suddenly, as the idea struck him, he turned to my parents and suggested, quite seriously, that they should start a Pony Club. 'Much better than a puppy-dog club,' he said. Within a year the Pony Club, a junior branch of the then Institute of the Horse of which my parents, Harry Faudel-Phillips and Colonel

Guy Cubitt were all council members, was founded. Three branches came into being in 1928, the Crawley and Horsham run by Guy Cubitt, the Grafton, run by my parents, and one in Shropshire run by Mrs Corbett. Within three years there were a hundred branches – and the rest is history.

Already, in a subconscious way, I was beginning to be aware of the split in my personality, the divergence in my interests. I loved reading, and writing, and it was at about this time that I embarked on a play entitled *Devil's Luck*, but it grew to be so similar to Patrick Hamilton's *Rope* that I abandoned it. But I loved, too, everything connected with the countryside, indeed had little doubt that I would finish up as a farmer, landowner – and Master of Foxhounds. I used to go for long walks round Greens Norton, often by myself, but usually with my brother Maurice, who also had a literary turn of mind so that we were able happily to indulge in both our interests. While hunting obviously dominated the winter holidays, Pony Club activities, gymkhanas, rallies, paper chases and horse shows dominated the Easter and summer. Before long I was introduced to show jumping, largely through another friend of my father's, Colonel 'Ted' Lyon. Many, many years later I succeeded him as editor of *The Horseman's Year*, an annual that he founded with great success after the war. When I was in my early teens he asked me to ride a 14.2 h.h. pony of his in show jumping events. Bengal, as the pony was called, knew it all and quickly taught me much.

In those days, of course, show jumping bore little resemblance to show jumping that we know today. The courses for the most part consisted of gorse hurdles, white poles, a gate, and usually a water jump. Certainly it was not taken seriously, such rules as there were being very haphazard, the judges usually making their decision more on style than anything else. Nobody took it very seriously, and so everyone had a go. I well remember at Hemel Hempstead, in the pair jumping, which was invariably part of the programme at most shows, the local M.P. and his wife competing. He was J. C. C. Davidson, then Parliamentary Private Secretary to Stanley Baldwin. His wife, who succeeded him as Member when he was raised to the peerage, was Joan Davidson, now a life peeress in her own right. As the show was a Conservative Fête they not surprisingly won, scoring a highly popular victory!

Jumping at the top was rather better, thanks almost entirely to the efforts of my father and a few friends including Colonel Taffy Walwyn, father of Peter Walwyn the trainer and his sister Jean, the sculptress. In 1926 they founded the British Show Jumping Association. Riders such as Tommy Glencross, the Taylor and Foster brothers, Phil Blackmore and others and, of course, many of the soldier riders such as Malise Graham, Joe Dudgeon and Mike Ansell always attracted the public and were worth going a long way to see. But the one that we would go farthest to see was Miss Bullows, the leading lady rider of her day. Her popularity, as far as we were concerned, was largely due to her tremendous 'hup' when she wanted her horse to take off. She always used to ride in a brown beret with, jutting out at the top, a little stump which nicely matched the short stumpy tails of the horses she used to ride. We thought her great, and became her most devoted fans. It was, if I remember rightly, at Tring Show, claimed then to be the greatest one day show in England, held regularly on August Bank Holiday Tuesday, that we discovered that we too could make her horse take off if, from the ringside, we called out 'hup' at the right moment, or the *wrong* moment, as was sometimes a great temptation. If Miss Bullows said 'hup' at one moment and we said 'hup' at the same moment, all was well, but if Miss Bullows said 'hup' at one moment and we said 'hup' at a different moment, then anything might happen. A course which had a water jump in it had great attractions for us. A carefully timed 'hup' could almost certainly guarantee an 'incident'. Fortunately Miss Bullows survived our outside assistance, and is still alive today as Lady Wright.

Needless to say, my show jumping efforts did not aspire anywhere near to the standards of those names I have mentioned, as I was still very young, but such riders were a great inspiration and I was soon nursing ambitions to follow in their footsteps. Indeed, so keen was I that I was able, a year or two later, to make history at Harrow by persuading the Headmaster to allow me a day off to go to the International Horse Show at Olympia. After all, I argued, others were allowed to go to the Motor Show, or the Victoria and Albert Museum; Kings and Princes even to State functions, so why should not the son of the Master of the Grafton Hunt and Secretary of the British Show Jumping Association be allowed to go to the International Horse Show? – logic which reluctantly Dr Norwood had to accept, but only after being told by my Housemaster that I had hunting pictures on my braces.

My father was on the Committee of the International Horse Show, so I was able to do it in style, sitting in the 'gold chairs' area. He should, in fact, have been a Director of the Show at this time, in due course becoming Chairman, but he had, apparently, had a row with R. G. Heaton, the Senior Director, who blocked him. This had taught him, he later told me, never to make an enemy: it is certain to rebound on one eventually. Again this is a precept – a very difficult one – that I have tried to follow in my own life.

My father may not have been a Director, but he was considered important enough to be included in a page of caricatures of show personalities in *The Tatler*. The caption underneath read ' "Pudding" Williams, one of the big bottoms of the Grafton' (a bottom, for which the Grafton is famous, is a big ditch with land either side sloping steeply down to it). The implication was really no fairer than his nickname. He was a big, strong figure of a man, but certainly not fat; though it has to be admitted that my family all have concave backs which result in our being slightly S-shaped. My father loved to tell the story, against himself, of his tailor remarking that it was always a pleasure to build a suit for a gentleman with such a fine figure, adding, 'Plenty to hang your trousers on, sir.'

My father did eventually become Chairman of the International Horse Show, in 1947, when he was largely instrumental in starting the show again after the war, at the White City. Ironically it was I who became Chairman of the Show at Olympia, but that was nearly fifty years later, and it was a very different show from the old Olympia International. My show was the Olympia Christmas Show. It was probably as well that my father did not become Chairman in the late twenties. Knowing how he had to throw himself whole-heartedly into anything in which he was involved, it would inevitably have conflicted with his hunting which now, as Master, absorbed him completely.

Chapter 3

'Great days in the distance enchanted'

A few days after my father had divulged to us his acceptance of the Grafton Mastership – for me such an exciting decision – I had to go back to school. It was, in fact, for my first term at Harrow. For a boy of twelve or thirteen to start at a large public school after the much more sheltered existence of a comparatively small preparatory school, where at least in one's last year one has imagined oneself to be quite important, can be an unnerving experience. It was softened to a certain extent for me by my being placed for a term, owing to the over-full school at that time, in a small 'waiting' house, Garlands. Nevertheless within weeks I had been subjected to one of the most dramatic experiences in my whole school career.

In Garlands was a certain swarthy seventeen year old called Ghazi. In fact, he was the young King of Iraq, and for the most part he was pleasant enough and seemingly quite normal. He was already obsessed with fast cars, in particular a Lea Francis that he was allowed to keep at Harrow in order to drive to London for State occasions. Though excitable, he was generally quite popular with everyone, including the Housemaster 'Tubby' Bradshaw and his no less tubby wife, Betty. One evening I was in his room chatting when he made some rather strange advances which, in my innocence, I found completely confusing. When I refused to comply with his bewildering suggestions he flew into a rage, suddenly opened the bottom drawer of his wardrobe and brought out an ornamental dagger. I made a dash for the door but, unbelievably, the dagger arrived there first; it had whizzed past my head and, quivering, was pinned to the door, as in a Western!

'Look!' he hissed through his teeth – it really was as melodramatic as that! Turning I found him, to my horror, brandishing a jewelled scimitar.

'See how sharp it is!' he snarled, and with one swipe slashed off the corner of the wardrobe. He then advanced on me, pinning me with his body against the door. I let out a frantic yell which was fortunately heard by my Housemaster's wife whose quarters were on that landing.

'Who is it? What's the matter?' she called.

Immediately Ghazi withdrew and Betty Bradshaw burst in. Ghazi, who always had great respect for her, quickly retreated, hanging his head, the scimitar dropped to his side.

'G-ghazi!' said Mrs B., who had a very bad stammer. 'G-ghazi! What on earth d-do you think you're d-doing? How d-dare you b-bring out that horrible weapon?'

Ghazi looked suitably shamefaced and mumbled an apology.

'You must p-pray to Allah f-for f-forgiveness,' Mrs B. continued, 'n-now, I insist.'

But that was the trouble, Ghazi explained. He could not pray, and he had not been able to pray since returning to school – he had mislaid his prayer mat.

'Then you m-must g-get a new one,' said the ever practical Mrs B.

'How?' asked Ghazi sulkily.

'Can't you b-buy one?'

'I suppose so.'

'Do you know where?'

To which, to my surprise, if not Betty Bradshaw's, Ghazi replied immediately: 'Harrods', thus upholding the bold claim that is always made for the famous emporium!

After that alarming experience, I was, not surprisingly, relieved to join my proper house, The Park, where I was as happy for the next four years as I had been at Hawtreys. Indeed, I loved Harrow altogether. Perched on top of its hill, it had a village-like atmosphere which immediately appealed to me, nor did its charm ever diminish. The romantic view from my room across to the lights of London never ceased to enthral me. If for the most part the buildings were of no great architectural importance, they were so full of history and tradition that one could not help but be impressed as, inevitably, one was by the famous songs, which a decade later were to prove such an inspiration to Winston Churchill. Like him, I was soon to know many of them by heart. A few weeks after my arrival at Harrow I found myself on the short list for the soloist in 'Five Hundred Faces', the new boy's song. Though disappointed in one way, I was on the whole relieved that I was not selected. However talented one might be, it must be a desperate ordeal to sing a solo in front of the whole school and as many parents. Nevertheless, it has a hauntingly beautiful tune by John Farmer, composer of most of the best Harrow songs, and some movingly evocative lines:

Five hundred faces and all so strange
Life in front of me, home behind.
I felt like a waif before the wind
Tossed on an ocean of shock and change.

Chorus: Yet the time may come though you scarce know why
When your heart will thrill
At the thought of the Hill
And the day that you come so strange and shy.

and the final Chorus:

Yet the time may come though you scarce know why
When your eyes will fill
At the thought of the Hill
And the wild regret of the last good-bye.

Prophetic enough words for me.

Another favourite verse for me came from 'The Silver Arrow':

Their spirit today is dead, men say –
Dead as their stalwart frames –
Their blood now runs in idler sons
Loving less manly games.
Can this be the truth? Arise, our youth,
Rise in your strength and show
By word and by deed ye are worthy seed
Of your sires who drew the bow.

Prophetic words again. In all there are some sixty songs, the most famous and well loved, not only amongst Harrovians, being 'Forty Years On'.

My four years at Harrow were not particularly distinguished, but left me with a rich legacy of friendships and, I believe, standards, if not, particularly high academic ones. I had passed into a form called, oddly, 'Shell', I have no idea why, immediately below the 'Remove', the form in which those who won scholarships were placed and from which one took the School Certificate. It was in the Remove that I met my Waterloo, yet it may, in retrospect, have proved a blessing in disguise. In those days one could only get one's School Certificate if one gained passes in English, Latin and Mathematics. At the latter I was congenitally hopeless, as I had been at my prep school. I took my School Certificate, on the second occasion gaining seven or eight credits, but never a pass in Maths, so there I stuck. Eventually my Housemaster, Malcolm Venables, 'E.M.V.', realized that it was a ridiculous situation, and from a psychological point of view, could not be doing me any good, sitting down in Remove with boys two years younger than myself – even Maurice, my younger brother, actually being in a form higher – just because I could not achieve a pass in Maths; I was simply marking time, denied the opportunity of progressing at all. Accordingly, E.M.V. arranged with the Headmaster that I should be in a special form – of one. Most of my lessons took place in the private study of my Housemaster, who quickly implanted in me his own enthusiasm for literature, in particular for Shakespeare. As a result, in my next attempt to get my School Certificate, I managed to collect 98 per cent in Julius Caesar, that year's Certificate play, but still failed in Maths!

Venables was not universally popular at first, perhaps because he was an idealist who took his job very much more seriously than his predecessor, Bernard Middleditch, 'B. Mid', a dear, old-fashioned Housemaster whom everybody loved, including parents. At the end of my first term in the Park he wrote in my report '*Un peu distrait*. So looking forward to seeing you shooting at Pendley next Saturday.' The French meant less than nothing to my father, but the remainder of the report endeared him to him for ever. B. Mid was keener on games than E.M.V., though, due more to the boys, in particular Charles Laborde, who later became Housemaster of the Park himself – and captained rugger at Cambridge – and Roger Pulbrook, a first-class cricketer and rackets player, games had once again, before I left, become very important.

I managed to get a trial for the School Rugger XV, but never achieved my 'Lion', having to content myself as scrum half for two years with the second XV. It was, however, in athletics that I was the most successful, representing the school for four years, in Cross-Country, the Mile and the High Hurdles. The reason for my success in athletics was almost entirely due to the fact that from my earliest childhood I had suffered from a form of dermatitis which reacted to anything in the least irritating coming into contact with my very sensitive skin. I have always been given to believe that I have one skin less than is normal. My mother used to warn me never to expect any sympathy when I was ill as my ruddy complexion would always disguise it as, over the years, has proved to be no less than the truth. This wretched and often extremely painful condition was always worse in the spring and summer – I remember having to have both arms in slings for my last Eton and Harrow match at Lord's – which meant that it was virtually impossible for me to wear football stockings in the Easter term. This, frankly, did not greatly worry me, as I always disliked Harrow football, a hybrid game that was neither one thing nor the other. In particular it enabled me to spend most afternoons on the track, thus gaining a considerable advantage over others. In 1932 I broke the then record for the mile at Harrow which resulted in my starting favourite for the Public Schools Mile at the White City. From the gun a little chap in black shorts, wearing big, black glasses, set off in front at a pace which seemed to me absurd. It was so obvious that he would run himself out that I did not trouble to go after him. In the third lap I decided that I had better cut him back, but he just went farther and farther away, finally winning by a distance. It was not, perhaps, altogether surprising as he turned out to be Sydney Wooderson, who was later to hold the world record! Eventually I finished a moderate fourth.

The only other sphere in which I scored any success, also largely by chance, was acting. I had no real interest in acting even after I had been selected to play Calpurnia in the Speech Day production of scenes from *Julius Caesar*. The Caesar was Terence Rattigan, for whom my first year I had been 'on boy' – fagged. Although older than me, we had always been friendly, not in any undesirable way as would probably now be assumed. His intellect and obvious literary ability were something of an inspiration to me. It was he who had suggested the idea behind 'Tranquillity', the poem quoted in the last chapter, and it was also he who proposed me for Calpurnia, which inevitably led to a good deal of good-natured teasing. A year or so ago when he was packing up his Albany flat before leaving to live – and die – in Bermuda, he came across a photograph of Caesar and Calpurnia and sent me a copy. His Caesar, as I remember it, was aloof, authoritative, beautifully spoken. (My Calpurnia was reduced to just one line: 'Here, my lord!') But even then it was writing rather than acting that was important to him. I can remember to this day a short story he wrote for the school magazine, *The Harrovian*, entitled 'The Laughter of the Gods', a brilliantly told story about trapeze artists.

His other love was cricket, indirectly responsible for what was probably the saddest moment of his school career. A week before the Eton and Harrow match he called for me, his fag, and asked me to send a telegram. He was weeping which, understandably, embarrassed me. 'You had better read it,' he said. It was a telegram to his father, who was a cricket idolator, telling him that he had been dropped from the XI: for two years he had opened the innings against Eton with Victor, now Lord, Rothschild. He was quite broken-hearted and appeared to me to be glad to leave Harrow a fortnight later. In November 1936, he sent me tickets for the first night of *French Without Tears*. It had a sensational success, with Rex Harrison, Trevor Howard, Robert Flemyng, Kay Hammond, Guy

Middleton and Roland Culver, all then unknown. Sitting immediately in front of me was that doyen of between-the-wars critics, James Agate, who left after the first act. In his criticism the following Sunday he damned the play outright, saying that he no more understood such rubbish than his cat understood Thucydides, but judging by the laughter behind him – me? – he guaranteed that the play would run for a year, and it did.

It was two years after my appearance as Calpurnia that someone suggested that Harrow should have a dramatic society, which up to that time it had never had. A group was formed, and Drinkwater's *Abraham Lincoln* was selected as the play. Quite unexpectedly, as I was not even a member of the society, I was invited to audition for the title role, probably because I had a big nose. To my surprise I won the part. Drinkwater's play is very fine but, somewhat wordy, yet tightly constructed, presenting a considerable challenge for a school production. There is little doubt that we could never have managed such a play had it not been for our inspired producer, an eccentric but extremely talented retired actress, Marjorie James. She literally produced the play line by line, gesture by gesture. It is in six quite lengthy but very effective episodes, Lincoln himself having no less than 1500 lines; nearly as many as Hamlet, which has 1530 lines. To learn such a huge part was tremendously demanding, especially at the beginning when in many instances I barely understood what I was learning – 'if the South insists on the right to secede it will mean resistance inexorable' – language at that time quite alien to me; nor had I ever before tried to memorize long speeches. Once I found the knack of it, I learnt much more quickly. The whole of the last scene, one very long speech – 'Government of the people, by the people, for the people shall not perish from this earth' – was learnt in a coach on the way home from a school rugger match.

For some reason, from the very beginning the production stimulated a great deal of interest, all tickets for its week's run being sold well in advance. Right up to the dress rehearsal I had not the least idea whether the play would be a success or a failure. I knew that thanks to Marjorie James I was completely word and gesture perfect, but how a school audience would take it I had no idea, even how they would react to my make-up. This took over an hour in the hands of 'Bert', the famous wig-maker, a magnificent artificial nose, flatteringly considered necessary, being the highlight.

It was a simple, straightforward but brilliant production, helped by some exceptionally talented young actors. Particularly outstanding was John Profumo, who played the second lead. He was a great friend of mine, one of the most charming and amusing people I have ever met. On one occasion when our form had a temporary master he pretended, with his Italian-sounding name, to be a foreigner who spoke only broken English. The last laugh, however, was against him. The Headmaster, the extremely impressive Dr Cyril Norwood, stopped him in the High Street one day and spoke to him, John Profumo replying in perfect English.

'But I understood that you could not speak English properly,' observed the H.M. ominously.

'Er, well, sir . . .' stammered Profumo.

'Well, sir,' the Headmaster interrupted, 'you will speak your broken English for the rest of the term, and if ever you are heard not speaking broken English on any occasion, then you will be asked to leave.'

An even unhappier result of this episode came at the end of term. On the last day Jack and I went up to the unfortunate master to present him with, on behalf of the form, a gold pencil. As we approached him he yelled at us to sit down, expecting some prank, but we persisted, placing the pencil on his desk. For once there was silence, then very quietly he said, 'I would have preferred your decent behaviour,' and walked out, leaving the gold pencil on the desk and us speechless and humiliated; since when I for one have tried never to carry teasing too far.

Perhaps the most effective scene in *Abraham Lincoln* is the episode in which a young widow calls on Lincoln and pleads with him to stop the war. There was a problem in casting this role until I remembered a boy who had been persuaded to play a small 'female' role in a house production the previous term. He was a young friend of my brother's, but when I had approached him he had not been at all willing, thinking that to play a female role was effeminate, suspecting perhaps that it was his pink and white complexion that had made me think him suitable. Being two years older I was able to bring a certain pressure to bear and eventually, somewhat reluctantly, he agreed. As he had made quite an impression in the house play it was logical that I should propose him for the part of the young widow in *Abraham Lincoln*. For a sixteen-year-old boy he gave a performance of remarkable sensitivity which was greatly admired and resulted in his taking up the theatre professionally. His name was Michael Denison. In 1977 I contributed to his *This is Your Life* programme, in which he suggested that it was I who was entirely responsible for his going on stage.

The complete hush at the end of this moving scene half way through the play – it was at least twenty seconds before the applause broke out – was convincing evidence that the play was a success. The end confirmed it. Lincoln makes his great Gettysburg speech – transferred by Drinkwater to the last episode of the play – in a box at the theatre. It is his hour of triumph. While the stage audience can still be heard cheering and applauding the fanatical out-of-work actor, Wilkes Booth, creeps up to the box, opens the door and shoots him. After a few moments of pandemonium Stanton, his Minister of War (Jack Profumo), comes slowly from the box. Obviously stricken, but still with dignity he speaks: 'Now he belongs to the ages', the final line of the play. As the curtain fell there was complete silence. It seemed to last minutes. Then suddenly there was a crash of applause. As the curtain rose again the whole audience was on its feet. The applause went on and on and on. For schoolboys it was an unforgettable and overwhelming experience to be part of a smash hit, something that few enough professional actors are privileged to enjoy.

Even *The Times* was adulatory: 'They possessed the talent necessary to bring a great undertaking to a successful close. The three actors who stood out above the rest were J. D. Profumo, who in the person of Stanton brought some delightful comic relief to a grave Cabinet meeting; W. Morris, who gave the negro, Douglas, an irresistible grin and naïve pathos; and lastly Dorian Williams, who dominated the stage, as he was meant to, with a gruff kindliness and a dignified earnestness which made the audience share with him his great burden. Michael Denison as Mrs Otherly brought pathos and restraint which contrasted well with T. G. H. Asher's Mrs Blow.' The *Daily Telegraph*, too, was complimentary: 'his clever and sympathetic portrayal of the "Last of the Kings" was the result of much thought and study' – and much midnight oil! – 'he had a bearing and presence comparable with that of George Arliss's study of Disraeli' – who also had a big nose! The *Harrovian* was almost euphoric, with a special mention of Lincoln's remarkable clearness of diction. 'The School Dramatic Society has established itself firmly and favourably in the eyes of all.' The producer, deservedly, received the most praise of all.

For the rest of the term the production of *Abraham Lincoln* was the talk of the school. The Headmaster even preached a sermon on the 'last of the Kings' in Chapel, not a little to my embarrassment. Even today I meet people who tell me they remember that production. It was certainly the highlight of my school career, though at the time it seemed just as important, if not more so, to do well in the School Sports which followed almost immediately.

Encouraged by the H.M.'s sermon and the fact that my great friend, John Wyld, was in Dr Norwood's Classical Sixth, we decided to invite him and his wife to Sunday breakfast. Entertaining at breakfast was a Harrow tradition, but at that time at any rate to invite the

Headmaster was unheard of. To our surprise and delight they accepted, appearing fully to enjoy the magnificent breakfast of grapefruit, cereal, eggs, sausages, tomatoes, bacon, coffee, toast and marmalade which we provided at the cost of 16*s* 6*d* for four! Indeed the breakfast party was so congenial that we were almost late for Chapel.

Though so happy at Harrow, one could not help resenting the time that a boarding school kept one away from home. I remember thinking, as a boy, that it would be much better just to have two long terms and two long holidays. The Christmas and Easter holidays, in particular, seemed far too short. Eight weeks in the summer was not quite so unsatisfactory except that most of our friends went away for their holiday while, as explained earlier, we never did, there always being so much to do at home. At Christmas and Easter the end of the holidays always came far too soon, seeming to cut short the busy and satisfying social life that we were all the time developing in the Greens Norton area. Never in any sense a clique, there was nevertheless a large group of us who, with similar interests, tended to spend much time together. Our closest young neighbours included the Courages at Edgcote, where now the crippled Edward trains so successfully; the Close-Smiths at Boycott, their grandmother, the Countess of Kinloss, being the last person to live privately at Stowe, now the famous public school; the Prices at Akeley, now a preparatory school; the Beales at Potterspury, also a school now – Billy, or Sir William as he is today, is a fellow M.F.H., of the Tedworth; the Wakes at Courteenhall where the distinguished Sir Hereward presided over a large and very attractive family: Diane, the most attractive, was later killed in a point-to-point; Mary is married to James Weatherby; Daisy, the mother, looked young enough and pretty enough to be the eldest daughter.

We were very friendly too with Janet and Gay, the daughters of David Margesson, Conservative Chief Whip, later a Minister. Gay married Sir Martin Charteris, recently elected a Life Peer, Private Secretary to the Queen. The Hillingdons, Pelly and Ursula, were naturally very close, their father being Master of the Grafton for most of our childhood. Our nearest friends were the Hoskins. The father was Rector of Greens Norton and idolized my father; Betty, or Boskie as we called her, was my sister's best friend, while Paul, the elder brother, was later, as will be seen, to have a great influence on my life. At that time we shared an interest in athletics, hunting and racing. A somewhat distant cousin, George Rodwell, became almost a part of the family, spending so much time at Greens Norton that he had his own room – and his own horse – repayment for all the kindness I had received from his parents, who lived at Harrow. After the war he was, for a short time, a joint Master of the Warwickshire. If it all sounds somewhat exclusive, one has to admit that in its way it was, social barriers in those days being much more rigid. One has to remember, though, that hunting, and in particular the Pony Club, was bringing young people of all backgrounds together in a way that would have been unheard of before the First World War when there was, of course, no Pony Club and children were not seriously encouraged to hunt. It is, in fact, true to say that in the late twenties and early thirties a minor social revolution was taking place.

Apart from the hunting, so much that we did in the holidays in those days we all did together: parties, Pony Club rallies, dances, terribly 'with it' cocktail parties; tennis – no hard courts then, yet we always seemed to be playing, which suggests that those summers of our childhood must have been as good as one has always imagined. Nor were there any swimming pools, but there was plenty of bathing in the river or canal. Car treasure hunts were particularly popular and, as I have already suggested, visits to the old Northampton Rep, or occasionally the New Theatre at Oxford for musicals; even more occasionally, but the greatest treat for me, Stratford-on-Avon for Shakespeare with Randle Ayrton and Giles Isham.

We were fortunate, too, in that people much older than ourselves frequently went out of their way to be kind to us. Ted Lyon, mentioned earlier, always loved young people around, entertaining in a cleverly off-beat way in his, to us exotic, man-about-townish flat above the Butchers Arms on the green at Greens Norton. He shared it with his artist friend, Humphrey Dixon. As he was, in addition to his other qualities, a brilliant pianist they created a fascinating environment for youngsters such as ourselves, making us feel grown up and sophisticated.

The remarkable Atkinson family, too, was wonderful with the young, though in quite a different way. They lived in a beautiful house called Cosgrove Priory. The two sisters, Mary and Guné, never married, their brother Philip only late in life, long after we had left Greens Norton. The 'gals' as they were known, though approaching their fifties – 'Mighty' and 'Kid' to each other – seemed to live for children, giving wonderful parties at Cosgrove, entering into all the fun and games as though they were our age. The Grafton Hunt was their world. They never missed a day, though frequently they had to ride twenty miles to meet, possibly even further home. Guné was one of the first women to hunt astride – she wore a long split skirt concealing her breeches! She also had an exceptionally beautiful singing voice and used to give recitals accompanied by her very old mother on a harp, which we found a bit spooky.

From time to time as we grew older in that brief, serene period of our lives there were smarter occasions, an invitation to Henley, Ascot even, the Fourth of June at Eton: for ourselves of course, the Eton and Harrow match at Lords – an adult social scene that we were diffidently yet complacently entering, unaware that it was the end of an era. But for the most part it was one long, carefree merry-go-round of simple pleasures – gaiety, laughter, fun, and love. Yes, love, but wonderfully innocent. Billy loved Barbara, as did Paul; Richard loved Venice; I loved Diane and Gay; Pelly loved me; Ursula loved Maurice, as did everyone, just as they all loved George.

Being in our late teens we should, doubtless, have been much more concerned with world affairs, less concerned with our own enjoyment. Reprehensible, no doubt, but we found the grown-ups' talk of budgets and New Deals, Snowden and Macdonald, Roosevelt and Montague Norman, and Maynard Keynes utterly boring. We seldom read the newspapers, other than the *Morning Post* which, with *The Times*, carried daily hunting reports, having by now grown out of the *Daily Graphic*'s 'Tailwaggers'. Our unconsciously escapist attitude to everything that was happening anywhere except in our own little world left us quite unprepared for the shocks that lay ahead. As far as my own family was concerned they came in two phases, the first involving my home life which for more than twelve years had given me such security. We had spent New Year's Eve at a lovely but quite informal party at the Beales' at Potterspury Lodge. Although it was very wet, we had had a marvellous day's hunting, which I remember particularly because it was one of the first days on which I had ridden Tollgate. This horse, standing just under 16 h.h., had been bought by my father as a two year old with the express purpose of providing me with a point-to-pointer. A bright bay, it was one of the most attractive horses that I have ever known, as quick as mercury, a brilliant performer, and with a most lovable personality. It was now five years old, and for me to be hunting him was quite an advance after Tinker, which had carried me so well since I had been promoted three or four years earlier from Freckles. (Oddly enough, in my father's diary for that day he writes, in brackets: 'Dorian going very well indeed on Tollgate,' the only time so far as I can discover that he ever mentioned a member of his family in his diary.)

Feeling well pleased with myself that evening – in a new dinner jacket to boot! – I had a particularly enjoyable and, as I thought, successful evening. I was really sorry when it all came to an end and we had to drive home in our old bull-nosed Morris, my poor brother being relegated, huddled under a rug, to the dicky! Once home we warmed ourselves in front of the stove in the hall and went to bed well-contented.

Next morning we exercised our horses at the usual time, no allowance being made for our having had a late night. We did the regular round – Caswell, Foxley, Blakesley, Bradden. Even the day after hunting my father never expected the horses to do less than five or six miles on the road. Jogging along, we pointed out places that on one occasion or another we had jumped, picked out possible places for the future, generally imagining a hunting situation, as was our invariable practice.

As it was wet again in the afternoon we decided to play Mah Jong. Halfway through our game my father entered the drawing-room, somewhat cursorily dismissing us to the school-room. We were not best pleased, but in those days it never occurred to children to question their parents' orders. My mother had recently had her bad hunting accident, so was reclining on the sofa. We left my father alone with her. Half an hour later we heard him calling us. Not a little disgruntled, we went downstairs. My father never, or very rarely, showed his emotions, but my mother looked decidedly distressed. We felt a little embarrassed. Almost as soon as we had entered the room my father started speaking. It was obvious from the way he spoke that he too was upset.

'We thought that you had better know at once,' he said. 'I'm giving up the hounds. This is my last season.'

We gasped, speechless. It was as unbelievable as it was unexpected.

'No!' I stammered. 'Giving up? but everything is going so marvellously.' It was a fact that the Grafton was having one of the best seasons ever – to quote from my father's diary: 'The best season for many years: compares favourably with any pack in England.'

He then explained, haltingly, that it had all cost much more than he had anticipated. Arthur Guinness was not prepared to put up any more money, and Lord Hillingdon had been persuaded to take over again.

One did not, of course, appreciate it at the time, but there may well have been more to it than my father was prepared to admit to. 'Bear' Hillingdon had enjoyed enormous popularity, whereas my father's somewhat revolutionary efficiency obviously did not go down well with everybody, especially, I imagine, the old guard which exists in every hunt, which always has and always will, exert great influence. More, there could well, almost unbelievably, have been a social implication. There was in the countryside at this time a last, almost despairing, effort to retain the old order. Masters of Hounds should be great landowners, preferably titled, ideally belonging to old aristocratic families, as they always had been. Our neighbouring Hunts were still fortunate in having Lord Willoughby de Broke as Master of the Warwickshire, Lord Chesham as Master of the Bicester, Lord Rosebery as Master of the Whaddon Chase, Colonel Jack Lowther, the immensely successful Master of the Pytchley married to the daughter of his eminent predecessor. Lord Annaly. Was it not more fitting, however able a retired cavalry officer might be, that the Master of the Grafton should be Lord Hillingdon, as it had been so happily ever since the war? Previously it had been the Dukes of Grafton or their kinsmen who had held office. Years later members of old Grafton families confessed to me that there had been this feeling.

Indeed, similar situations were being experienced all over the country, but that this clinging to the past was a last despairing gesture is shown by the fact that in that final decade before the war many of the most famous packs of hounds in England found that they could only survive with an injection of money from *nouveaux riches* who now, for the first time, were not just content to contribute anonymously, but insisted on donning the velvet cap, the traditional badge of office. This was, perhaps, the biggest revolution in the world of foxhunting since the formation of subscription packs a hundred years earlier, a development which had enabled many of the great family packs to survive then. The new arrangements did not by any means always work harmoniously. As with the first subscription packs there were frequently clashes between those who paid the piper and those who liked to call the tune. A happy exception was the Grafton where, somewhat ironically, my father persuaded the charming old George Beale, of Greens Stores, now living at Potterspury, to become 'Bear' Hillingdon's Joint-Master and Paymaster.

There was concrete evidence of this attitude suggested above, unspoken though probably fully appreciated by both my father and his Joint-Master Arthur Guinness, at the Annual General Meeting a few weeks later. After the Treasurer had presented the accounts, the Chairman's announcement that Lord Hillingdon was returning as Master was greeted with enthusiasm amounting almost to euphoria. The Chairman then declared the meeting closed. Everybody rose to leave, chatting happily as they made their way to the exit. Suddenly an old lady, Mrs Barnard from Duncote, who had just celebrated her fiftieth season hunting with the Grafton, stood up and called out in a voice, shaking with emotion: 'Please, ladies and gentlemen! As it appears that no one else intends to do so, may I ask you to record a vote of thanks to our retiring Joint-Masters. In fifty years I have never enjoyed better sport or known the hunt in a healthier condition.'

There was a moment's embarrassed silence, then a murmur of 'hear hears'. The Chairman hesitant and embarrassed, made a formal proposal which produced raised hands and more 'hear hears', as the assembly hurried out.

'Bear' Hillingdon was the kindest, most genuine person that ever was, and devoted to my father; indeed knew the debt that he owed to him. He telephoned that evening: 'Can you ever forgive me?' he asked, and apparently broke down. It was one of the rare occasions on which I ever saw my father allow himself really to show his feelings; he had been very hurt.

His last day as Master was on 4 April, deliberately delayed to allow us to be home from school. The meet was at Greens Norton, and my father's report was characteristically factual: 'To finish the season. A very large crowd out. Found at Kingthorne and hounds ran very fast to the Delph, right-handed to Abthorpe, then with Silverstone on the right to Seven Copses and back to kill him in the open below Whittlebury. Thirty-eight minutes of the very best.' And the very best had come to an end. For us it appeared to be the end of a way of life. In a perhaps unconscious tribute to the retiring régime everyone was there, all superbly turned-out. The great cavalcade as it swept from Kingthorne was an unforgettable sight; more accurately an unforgettable experience of which to be a part. The odd thing is that I have no recollection of it being an ordeal for a child to be a part of such a vast, hard-riding concourse. This, doubtless, was partly due to the fact that in those days of wire-free, beautifully trimmed stake and bound fences, it was possible to jump anything between fifty and a hundred abreast, and there was little queueing.

Because it was almost socially obligatory to go hunting in a hunting country in those days, the field was very quickly reduced in size as large numbers having put in an appearance made for home at the earliest opportunity, leaving a field of manageable proportions. If one were lucky enough, even as a child to be mounted on an animal as bold and brilliant as Tinker or Tollgate, one was not for long worried by the crowd. But one young man could still be worrying today, if still alive, after his experience at the famous Battle of Padbury on 10 January 1932, when the Whaddon Chase and the Grafton held a joint meet. As the huge field surged down towards the little hunting gate at the corner of Padbury Gorse – it is still there – this young man, quite out of control, charged between the two Field Masters, Lord Rosebery and my father. In so doing he wrenched off one of the former's stirrup leathers, which was then trampled on by some five hundred horsemen. I doubt if it was ever seen again! Nor, at least for a long time, was the young man. It was not, thank goodness, myself, though it might well have been, for Tollgate, especially at the beginning of a hunt, was just about as much as I could manage.

By now my father had made it quite clear that he was not only giving up the Mastership, but he was giving up hunting altogether. He implied that this was because of the deteriorating health of my mother who had been advised a warmer climate, but one knows in retrospect that the real problem was financial. In his three seasons as Master he had spent very lavishly – only the best in such circumstances was good enough for my father, who in any case must have been aware of the feeling that a mere 'commoner' would never be able to do things in the style of His Lordship. He had been living far beyond his means for some time, probably ever since he had taken up showing in a big way and started his stud with some seven mares in the mid-twenties. The situation had been aggravated by the fact that when he inherited from his uncle in 1922, he found that he not only had to maintain his aunt at Pendley during her life time, but that he also had to provide her with an income of £5000 p.a. *tax free*. His inheritance was, in fact, of little benefit to him, though he did not fully appreciate this until circumstances forced him to.

His announcement that he was selling all the horses came as a fearful shock to us. At the time it seemed appallingly callous, though, looking back one realizes what an almost unbearable decision it must have been for him. Apart from the hurt to his pride, he had a deep and genuine love for his horses, particularly those he had bred himself. To sell the hunt horses was bad enough, but to sell all our own horses! The Judge, one of the finest horses my father had ever hunted; the famous Wait and See, twice champion at Olympia; my mother's Nanette; Miss B, the first horse that my father ever bred, my sister's Whitwell, my own Tinker and Tollgate and our darling old Freckles. It was unthinkable, too terrible even to contemplate. Freckles, in fact, was mercifully put down: but the others – ! We were distraught, yet, unbelievably, worse was to follow. Ossa on Pelion indeed!

How we heard the news I cannot now remember; we were probably so shocked that the details became blurred. My father had reached the irrevocable decision to sell Greens Norton, and further, to live abroad with my mother and sister, just leaving my brother and me at school in England. The crash and crisis of the thirties had now well and truly overtaken us. Thousands of others, doubtless, were finding themselves in situations similar to or much worse than ours, but others' misfortunes, sadly, mean little to teenagers. We were concerned only with the loss of our home and everything that we loved. How long it took to sell Greens Norton I do not know. It went eventually for a little over £3000. This lovely home that had given us a hundred thousand pounds' worth of happiness: the two model stable yards by themselves worth that alone, surely; the twelve acres of gardens, the paddocks, the perfectly laid out cinder *manège*, which had done so much to make my father's reputation. Presumably my father, like so many others, had had to accept what he could get.

Being by nature emotional – frequently the National Anthem brings a lump to my throat – I have attempted always to be undemonstrative, anxious not to betray my feelings. I was horrified, therefore, when shortly before getting into the car to depart for my last term at Harrow – and to leave, of course, for the last time our beloved Greens Norton – my father called out: 'Aren't you going to say goodbye to your horses?' This above all was what I had dreaded. I try, in life, never to look back, rather to accept the inevitable, thus so fully involving myself in the present and the future that anything of the past that is painful or best forgotten is obliterated. This was my philosophy even as a boy. But now I could not practise it; there was no escape. I went back through the house to the yard. One is more distressed at crying at the age of seventeen than at any other time in one's life: children cry, men control themselves; at seventeen one plays at being a man but one has the frailty of a child. How could one possibly control oneself? Mercifully I was on my own.

Tinker was at the back of her box when I called her. She came languidly forward, and momentarily I fondled her grey, friendly, almost white face. In reply she nodded her head repeatedly, nibbled at my fingers. Tollgate as always had his head over the stable door, intelligent, alert, and ready for anything. He greeted me with a soft murmur and licked the palm of my hand. I stroked him, patted him, kissed him gently on the nose, then walked away. He watched me, head high, ears pricked, waiting, and whinnied quietly. His look as I left the yard haunted me for years to come: even now as I write. . . Tollgate was sold for 50 gns to a stupid woman who, understandably, fell in love with him at first sight. Run away with the first time she rode him, he crashed into an iron gate, breaking both forelegs. Tinker at the sale at Leicester made 41 gns. Even the legendary Wait and See, sold as a brood mare, fetched only 200 gns; her yearling colt by a first-class stallion, The Vizier, made 43 gns. The Judge, my father's most brilliant hunter, 100 gns. The total for thirty-four horses, including young stock, came to £3800. The thirty hunt horses which had cost, initially, £2000 fared minimally better going for £3500 – an interesting comment on the value of horseflesh in the thirties, remembering, of course, the slump. Today it is not unusual for a single top class hunter to be sold for as much as my father sold the whole of his stud, or his home.

I returned to Harrow for my last term. There I was soon so busy that there was little time for moping. There were the house plays; there was the training on the track, not only for the School Sports, but for the Public School Meeting at the White City; there were the responsibilities of being a House Monitor and a member of the 'Phil' (Philathletic Club, the Harrow equivalent to Eton's 'Pop'). Time permitting I was half falling in love with one of my Housemaster's very attractive daughters, and, time permitting again, I was still struggling with my Maths for the elusive School Certificate. It was only at the very end of the term that my precarious situation began to dawn on me. Harrow, for so long my alma mater, I was now leaving behind: I had no home, my parents were abroad. Apart from the two weeks when I was joining them at Lisbon, I had little idea of what lay ahead. My future was totally obscure.

The last day: speech room, Chapel, songs, goodbyes, the usual exchanging of leaving photographs, a forced gaiety, a final late night session with a few of my closest friends. I had deliberately ordered my taxi for 9.30, by which time most of the boys would have departed, thus sparing me the awful finality of 'the wild regret of the last goodbye'. I now found myself alone on the pavement, waiting, a little self-conscious in my new Old Harrovian tie, for my taxi – and what? Suddenly I realized that everything that had ever meant anything to me now lay behind me, that I was on my own:

> Forty years on, when afar and asunder
> Parted are those who are singing today,
> When you look back and forgetfully wonder
> What you were like in your work and your play,
> Then, it may be, there will often come o'er you
> Glimpses of notes like the catch of a song –
> Visions of boyhood will float then before you,
> Echoes of dreamland shall bear them along.
>
> Oh the great days in the distance enchanted
> Days of fresh air in the wind and the sun,
> How we rejoiced as we struggled and panted –
> Hardly believable, forty years on!

Visions of boyhood – the distance enchanted! Lost and confused, with a gnawing sense of anticlimax after the hectic end-of-term whirl I felt bewildered, suddenly unsure of myself. Forty years on! – I could scarcely imagine forty days on. Had I realized that it was to be some twelve years before I was once more sure of myself I would have felt even more insecure.

Chapter 4

Pendley Manor

The twelve long, shifting, indeterminate years ended, less by design than by force of circumstances, even luck, at Pendley Manor, my old family home. It was 1 November 1945. 1 November is traditionally the day associated with the Opening Meet of a new season's foxhunting, but on that glorious autumn morning as I walked in the grounds at Pendley my thoughts were in no way connected with hunting and horses. It was not the Opening Meet that I was thinking of, but the opening of Pendley Manor as a Centre of Adult Education, for in a simple but effective ceremony the previous afternoon Pendley had been officially opened as the first Residential Centre of Adult Education of its kind in the country.

How was it different from other Adult Education Centres? What, in fact, was Pendley? The original Pendley Manor is mentioned in Domesday. William the Conqueror, who was offered the crown of England in 1066 at Berkhamsted, confiscated it from Edeva, a Nun who then inhabited it, giving it to his brother-in-law, Earl Moreton, who was his treasurer. For five hundred years it remained the property of the King's treasurer, then a hereditary position; but due to female inheritance it passed first to the Whittington family, then to the Verneys, finally to the Andersons and Harcourts. Sir Simon Harcourt, disturbed by the construction of the railway and canal, abandoned Pendley at the beginning of the nineteenth century, leaving it deserted and crumbling until it was destroyed by fire in 1835. The estate was then absorbed into the neighbouring Tring Park estate, which comprised a delightful Christopher Wren house and some four thousand acres leased from the Crown by my great-great-grandfather, Joseph Grout. My Dutch ancestors, then named Grout (de Groot), had originally arrived in England in the sixteenth century, being granted a coat of arms by Henry VIII. My own branch of the family probably arrived later as there is evidence that their wealth still came from Dutch crêpe at the beginning of the nineteenth century, as well as from coal in South Wales. It was in 1838 that their coat of arms was granted, identical to the original but with the addition of a crest and a motto, 'ingenio et meritu'.

Greatly attracted by the English sporting way of life the family settled happily at Tring, doubtless intending to stay there permanently. In the late 1860s, however, Tring Park, which up till then still belonged to the Crown, was put on the market and sold to the Rothschilds, who easily outbid my predecessors in their anxiety to have a mansion in the same part of the country as their other great houses, Halton, Waddesdon, Aston Clinton, Ascott, Mentmore. I still possess a book, however, in which are entered the subscriptions made by the Tring trades-people towards a fund opened in an effort to raise the difference between my great-grandfather's bid and that of the Rothschilds. Predictably the few hundred pounds guaranteed was totally inadequate, and so Tring Park passed to the Rothschilds. Sensitive to the local feeling, however, the Rothschilds agreed to sell the original Pendley estate at a very reasonable price to my great-grandfather, the Reverend James Williams, who had by this time been naturalized and taken his Welsh wife's name, and who before the death of his father, Joseph Grout had, interestingly, been curate at Patishall where for many years the Grafton point-to-point was held. An old Tring resident, Arthur Macdonald, once told me, shortly after Pendley had been opened as a Centre of Education, that he remembered the Reverend James showing him, as a boy of ten, just where he was going to build the new Manor. Unfortunately, though comparatively young, James died almost before the building had started. His twenty-two-year-old son, my great-uncle Joe, inherited the estate, living – and becoming engaged to be married -- at Chequers while the house was being built and the park and gardens laid out, at the same time buying for his younger brother, Stanley, my grandfather, Brooksby Hall in Leicestershire, now an Agricultural College.

As already described, Stanley, my father's father, died, again comparatively young, with the result that his children were brought up at Pendley with Uncle Joe and Aunt Katy. Uncle Joe, who was greatly respected locally, being a J.P., High Sheriff and County Alderman, but who turned down a peerage because it was offered to him by a Liberal Prime Minister, was also, as a member of the Rothschild Staghounds Committee, one of the founders of the Whaddon Chase Hunt as it exists today. Originally the southern half of what is now the Whaddon Chase had been hunted by the Rothschild Staghounds, the northern half, on loan from the Grafton, being hunted by the Selby Lowndes family. When the Rothschilds realized that hunting the fox was considered more acceptable in fashionable circles than hunting the carted stag they converted their pack to fox hounds with Lord

Dalmeny, later Lord Rosebery, as Master. This led to the famous and best-forgotten row after the Second World War when two packs of hounds hunted the same country. It was resolved by both Lord Dalmeny, as he then still was, and Colonel William Selby Lowndes resigning, the Mastership being taken over by Lord Orkney. But in 1923 Dalmeny returned as Master, and Colonel Selby Lowndes became Chairman shortly afterwards. Thus it is that I have a long family connection with the Whaddon Chase.

Uncle Joe died in 1923, but his widow lived on, in considerable style, until her death at the age of ninety-two in 1943. By my great-uncle's will she was entitled to live in the house for as long as she wished, though apparently he had never expected her to do so, certainly not for twenty years, making it quite impractical for my parents ever to live there, though it is doubtful whether they would ever have wished to. To begin with, with nearly a hundred rooms and grounds and gardens requiring eight gardeners, it was far too big. In addition, my father, whose boyhood associations had never been very happy, had little affection for Pendley, while my mother had always disliked it, finding it all far too formal compared with her own simple, unsophisticated home at Aldbury. I, on the other hand, despite the fact that childhood visits had always been something of an ordeal, had always loved Pendley. The trees, the spaciousness, the panelling, the lofty ceilings, the great fireplaces, all appealed to me, as did the dignity of the front hall with its magnificent staircase, the library with the endless shelves of leatherbound books, the huge billiard table and the solemn, hushed atmosphere. Best of all I liked the long carriage drives with the walks leading off through the woods, the beautifully laid out park with its magnificent avenues of oaks and beeches and brilliant clumps of copper-beeches.

Pendley had always impressed me, even as a child. It impressed me even more when I returned to it grown up. I am not quite sure why, but more so than any other member of the family I managed to establish an easy relationship with the somewhat intimidating Aunt Katy, who seemed genuinely to welcome my visits. Towards the end of her life I even had my own room there and used the old school-room, with its cases of guns and its hunting prints, as my own study. It was at this time that I came to appreciate the marvellous peace of Pendley. Perhaps it was our mutual appreciation of the beauty and peace of Pendley that drew us close together. During the war, while scarcely disturbing Aunt Katy in the main rooms, the Land Army, for whom the house had been requisitioned, could not have treated the house with greater respect. And at Government expense they did much to convert the house, dividing the rooms, putting in bathrooms and so on, so that it could, after the war, easily be adapted to some sort of institution – a residential centre of adult education, for instance.

Strangely enough it was not this material fact that influenced me in turning Pendley into a centre of education. Much, much more it was the environment and atmosphere. It may have been the contrast between Pendley and war-time London with its black-outs and bombs and wailing sirens that made me find Pendley so inspiring on my war-time visits. Always it 'lifted' me, and I came to believe that others would be similarly 'lifted'. Just to spend a few days in such surroundings and in such an atmosphere, especially when they contrasted so dramatically with London or any other industrial city must surely, I thought, be a kind of spiritual experience, if not an educational one. But I personally was of the opinion that such an experience *was* of educational value, simply because of the impact it made on one's outlook, even one's way of life. This was implicit in the first draft of the aims and objects of Pendley when it came to be written a few years later: 'To establish, in a house attractively equipped and situated, a residential centre of adult education (open also to non-residents) offering interesting courses and lectures of a liberal, educational character taken from as wide a field as possible, all within the scope of the ordinary man and woman.'

But in what way was this really different from other adult education centres? The answer lies in the inclusion of the word 'ordinary'. There had always been ample provision of educational opportunities for those of intellectual persuasion. During the war years I had come to believe that quite ordinary men and women, too, were capable of learning a great deal more, having reached adulthood, and with their own experience of life. More, I was convinced that most people had a latent desire for knowledge, and it was only because they had left school at an early age, going straight to work, that they had come to believe that their learning days were over. They had little desire, certainly, to go back to school. If, however, the opportunity for them to further their knowledge was presented in an informal manner, in a congenial environment and, most important of all, in such a way as to allow them to feel that they were being treated as adults rather than children, then, I believed, their suspicion of adult education, their reluctance to seek further knowledge, other than that which they acquired through normal contacts, might be overcome. My work with Services' education during the latter part of the war had convinced me of the truth of this. I became convinced, too, that there was an additional value in education of this nature being residential. If people were all living together then their opportunity of acquiring knowledge extended far beyond the actual lectures and formal sessions.

In argument and discussion at meals, at the bar, even in their bedrooms, they could be learning as much as from a formal lecture.

Those with a more conservative approach to education were, not surprisingly, sceptical at the idea that anything could be taught in a course lasting only a weekend, three or four days, a week at the most. I, and later my colleagues, looked at it differently. We did not expect to teach people very much, rather to stimulate them, so that they would want to learn more by themselves. Pendley, and places like it – if, as we believed, the idea caught on – would provide an impact which would help them to realize that they were capable of enjoying and learning about subjects which normally they might have thought to be beyond them. New vistas would be opened to them, their horizons extended. Today, of course, all this is taken for granted. Surprisingly it was completely novel in 1945. There had, of course, been colleges running courses of a specific nature such as Ruskin College, the Conservative College at Ashridge, later at Swinton, and the Lamb Guild House in Manchester where a group of people came together regularly to discuss some particular project. There was, too, the Workers' Educational Association which for many years had catered for members of the working class who had either been denied proper educational opportunities or who had the intellect and inclination to go much further than leaving school at thirteen permitted them; but these latter, of course, were of a non-residential nature.

It is doubtful whether I would ever have attempted to put forward these ideas that for a year or two had been fermenting in my mind had not, in 1943, Aunt Katy died. It was obvious that my father and his trustees would waste little time in putting Pendley on the market. Alternatively one or other Government department might requisition it, which would mean that it might be years after the end of the war rather than months before Pendley was released; or that the house would be returned in such a poor condition that it would be a long time before it was habitable. The Land Army were ideal tenants, keeping the house beautifully and unlikely to remain long on the land after the end of the war with the demobbing of the Forces.

It seemed essential, therefore, to stake one's claim, as it were, as early as possible. As will be seen later, there were many factors and a variety of circumstances that eventually led to the founding of Pendley. Suffice it to say here that despite enormous problems, many of which seemed quite insuperable at the time, it did get off the ground, in 1945, remarkably within a few months of the end of the war. That this was possible was largely due to the Director of Education for Hertfordshire, John Newsom, and to such people as Edwin Barker of the Y.M.C.A., William Hazelton of Education Settlements, Harold

Clay, of the Transport and General Workers' union, Dr M. W. Jack and Dr Colin Cooke, of Oxford University, Sir Fred Clarke, of London University, Lady Elliot of Harwood, Miss K. T. Butler, of Girton College, Sir Colin Jardine, the Earl of Verulam and our Member of Parliament, Lady Davidson, all of whom had the perspicacity in their different spheres to appreciate the value of what we were trying to do and were, to the best of their ability prepared to help us. Most helpful of all, of course, were my colleagues Roger Pulbrook and Kenneth Bowden who had joined forces with me when with my usual impetuosity, which on occasion has proved both to my advantage and to my disadvantage, I had suddenly decided, in 1944, to go ahead with the Pendley Plan as we called it. Roger had been a friend of mine at Harrow, and was already involved in adult education; Kenneth was a brilliant if sometimes erratic person interested in the welfare and personnel side of industry and a burning idealist. For a year the three of us had thrown ourselves into the project with unflagging enthusiasm despite the setbacks and disappointments. At last with the assistance of the Chairman of the County War Agricultural Committee, Major 'Mo' Barclay, who was also Master of the Puckeridge Hunt, which helped, we managed to get the Land Army ejected from Pendley on 1 July – my thirty-first birthday – and Pendley was opened just three months later.

John Newsom, later eminent as the author of many important educational reports, and Douglas Cooke, the Buckinghamshire Educational officer, persuaded the great Sir Richard Livingstone, whose books on adult education, in particular his books on the Scandinavian Peoples Colleges, had done so much to inspire me, to become President. Inevitably his name gave Pendley a respectability, a status even, that it would otherwise have lacked. On 31 October 1945, he presided at the opening, before a large gathering of local and educational worthies.

In his address he made two particularly telling points. The first related to a letter he had recently received from a woman who had left school at thirteen and who now, at fifty-five, felt that her lack of education denied her self-confidence. In Sweden or Denmark he could have advised her to go to an adult college, but in England there was no answer until – Pendley. His second point related to another letter, one that he had received from a prisoner of war who told how he had only found his latent yearning for further knowledge gratified in a prisoner of war camp in Germany where they had formed themselves into discussion groups.

These two points made by Sir Richard seemed to me to reach the very heart of what we were trying to do. First, lack of self-confidence inevitably causes unhappiness and frequently leads to trouble-making. Secondly, if adults are really going to enjoy learning then they must be treated as adults. People are likely to learn far more from a well led discussion group, in which all contribute, than from a straightforward lecture: a point fully appreciated during the war by A.B.C.A. (The Army Bureau of Current Affairs). This was why the atmosphere of Pendley was so important. It seemed to me vital that those attending courses should never feel that they were attending an institution, rather that they were coming to someone's home, or at least joining a club; never that they were going back to school. This could be so much more easily achieved, perhaps could only be achieved, in a congenial environment. Although obviously the gardens had not been properly maintained, the grounds and the park were even then delightful, as was the house itself. Much of the furniture having unfortunately been sold, to pay death duties; there had obviously been problems in equipping the house in the style of a private house or a good class hotel. We had of necessity only partially succeeded, but in those early days after the war people expected very much less than today. At least they were going to be comfortable and well fed.

Hoping for maximum publicity, every effort had been made to get someone really important to perform the opening ceremony. We had been unsuccessful with Royalty as, regrettably, has always been the case at Pendley. The Archbishop of Canterbury had been unavailable, the Prime Minister otherwise engaged, though later he and Lady Attlee frequently attended the Pendley Shakespeare Festival when they were at Chequers. We had been no more fortunate with the Minister of Education, though he too, as George Thomas, came later. Others unable to accept the invitation despite considerable string-pulling, included Lord Beverage, Lord Beaverbrook, Bernard Shaw, Lord Mountbatten and other Services top brass. Even leading theatre personalities had turned us down.

It was when I was giving a talk one evening at the Nuffield Centre, only a week or two before the opening, that I solved the problem. The whole object of Pendley was to provide educational opportunities for ordinary people, so why not have it officially opened by an *ordinary man*. Just as the unknown warrior in his tomb symbolized the ordinary serviceman who had given his life for his country in the war, so an anonymous ordinary man could symbolize the ordinary people who, it was hoped, were going to benefit from this new kind of adult education. I had noticed a young sergeant regularly seated in the same corner at my talks and musical appreciation sessions at the Nuffield Centre; he seemed ideally to fill the bill. When, later that evening, I approached him and explained he readily agreed. It was he, therefore, who was introduced by Sir Richard Livingstone to perform the opening ceremony that 31 October. He spoke briefly, but most effectively:

'Due to the war,' he concluded, 'people have missed many opportunities, yet have acquired a definite interest in education and citizenship. For people like us Pendley will play an important part in our lives and be the forerunner, we hope, of many similar institutions.

'We have seen much, we have travelled much, we have lost much. It is my great honour and pleasure, therefore, to declare Pendley open – for people like us.'

He turned out to be a most unordinary ordinary man: John Pritchard, a R.E.M.E. Sergeant, he wore the ribbons of the Africa Star, the Defence Medal and the British Empire Medal. Later he was to become a successful and highly respected Headmaster in Shropshire at a place called, strangely enough, Penley (without the d).

The opening was a great success and the assembled company were impressed by our initiative, by the programmes that we had planned, by Pendley itself and by the general organization. Above all everyone wished us well, seeming genuinely anxious that we should succeed, with what was probably the first wholly new venture to be launched in any field after the war. I had no doubt, whatever, that we would succeed, though looking back I wonder why. I was, for some reason completely confident. I knew that what we were doing was right – and needed. I was convinced, too, that in creating Pendley I had made for myself a niche that was also completely right – in founding Pendley I had found myself. Pendley, I believed, after the unreality of the thirties, the wretchedness of the war years, could provide the answer to many problems, including my own. My feet felt firmly on the ground again; after twelve years the way ahead once more seemed clear. I knew where I was going, which for so long I had not. Now more than thirty years later it is not easy to justify the confidence I experienced at the opening of Pendley, let alone explain it, but it was real enough at the time. It was almost as though I had been reborn. The entry in my diary for 1 November 1945 reads: '1945 may well later be regarded as a crucial point in my life: the year that the Pendley scheme was crystallized and born. It is up to me to see that it is nursed into health, strength and reliability. There must always be a readiness to experiment. Doubtless there will be many failures and disappointments, from which we will have to learn.'

During the next five or six years Pendley was firmly established as a new kind of Centre of Education. In the same period I launched the Pendley Shakespeare Festival, also very successful, and I then took up commentating on show jumping for television and became a Master of Foxhounds. Teaching, acting, show jumping, hunting: a group of apparently only most loosely connected activities, but they all stemmed from experiences and developments in my life during that twelve years between leaving school and starting Pendley – unsettled years in which I seemed to have very little sense of direction. Yet surprisingly those years were in many ways to prove a useful background when, after starting Pendley, I settled down to an existence which was certainly full of variety, but, as will be seen, not quite as fragmented as people have often thought. In fact, there are clearly identifiable links between most of my activities at that time – activities which were gradually to develop into my way of life for the next quarter of a century.

Chapter 5

The uneven path to Pendley

Friends and acquaintances of my parents, and indeed many of my own contemporaries, could never quite understand my extraneous interests as a boy and as a young man – drama, poetry, education. My father certainly was totally absorbed in horses, as was his own father, which resulted in our living in a horsey world, but my mother came from a totally different background. Her branch of the family was directly descended from the Wedgwoods of Staffordshire, originally Wedge Wood, and on her mother's side she had connections with the Hawtreys, a name famous in both scholastic and theatrical history.

I myself had always been interested in education as well as in the theatre. On leaving Harrow I was frequently invited back to the school to help in the training of athletes or to produce house plays – a form of education in itself. I spent much time at Hawtreys, especially when for a few months I was at a crammers at Westgate-on-Sea attempting to improve my mathematics, always hoping that there might be an opportunity to take a class if some master was laid up, or to coach a team or, again, to produce a play. I also used to give talks to various groups on drama or mediaeval castles, my hobbies at that time. My first effort as an author had been a short treatise on education which, very much to my surprise, as it was published privately, had received encouraging notices in such papers as *The Spectator* – 'a very sensible little book which might well be read with profit by many educationalists', and *Truth* – 'Many volumes have been written about education: few are as worthy of attention as this wise and thoughtful, yet original and provocative book'. Even Sir Cyril Norwood, my late headmaster at Harrow, had written: 'I have gained from reading this treatise. It shows freshness, enthusiasm, integrity of mind.'

All this, doubtless, had been responsible for old Mrs Hawtrey, my great aunt, suddenly informing me in 1935 that she intended shortly to make over the school to me and to my brother. Her son and daughter had both died, she herself was nearing ninety, and she had never wholly accepted her son-in-law, Frank Cautley, himself approaching sixty. This must have made his task as headmaster extremely difficult, for she was not only the proprietress of the school but also a very dominating character. My brother was, by that time, already firmly embarked on a legal career, which meant that it was I who would be involved. I was twenty-two and had had no proper teaching experience. Yet, obviously, it was an offer that I could not ignore. The school was, after all, a family concern, and there were no other available relatives to take it over.

I immediately found a job at a neighbouring preparatory school, Beachborough, near Folkestone, where I had two extremely happy years, spending any spare time that I had at Westgate familiarizing myself with the school and the staff. It was eventually decided that I should join the school in April 1938, first in partnership with Frank Cautley – a prospect that had little attraction for me, he being my own ex-headmaster – and then gradually taking over from him.

I was sad indeed to leave Beachborough, first because, with only minimal responsibility, I had found the happy, carefree atmosphere very stimulating, secondly because I liked enormously and respected the Headmaster, Fred Chappell. He was a very human, amusing, elegant person who, I am glad to say, is still alive, and at ninety-five has just had a book published. He was kind enough to write when I left that he considered me a born teacher. Later I have preferred to substitute the word communicator for teacher. In all my activities, Hawtreys, Pendley, the B.B.C., even hunting, I have tried to communicate something of my own enthusiasm and such knowledge as I have to people initially less informed than myself, a kind of middleman interpreting the skills of the expert to the layman.

Thirdly I regretted leaving Beachborough because I was well aware that I was far too young, and much too immature, to accept the responsibilities of being a headmaster and to take over a great school, the fame of which was beginning to decline. This was partly because of the age of those in charge, partly because there was, obviously, some uncertainty about its future, but particularly because it was, geographically, in a most vulnerable position should war break out, as, in 1938, seemed increasingly likely. Moving to Hawtreys was, therefore, a daunting prospect for a young man of twenty-three. It would have been even more daunting had I not just married Moyra, despite the fact that she was not yet twenty-one. Though her family was not amongst our closest friends, yet hunting together, in the same Pony Club and so on we had more or less grown up together. After I had left school I had seen a good deal of her. In 1935 we had been in a ski-ing party together, shortly after that becoming engaged. Our interests seemed to be very similar and we were rather more intellectually inclined than most of our friends. In fact her intellect was immensely superior to my own. Her grandfather, the first Lord Avebury, was an eminent scientist – he also invented Bank Holidays – and most of her family were extremely clever. Moyra herself was a born student, always fascinated by research, a field in which she was later to have great success. Whereas I was impulsive, occasionally seeing straight to the relevant core of a problem, she was immensely thorough and painstaking, always more ruled by her head than her heart.

Only nineteen when we became engaged, she had no intention of getting married for five or six years, while with my usual impetuosity I was prepared to marry immediately. Hawtreys falling into my lap played right into my hands, and I persuaded her that she was an essential part of the whole plan. Generously, if reluctantly, she agreed. We were, of course, far too young, though the intensely busy life of the next few years effectively prevented our fully appreciating our incompatibility. It is possible that had we led a more normal life, had I been a stockbroker or a soldier, it might have worked all right, though I am inclined to think that her reluctance to have a home or a family, preferring her student-like life, would always have prevented a lasting happy marriage. In fact, we never had rows: she was not that sort of person. We just tended to go our own ways. When we parted she wrote: 'You may think that I have never trusted you or wanted you to succeed, but if this is so it is only because I have felt that the further you succeeded in obtaining your ambitions the further removed I should be from obtaining mine.' When later I married again she wrote, characteristically kind: 'I cannot imagine anyone making a worse wife than I did; there must be quite a lot to be said for matrimony, but I am still not sure that I am the right person for it.'

She was, to be fair, a better wife than I was a husband, being so practical, so level-headed, never ruffled or put out, despite her youth. Which was why she was so helpful in those early days at Hawtreys when there were certainly problems great enough to defeat many couples much older than we were. Numbers were falling, war was approaching and Frank Cautley refused to agree to our moving the school at the time of Munich. When evacuation was forced on us in September 1939, we had just two weeks to find a new home and move the school. On the advice of a school parent we saw, amongst many other properties, Llangedwyn Hall, near Oswestry, the home of Sir Watkin Williams Wynn. We started the Michaelmas term on 26 September, only a week late, but with fewer than forty boys.

Llangedwyn had a unique magic about it, set in its gentle valley by the Tamat that ran through the Berwyns. It was ideal for a school evacuated from the front line, but from a personal point of view, though I came to love it as much as I have ever loved any place, I found that before long it produced within me a disturbing conflict. It was too peaceful, too beautiful, the job was too attractive. The day after war broke out I had driven over to Canterbury to enlist in the Army, only to be informed brusquely that I was in a reserved occupation and told to return to my teaching. I would be informed when I was wanted. Two years later I was called up only to fail my medical because of my skin condition, which had been giving some trouble again. The following year I had another medical and was again rejected.

Such was the remoteness of Llangedwyn that it was impossible to believe that the country was locked in a terrible war. One's experience was limited to distant explosions and flashes fifty miles away when one was doing one's twice weekly Home Guard duty, and the odd bombing when one was visiting London. By contrast one was living an almost idyllic existence doing an ever rewarding job in perfect surroundings, which inevitably led to a feeling of something very like guilt. There is no one more attractive, more responsive, more enthusiastic, more co-operative than the child of ten to thirteen; it is the ideal age. A preparatory school, therefore, is naturally a happy, relaxed, rewarding community. Hawtreys at Llangedwyn was even more delightful than most. This was partly because the school was evacuated, more because of Llangedwyn itself, but most, I believe, that because of my own philosophy the atmosphere was completely informal. There was only one rule: boys could do more or less anything they liked but if ever they did anything that resulted in inconvenience, let alone misery, for anyone else then they were not spared. In every society there are too many rules: fewer and simpler are often more effective. In this case it had the considerable value of teaching young people to think before doing. (Recently, addressing a motoring organization, I suggested, in a similar vein, that most motoring offences should be abandoned, except for dangerous driving, for which the penalties should be extremely severe. Somewhat to my surprise I found that the majority present, including many senior police, agreed.)

Naturally one threw oneself energetically into every local war effort; the Home Guard, War Savings, various charities, all of which kept one busy and at times almost over-stretched, even in the holidays. Just how it all started I cannot be too sure, but every holidays the house filled up with old boys, parents, teachers, their friends and connections, servicemen on leave, who for one reason or another had nowhere else to go. As a rule there would be at least twenty people in residence. With no transport, no local cinemas, no television, it was logical that we should organize activities of one sort or another amongst ourselves. So it was that each evening we arranged play readings, poetry recitals, lectures, discussions, musical appreciation, concerts even. Those involved were, for the most part, anything but sophisticated, yet all seemed to enjoy enormously joining in. Obviously at the time I did not appreciate it, but the seeds of Pendley were there being sown: adult education of a most informal kind, in pleasant surroundings.

Before long I found that these holiday activities were giving me more tangible satisfaction than the ordinary school term time. I began to feel that being a prep school master, in these conditions, was almost too easy, almost too straightforward, the scope too limited. What went on in the holidays was more of a challenge and ultimately, therefore, more rewarding. One expected boys to progress, develop, mature: it was inevitable; but when one saw that a flame had been lit within an adult it was really exciting, because one knew that such people so often believed that they were incapable of finding satisfaction from anything of a cultural nature. The term time and the holiday activities, though complementary in themselves, were nevertheless conflicting in that the one, the less official one, was proving more satisfying than the other; possibly at the expense of the other. After a year or so I felt increasingly unsettled. I had hoped that this unsettled feeling, which had so beset me ever since I had left school until I married and came to Hawtreys, was something of the past. But now I was restless again, just as I had been in those years after leaving Harrow when I found it impossible seriously to get down to anything, or even to know what it was I wanted to get down to.

I cannot say that this was the cause of my illness, but it could well have been a contributory factor. At the end of 1942 I had a very serious attack of jaundice, serious enough for my family to be sent for. I have always said that I owed my life then to an old friend walking seven miles down the valley to get some brandy from a farmer. I was convinced that I would recover if I could find the strength to keep anything down. The brandy did the trick and I recovered, but being war-time it was not possible for me to go away anywhere to recuperate, with the result that I started work again far too soon. By the end of the year I had a proper breakdown, necessitating my going into hospital where it was discovered that I had some sort of internal growth which was naturally suspected of being malignant. Diagnosis was not so accurate in those days, so whether it really was malignant, or whether it was just an ulcer gone septic I do not know, but it meant many months of treatment in a London hospital. Naturally I was not entirely idle. I worked at various Service Centres, in particular the Nuffield, Leicester Square and the Gordon in Vauxhall Bridge Road.

In these I pursued the lines that I had been developing in the holidays at Llangedwyn – educational activities of a very informal nature: discussions, talks, musical appreciation. I had the opportunity of co-ordinating it all when I was invited to run a Centre at Sloane House in Chelsea, but I did not feel ready to accept the challenge. I was still in something of a turmoil, unsure what to do next. I only knew that I could not go back to Hawtreys. Already I had appointed a caretaker headmaster. Indeed, I could never bring myself to go back to the school even when I had recovered, though after the war I returned frequently to renew friendships that I had made in that lovely valley, mostly in the Home Guard.

It was to Pendley that I turned whenever I could escape from London, and it was not long before Pendley began to assert its own magic. Old Aunt Katy had died; most of the contents had been sold to help my father pay the heavy death duties which then became due; the Land Army was still in residence, yet weekend after weekend Pendley provided just the peace that I needed, helping to assuage the restless dissatisfaction with myself, brought on for the most part by the fact that I felt inadequate and frustrated while Maurice and all my contemporaries were in the Services, many of them now in France. Oddly enough, probably because I had not yet properly formulated my plans for an adult education centre, I was not seriously thinking, at that time, of using Pendley for the purpose. In fact, I had no idea what would happen to Pendley. For the present all that concerned me was that it was a haven from the doodle-bugs in London and my hospital treatment. I was becoming very attached to it, enjoying every moment I spent there.

Nevertheless, that August I was easily persuaded to join a few friends on a bicycle tour in North Wales, little expecting that I was to have an experience which I genuinely believe altered the course of my life, or at least gave me the push that I needed to get out of my self-pitying lethargy, the stimulus to stand up and fight.

We set off by train for Gobowen, then proceeded through the villages and over the mountains, already tinged with a hint of autumn, putting up at different little pubs en route for Penryndeudraeth, where I visited for the first time the famous Port Meirion, before staying for a couple of nights at Larne with the author, Richard Hughes, who had a son at Hawtreys and with whom I had become friendly. His delight was to bathe in the nude, insisting that we all did the same, bringing back memories of Ducker at Harrow, excẽpt that at Larne it was mixed bathing.

The weather was ideal, but before long I realized that I was not really strong enough to be bicycling up all those hills, lovely and tempting as they were. I managed to get as far as Bedgellert with the others, then while they toured around I stayed in a hotel, arranging to meet them two days later at Capel Curig. It was 9 August, a soft, damp, typically Welsh day, and very peaceful. Arriving by taxi I had several hours to wait before I could expect the others; but was content to be on my own in such beauty and stillness. It seemed as though I was the only person within miles. I wandered around, ate the sandwiches that I had brought with me from Bedgellert, then when in the afternoon a very gentle, fine rain began to fall I went into the church, partly for shelter, partly to look at the famous mosaics. Time passed very slowly so, realizing that there was still an hour or more to wait before I could expect the others, I sat down in one of the pews and decided to have a good think, about myself, about my future, even to try to pray. For several minutes I sat there, silent, with my head in my hands, hoping that I could discover the way to pray properly for, as with so many – the majority, perhaps – praying in church had been very much a formality, saying my prayers something abandoned since childhood, despite my upbringing and my clerical forbears. A religious experience was, for me, something created by atmosphere, something indefinable, almost impossible to understand. Praying was – what? Words seemed out of place, rather it was concentrating, and waiting; which presumably is what is meant by meditation. But is that prayer? I did not know. Nor do I now.

Sitting there, depressed about my health, worried at the failure of my life so far, uncertain of the future, I tried my very hardest to pray, yet aware that there was something wretchedly hypocritical about it, only praying when I was in trouble. Suddenly, breaking in on my concentration, I heard someone speaking behind me. The voice was clear and immediately recognizable. It was my brother, Maurice.

'Don't give up,' he said. 'Keep going and everything will come right. I promise you.'

That was all. I sat up quickly and looked round. He was not there, of course. I knew that he would not be; could not be. He was in France, yet it had been his voice that I had heard. It was no illusion. Maurice had been speaking to me as clearly, as naturally, as he had a hundred thousand times in all our years together. He had spoken to me – now. Just how I did not know, but that he had been with me at that moment I was absolutely convinced. Nor in view of our closeness was I really surprised. Although he was a year younger we had always been more like twins, and many people assumed that we were. Tall for his age, he had caught me up in height while we were at Harrow, finishing up about an inch taller. His intellect was superior to mine; as I have mentioned earlier he was at one time in a form above me, thanks to the ridiculous School Certificate situation. This could so easily have led to strained relations, but if I ever felt any resentment his charm, his understanding, his humility soon overcame it.

We did everything together, our interests being almost identical: the theatre, literature, horses, hunting and racing, the use of words, clothes, politics, though he was much more involved than I was. His only ambition, from an early age, had been to become Speaker at the House of Commons. The quality that most closely united us, however, was his wit. It was ready, sharp, subtle. He could see humour in everything and everybody, but his wit, however to the point, was never barbed. He wallowed in quotations, flattering himself that he could produce a suitable quotation for almost any circumstance. For hours we would vie with each other, trying to out-quote one another. Our sense of humour was identical, too, making for a wonderfully close companionship. We could discuss everything with each other and, not always common in families, could always see the best in each other as well as the faults – which in his case, thanks to his nature, were few. He treated mine with great generosity. As the unquestioning devotion of a dog can be uplifting to the biggest villain, so the admiration of someone whom one holds in high regard can stimulate and encourage one who is only too aware of his shortcomings and, therefore, lacking confidence.

To anyone not knowing Maurice hearing him described in such terms might get the impression that he was almost too good to be true. That this just was not so is borne out by the fact that his friends, of all ages, both sexes, all classes, were legion. I am convinced that when I say that he never had an enemy I am speaking the literal truth. Everyone loved him. Even Frank Cautley, the Headmaster at Hawtreys, who never to my knowledge showed any sign of affection for anyone, appeared to love him. When Maurice left the school Cautley wrote to my father, 'it is as though the sun has gone in. His attractiveness is almost uncanny. He has never caused me a moment's anxiety with his wholesome manly outlook on life. What a trier too – I shall miss him terribly, he has been such a friend.' On leaving Harrow his Housemaster wrote: 'This house is the richer for his influence. His selflessness, his humour, and constructive endeavour have added enormously to the unity and happiness and success of the house. For myself – I can only say that I shall miss him dreadfully, and that I thank him for all he has done.'

Almost the worst part of the war for me personally was the inevitable separation, though I was fortunate in that he did not go overseas until 1944. Wherever I was, Hawtreys, London, convalescing at my parents' home in Somerset, he always came to spend part of any leave

Pendley Manor

1. Family home: the drawing-room of my childhood

2. Centre of Adult Education: today

Childhood

3. Pearly King at three years old

4. Prep school at eight years old

5. New boy at Harrow, thirteen years old

6. Last term at Harrow, eighteen years old

Family

7. Bushranger brothers, 1918

9. Schoolchildren, 1923

8. Nursery Trio, 1920

10. En famille, 1928

Drama at Harrow

11. Terence Rattigan as Julius Caesar with myself as Calpurnia

12. Abraham Lincoln: second from right and inset; with John Profumo as Edwin Stanton, second from left

Hurdles: with and without assistance

13. All alone: winning Southern Counties Championship, 1937

14. With the help of Lantic: winning Whaddon Chase Hunter Trials, 1954

Home

15. Greens Norton Court

16. Foscote Manor

School

17. Hawtreys at Westgate-on-Sea: hardly the ideal environment

18. Llangedwyn in North Wales, which had a magic about it

Brothers

19. Maurice

that he had with me. For hours or days we would then catch up, joking, quoting, laughing, pulling each other's leg. The sound of his voice in the church at Capel Curig was a shock obviously, yet as I have said it did not altogether surprise me, such was our closeness. It seemed natural that he should want to help me, as he had so often before. I said nothing to anyone, of course, but even my friends, when they rejoined me, noticed how much more cheerful, more relaxed I was that evening and the next day before we all returned to London.

Although I was on my own in the flat for the next few days I forced myself to be busy. On the strength of my treatise on education I had, surprisingly, been invited to produce a similar work on Conservatism. Not surprisingly, it was rejected by the Conservative Central Office, but I was paid £100 for it and it kept me fully occupied for a week or so after my return from North Wales. It was very hot that week, which was no worry to me, though everyone else obliged to be in London was complaining. Thanks to my little holiday and the experience at Capel Curig I felt better than I had for months.

Early on the morning of 18 August I was in the bath when I heard the telephone ringing. Putting a towel round me I went into the sitting-room to answer it. It was Betty Elliot, who as Betty Hoskin had been my sister's greatest friend at Greens Norton. At the beginning of the war she had taken her small daughter to my parents' home in Somerset. I was aware of a quaver in her voice as she said, 'Hullo D,' and feared the worst. On the previous day my mother had been operated on for cancer. Then suddenly, as she said: 'Bad news, I'm afraid,' I knew the truth: it was Maurice.

She waited for me to say something, but I could not. It was the moment that I had dreaded above any other since the war had started.

'It's Maurice, I'm afraid.' After a pause, to pull herself together I am sure, she started to tell me of my father's courage. He adored Maurice. Now with my mother in hospital he had to bear it alone. Still I could not bring myself to speak, though, in a way which on such occasions is almost inexplicable, I managed to keep a grip on myself, did not break down.

Finally she told me that they had received only the barest information, did not even know exactly when he had been killed.

'I do,' I blurted out, to her surprise. 'It was the afternoon of 9 August.'

'But how – ?' she started.

'Don't worry,' I said. 'I'll be all right. I'll ring you back.'

I could not bring myself to go straight down to Somerset. My presence, I felt, would be an embarrassment to my father in the first few hours of his ordeal. I decided to go instead to Pendley, but could not go there until the evening as I had someone coming to see me about the adult centre at Sloane House, which project was still vaguely in the offing. It was a glorious, calm evening when I arrived at Pendley, walking up through the farm having travelled down by train. Pendley was at its most majestic, yet peaceful and lovely. Springham, the old Pendley butler, retired but, of his own accord, available on my week-end visits, brought me my dinner on the verandah that leads out from the library. The pigeons, always for me associated with Pendley, coo-ed gently in the evening air. I sat there, remembering, unable wholly to accept the fact that Maurice was dead. Only a few weeks earlier we had spent the week-end together here at Pendley; so much of our childhood had been spent here: tennis, cricket on the lawn, bicycling round the grounds and, until it was forbidden, up and down the passages in the house. It all flowed through me, our childhood, his appearance, his laughter, his jokes, his voice.

His voice: 'Don't give up. Keep going and everything will come right.'

Everything will come right; for his sake, now, it must.

In the fading light of that quiet August evening I wandered round the Pendley gardens, Maurice very close: through the rockery where we once produced a little play; round to the front lawn where we used to have a cricket net: across to the ha-ha from which we watched the Life Guards, all a-jingle, jogging across the park from the station on their way to Tring Show; back through the rose garden with its insidious smell of 'cherry pie' – heliotrope – from the borders.

By the time I returned to the library I knew that Pendley must be saved – that by saving it I would be making the effort that Maurice had seemed to be urging me to do. It is easy, at this distance, to oversimplify. Of the exact sequence of my thoughts and reasoning I cannot now be certain. I only know that before I left Pendley the following day I had firmly made my mind up to carry out here at Pendley, our own family home, the scheme that had for so many months been vaguely formulating in my mind. I am sure that Maurice's death influenced me in this decision, because, if it is not too fanciful, I believe that somehow he knew that unless I forced myself to get fully involved in some really worthwhile activity his death, at a time when I was already very low, could easily result in my going to pieces altogether and having another breakdown.

The next day I returned to London. As I expected there was a message to say that it was now known on which day Maurice had been killed. It was 9 August. I offer no explanation. There can be no explanation. I can only quote, as surely Maurice would have done, Hamlet's 'There are more things in heaven and earth, Horatio, than are dreamt of in your philosophy'. The longer one lives the more one realizes that so much is still beyond the comprehension of man.

For my father it must have been an agonizing time. Visiting my mother each day in hospital, he had somehow to conceal his grief. When eventually she was told, her fortitude was extraordinary. My father wrote: 'She was just too brave for words, an example to us all. It has made it so much easier for me as it has been a strain talking about him as if nothing had happened, fearing every moment that one would give oneself away.' My mother herself wrote: 'How dare I complain? You have been such a wonderful trio and I still have two thirds of you, all of us now knit closer still by the mutual love of M, apart from our immense love of each other. Y'r F [as we always referred to my father] is quite wonderful. I long to be home, under the same roof, living the daily life near him, helping him to relax. It is the quiet, lonely hours that must have been so difficult for him, but he faces it all so bravely.'

Can anything equal a deep family love at a time of unhappiness?

One is tempted to believe that my mother was aware of the fact that in a few months she would be joining him in the after-life in which her simple faith had taught her to believe. Thanks to my father being able to pull strings my sister was posted home from Italy, bringing great comfort to my mother in the last months of her life, and to my father in his double bereavement; and, indeed, to me. We had always been so very close.

I have known no sadness to compare with that I experienced when Maurice died. On learning later how he died it was hard not to be bitter. Standing up in the turret of his tank he had been hit by bullets from a machine gun, accidentally fired from one of his own tanks. Ironically his regiment suffered no further casualties the whole way to Berlin. The senseless waste . . . There is no doubt that his death was a great shock to the regiment. His Colonel wrote: 'He is an irreplaceable loss to the Regiment where he was loved and admired by everyone, and where he has done more for the Regiment in the last eighteen months than any other individual. Apart from being an exceptionally able Officer and undoubtedly the best adjutant we have had ever since I joined, his personal example, absolute unselfishness and charm of manner, however hard worked he was himself, were incomparable.'

From his Squadron Commander: 'He has left a gap which no-one can ever fill. As a soldier and adjutant he was incomparably the best I have ever known: his manner courteous and gracious, however trying the circumstances. He was the most unselfish human being I have ever met, while his wit and charm made him loved by everyone. He could never have had an enemy in the world.'

His godfather, General Sir Hubert Gough, who commanded the Fifth Army in the First World War, wrote in *The Times*: 'From his early school days until the day he fell on the battlefield he had cheered and encouraged all those he worked with by his personal charm, by his high sense of duty and his truly amazing unselfishness and sympathy. He was a most delightful companion with a polished wit and a very cultural mind.'

At the time of his death I found myself constantly reminded of some lines that I had written a few months earlier on the wrench of a final parting; indeed, haunted by them, as he always thought they were the best that I had ever produced. I did not know at the time that he was very much in love with a girl to whom he was more or less unofficially engaged. It was the one secret that he had kept from me. Only on going through his papers and belongings after his death did I learn of 'Joannie', eventually tracing her and in doing so giving her a horrible shock. Our voices, Maurice's and mine, were so similar that on the telephone we were frequently mistaken for one another; in fact, we often used to play rather unkind tricks on friends and on each other. When first I telephoned her she was convinced that it was Maurice and, understandably, was momentarily very upset.

I quote from this poem as it does seem very apposite to my mood at that time:

This is our last evening together,
And as we stand
For the last time hand in hand
We wonder whether
We have been too happy, now will be too sad
Remembering all the fun and love we had
Together.

I will wander this path tomorrow and will hear
The echoes of your thoughts and your dear
Laughter:
I will wander this path tomorrow and long after,
Sensing the endless memories where
We wandered this path today
And yesterday,
And yester-yesterday.

You are gone now. I know, for we arranged this –
That you should steal away with no last word, no kiss
To force the mists into our eyes, stifle our throats,

And now that you are gone
I must cry out. I cannot bear to struggle on
In this engulfing sea of memories
Alone,
For your life is more mine than my own:
You are my own.

Before very long I had made up my mind that I must quickly involve myself in work so much that there would be little time to think, let alone to wallow in my grief. The work, of course, would be Pendley. I sought immediately the co-operation of Roger Pulbrook, as great a friend of Maurice's at Harrow as of mine. It was he who introduced me to Kenneth Bowden. Soon we saw ourselves as the three musketeers, dashing hither and thither, soliciting support, gathering equipment, and gradually, once the Land Army had departed, establishing ourselves at Pendley. John Newsom, the Director of Education for Hertfordshire, who proved a tower of strength, used to refer to us as the unholy trio. Certainly we left no stone unturned, legitimate or not so legitimate, in our efforts to get Pendley off the ground. By the summer of 1945 we may have been physically exhausted, but we had all become convinced that we were engaged in something that was not only worthwhile, but inevitable. It is not without interest that being so busy I had abandoned my hospital treatment and experienced no further trouble whatever – another example, surely, of mind over matter.

Of enormous help to me at this time was Jean Venables, one of my old Housemaster's daughters, who, while her husband Tony Spafford, a doctor, was still overseas, devoted herself to assisting us. She understood what we were trying to do, appreciated the urgency. Furthermore, she shared my love of music, which was the one relaxation in which we could indulge. She also loved Pendley and, like everyone else, had loved Maurice. She could appreciate how necessary it was for me to succeed. Since leaving Harrow my life had so often been indeterminate, even dilatory, while for Maurice it had been a success story. He had been President of the Junior Common Room at Magdalen, a leading light in the Oxford University Dramatic Society, selected to keep wicket for the University, though not against Cambridge for, as at Harrow, despite his superiority as a wicket-keeper, a better bat had eventually been selected. He had also, on occasions, played for Somerset, being, I believe, the only wicket-keeper to stand up to the bowling of Reid, whom many considered faster than Larwood or Tyson. His legal career, too, had shown exceptional promise, as had his career in the Army. Now it was I who had to succeed, if only to justify the faith and belief that he had always had in me.

When eventually Pendley was successfully launched in that autumn of 1945 I was convinced that although the road to Pendley since my leaving Harrow twelve years earlier, had often been tortuous it was going to succeed; that we were doing something that was really worthwhile. So different from the uncertainty of the previous years, the failure of various projects, even the slings and arrows which seemed to have beset the last few years, this conviction in the future gave me great confidence. I believed that I had found the niche that was absolutely right for me. So completely absorbed was I in my work at Pendley that I quite failed to see the significance of a certain straw in the wind that wafted before me at about this time.

Mike Ansell had sent me tickets for the Show-jumping Victory Championship that he was organizing at the White City. We had always been very close, almost relatives: my father had become his guardian on the death in 1914 of his own father, who was my godfather. A few weeks after the Victory Championships when we were having dinner together at the Cavalry Club he asked me what I thought of the jumping – an almost entirely unknown sport in those days. I told him how much I had enjoyed it, but when he pressed me for criticism I admitted that I had found the public address rather unsatisfactory, to which he characteristically replied: 'Well, you can bloody well do it yourself next time.'

'Next time' proved to be the first International Horse Show staged after the war, also at the White City, with my father Chairman and Mike Ansell Show Director. Thinking that I was moderately articulate as well as fairly knowledgeable about horses they suggested that I might be able to interpret, over the loudspeakers, this little known sport to a largely lay public. As a result I took a few days off from Pendley to do so, and have been doing it ever since. Commentating on television followed naturally a few years later.

Nothing, however, could have been further from my thoughts at that time than any career other than Pendley. I was totally involved.

Chapter 6

'One man in his time . . .'

To be associated with Pendley in those early days was both exciting and rewarding. Not only were our courses well filled, but during that first six months or so we were fortunate in amassing a really magnificent list of speakers. These included Robert Speight, Dean Inge, L. A. G. Strong, Field Marshal Slim, J. B. Priestley, Sir Alfred Richardson, Professor Joad, Sybil Thorndyke, Seebohm Rowntree, Dr Glyn Daniel, Krishna Menon, Richard Elwes, Basil Henriques, and Dr David Mace of the Marriage Guidance Council. There being, as yet, no local evening classes, we also organized classes in various subjects at Pendley, hoping that the shortage of petrol, which was still strictly rationed, and lack of public transport would not prevent people coming. Apparently it did not, for that first winter we had anything between twenty and sixty people for the Drama, Music Appreciation, Current Affairs, Singing, Dancing, Art Appreciation that we organized each evening. The classes in Plastics and Pottery added a few months later were even more popular: as was the Women's Afternoon when a speaker gave a talk which was followed by tea: a mixture of the educational and social, as, of course, were the week-end courses. In addition these local classes helped to break down the 'big house behind the trees' barrier. Pendley was better known locally than ever before: indeed, there is no doubt that it was the opportunity to see inside Pendley that was part of the attraction in those early days.

Before long, however, I sensed a certain scepticism amongst those connected with the Local Education Authority. Despite the support of their Chief Executive, John Newsom, they felt, I suspected, that the whole scheme was merely a stunt to prevent Pendley being sold, thus, indirectly, providing me with a job. Anything new, of course, is suspect and what was being done at Pendley was very new in the eyes of the more orthodox teachers and organizers in adult education. Their attitude was summed up in the surprise shown by a local education officer at finding that there were no desks, benches, lockers and black-boards at Pendley. He could not understand how people sitting around in comfortable chairs, asking questions, arguing and discussing, could be regarded as of educational value. Nor can it be denied that in some cases there was a blatant distrust in the whole project because of my background. The leftish influence of A.B.C.A. was still rife in educational circles: it was a world dominated by intellectuals, and outsiders, especially from the 'country set' or public school background were not welcome. Frequently, when Pendley was used mid-week by a department of the local authority, I was made to feel something of a fish out of water, my offer to open proceedings with a talk on the past history and present aims of Pendley often being rejected: with my new colleagues in the world of education I was not altogether *persona grata*. This was by no means always the case, as is shown by the surprise proposal I received from the Chairman of the local Labour party that I should put myself forward as their candidate for the forthcoming General Election. When I told him that I supported our Conservative member, Lady Davidson, he was amazed: 'But surely,' he said, 'you cannot run a place like this and be Conservative.' The very idea seemed, to him, preposterous: my sort did not concern themselves with progressive ideas, either socially or educationally.

Oddly enough, towards the end of the war, a senior officer of the Liberal Party, Mrs Stratton Farrier, who had had a son at Harrow, tried to persuade me to stand for the Liberals in Kensington. Many years later I was invited to oppose Robert Maxwell on behalf of the Conservatives in North Bucks! Is this a record?

In my book *Pendley and a Pack of Hounds* (Hodder and Stoughton, 1959) I have told of the many vicissitudes, the triumphs and disasters, of the early days of Pendley. Suffice it to say here that although we inevitably encountered many problems during those first years, the whole conception of Pendley gradually became accepted and within two years we were firmly established as a Centre of Education. In 1947 we added a regular series of mid-week courses connected directly or indirectly with industry, which notably improved our financial situation. Most satisfactory of all, within a couple of years, similar centres, all in large country houses, the majority of them under the auspices of their Local Authorities, were established at Attingham Hall (Shropshire), Urchfont Manor (Wiltshire), Westham House (Warwickshire), Dillington House (Somerset), Missenden Abbey (Buckinghamshire), Burton Manor (the Wirral), Grantley Hall (Yorkshire), Knuston Hall (Northants), Wansfell (Essex), Balstead House (Suffolk) and Denman College (the Women's Institute Centre near Oxford), most of their first principals spending a week or so at Pendley prior to opening their own centre. In 1948 we convened at Pendley a short conference of all the heads of such centres to exchange ideas. This became an annual occasion and is now attended by the principals or wardens of some forty centres though, sadly, economic problems have recently closed one or two.

Another development in 1947 was also to play an important part in the future of Pendley. We held, in mid-July, in the gardens, an open day at which the various evening groups displayed their wares: the choir, the drama group, the art group, the dancers, the pottery and the plastics. The most successful of these groups appeared to be the drama, when scenes from Shakespeare were performed. The following year another open day was equally successful, with the result that something more ambitious was planned for 1949. This was a combined performance by all the groups of Shakespeare's great pageant play, *Henry VIII*. The actors acted, the choir sang, the dancers danced, the artists painted the scenery and props, the potters provided goblets, all combining to give audiences at three performances considerable entertainment. The production was an outstanding success, despite rain at the first performance of all and indeed, the success of our efforts exceeded our expectations. The following month we were invited to perform in the Priory Gardens at Dunstable where Queen Katherine of Aragon had learnt of her divorce, an invitation repeated the following year when the chosen vehicle was 'Falstaff'. It was an amalgam of the plays in which this magnificent character appears, superbly played at Pendley by Ronnie Evers, then Headmaster of Berkhamsted School: *Henry IV* Parts I and II, the *Merry Wives of Windsor* and, in an epilogue, *Henry V* (Mistress Quickly's description of Falstaff's death). Several years later a similar production was mounted at the Old Vic, and hailed as something entirely original!

In 1952, when for the first time two plays were performed, *A Midsummer Night's Dream* and *Julius Caesar*, it was billed as the Pendley Shakespeare Festival. Since then it has become increasingly successful, its eleven performances now attracting audiences of over 12,000, the whole Festival being sold out, except for the unreserved seats, more than a month ahead. On my retirement as the Director of the Festival in 1976 I had enjoyed the unique opportunity, for an amateur, of presenting some fifty productions of twenty-five different Shakespeare plays performed before a total audience of approximately a quarter of a million people. I am inclined to think that my favourite productions were *The Tempest*, *Hamlet*, *Romeo and Juliet* and my swan song, *Henry V*, which in that unique open air setting provided marvellously exciting opportunities for a producer. Over the years the Festival undoubtedly became the highlight of the Pendley year, though, however successful a tail it might be, it was never allowed to wag the dog.

Although involved in one way or another with many of the courses, either as Chairman or as a lecturer, and principally responsible for the planning of the programmes, it was natural that I should be most closely involved with the drama, something in which I had, all my life, been intensely interested. During my last year at Harrow I had taken singing lessons, originally because I had been cast as Don Alhambra in *The Gondoliers*, a part from which I had had to resign because of *Abraham Lincoln*. Both my teacher at Harrow and Roland Jackson, my great friend John Wyld's godfather, a very fine teacher – and singer – himself, who had given me lessons when I first left Harrow, persuaded me that I should continue with my singing, Roland Jackson arranging for me to become a pupil of Plunkett Green, a famous ballad singer, and an eminent teacher at the Guildhall School of Music.

This I did, but was soon inveigled into joining the Drama Class which, as usual, was short of males. It was taken by a remarkable old lady, well over eighty, Kate Rorke, who had acted with Henry Irving, Beerbohm Tree and Lewis Waller – 'embarrassingly handsome', as she described him. She also took private pupils at her flat in Westbourne Terrace, up-and-coming young actresses such as Peggy Ashcroft, Diana Churchill, Dorothy Hyson. Giving me no chance to refuse, had I wished to do so, she used to invite me round as a 'feed', someone to read Romeo's lines to a Juliet, Hamlet's to an Ophelia. Inevitably I learnt a great deal. Indeed she invariably paid as much attention to me as to her pupil.

After some months, anxious to prove that if the technique was right it was possible for young people to play convincingly the parts of much older people, she decided to produce a play at the Guildhall. The play was Alfred Sangster's *The Brontës*. I was selected to play the part of The Reverend Patrick, who during the play aged from the middle sixties to the middle eighties. After *Abraham Lincoln* I was becoming used to playing people old enough to be my grandfather. (As a matter of interest, one who played the part of someone nearer his own age, the office boy in the scene at the publishers' office, was Cyril Fletcher.)

The play was well received and reviewed: 'The performance demonstrated alike the soundness of her teaching and the value of the young talent at her disposal. The performance reached a very high level, and the absence of self-consciousness in parts demanding period treatment was very noticeable. Catherine Overstone played Charlotte with style and charm, Joan Curry's Emily suggested the burning spirit of the woman held in leash. Elizabeth Fergusson was a convincing Ann and Dorian Williams was very good as the Reverend Patrick' (*News of the World*). The author wrote to Kate Rorke to say how immensely impressed he had been: 'The whole thing attained a level of spontaneity that is often quite absent from professional shows and I learnt a great deal from many things that were done both in acting and in production. I am sure that both the Branwell and the Emily and the Tabitha and the Nichols could hardly be bettered anywhere. Mr Brontë also was a wonderful attempt. I hope to come again on Saturday.'

Branwell was played by a young man called Gordon Edwards. I still believe that he was one of the most brilliant actors I have ever watched. Why he never became a household name I do not know. His performance in another production, that beautiful play *Berkeley Square*, in which I played a small part far from convincingly, was even more impressive. Other plays in which I acted at that time were *The Twelve Pound Look* and *Dear Brutus* by J. M. Barrie, a dramatist for whom I developed a very high regard, and *Man of Destiny*, Bernard Shaw's play about Napoleon, which was at least partly responsible for my consuming interest in Napoleon, fired by Emil Ludwig's book which I read for background material; it also made me a great admirer of Bernard Shaw. The part that I enjoyed most was that of the Baron in *Candlelight*, but I was completely overshadowed by a marvellous Naunton Wayne-ish performance by a certain John Foreman, who unfortunately had no designs on the theatre as a career. As a result of these productions drama increased in importance and the school became known as the Guildhall School of Music and Drama.

Kate Rorke had invited to the performance of *The Brontës* a number of managers and producers, one of whom was Basil Dean, who had also seen *Abraham Lincoln*, in which his son, Winton, had taken the small part of Mr Slaney. Apparently he was quite impressed and assured Kate Rorke that he would bear in mind some of those who had taken part. It was nevertheless a great surprise when a month later I received a message to say that Mr Dean wished to see me. Naturally very excited, I went along to his office and after the briefest, one might almost say most monosyllabic of interviews, I was offered a part in J. B. Priestley's new play, *Cornelius*, in which Ralph Richardson was to star. I was told to report at the theatre next day and that my salary would be £9 per week, a fortune as it seemed to me.

I duly turned up at the Duchess Theatre, was given a script and started rehearsing. My part was small but quite effective, that of a young office employee who is sacked. Such experience as I had had, and goodness knows it was limited enough, did not really include playing a young man. I was very self-conscious, only too aware of my limitations, though hopeful, if not confident, of a quick improvement: a hope which was not, apparently, shared by the stage manager, who waylaid me in the lunch break. Today I would recognize him as an ageing pansy; then I just knew that he was the sort of person I disliked.

'I'm afraid you won't do,' he lisped, 'won't do at all.'

'But, surely . . .' I began.

'No, no you won't do,' he interrupted. 'I've given the part to so-and-so.'

'But Mr Dean gave me the part,' I said.

'No, dear,' he replied. 'He offered it to you, but he did not know then that Mr Richardson had already promised the part to . . .' and he mentioned the name of a young actor of whom I regret to say I have never heard since.

I was disappointed, but even more I was angry. I was not used to fiddles. All my life so far had been straightforward and honest, and there was something about this that I did not like at all. Uncertain for a moment as to how I should react, I moved away. He followed me.

'Wait a moment, Dorian' – the use of my christian name took me aback, illogically made my hackles rise – 'if you are prepared to co-operate I'll get you fixed up with an understudy,' and he took my arm.

I was nauseated and bewildered, completely unprepared for what I imagined he was suggesting. I had heard that girls were expected to sleep with producers if they wanted to get parts, but boys! My knowledge was as limited as my background. So sheltered and innocent, I was shocked and shaken, and disillusioned. Wrenching myself free I rushed from the theatre, bringing my promising theatrical career to a premature end!

Dear old Kate Rorke attempted to persuade me to try again, assuring me that I had been unlucky, but I had persuaded myself, a little unadventurously, that all in all my upbringing did not perhaps quite befit me for the stage. It was, however, through one of her pupils, Joan Curry, Emily in *The Brontës*, that I found my first employment. Joan did advertisements for Outdoor Girl Beauty Preparations on Radio Luxembourg. They consisted of little 'sketches' with the obvious pay-off line at the end. On one occasion, as a young man was required to play opposite her, she recommended me for the job. I was auditioned – there appeared to be no other aspirants for the role – and recorded two or three 'sketches' of the 'Who's for tennis?' type, for which I was paid three guineas. I was not immediately sacked, nor did the producer make advances; rather when saying goodbye, he remarked very pleasantly that I had a very nice speaking voice, and advised me to try for a job on the B.B.C. As a result, by pulling one or two strings, I managed to arrange two interviews with the B.B.C.:

the first was with Eric Maschwitz, later head of Variety, but then in the News. He made me read three bulletins, each with a number of foreign names, and one with a whole sentence in German, a language which I had not only never learnt, but which I disliked. Not surprisingly I heard no more from him.

The other interview was with Mary Summerfield, then head of Education. Despite the fact that she had become friendly with my parents on a cruise, she quickly made it clear, in the nicest possible way, that she thought that I had little or nothing to contribute either to education or to broadcasting. I was in no position to beg to differ. Not surprisingly I heard no more from either. One cannot help wondering whether, had I been given an opportunity to work for the B.B.C. at that time, I would have responded quite so readily to old Mrs Hawtrey's proposal a few weeks later that I should take over the school.

Being unemployed is inclined to make one believe oneself capable of almost anything that is proposed. When the crash had come in 1933 my father had told me that he could not possibly afford to send me to University. Instead when I left Harrow he had given me £200, telling me to put it to the best use that I could, making it last as long as possible. I had now made it last a year, supplementing it occasionally with a very small fee for an article accepted by some lesser-known magazine. Enrolling at the Guildhall School of Music, of course, had certainly proved an investment. Not only had I learnt to use my voice properly, but from Kate Rorke I had learnt a great deal about acting and producing, which later enabled me to help establish a cultural reputation for Pendley. It had also equipped me to produce the twenty or so pageants with which I had the privilege of being involved after the war, to say nothing of the displays for which I was responsible at the major horse shows.

£200 would not go far today, but in those days, having paid my fees, I was still able to afford to live very comfortably in a roomy bed-sit at No. 109 Warwick Road – I have not noticed the blue plaque! – go regularly to the theatre and concerts, enrol with two young ladies in Hertford Street who taught young men typing and shorthand, even to buy two new suits from my Harrow tailor, only to have them stolen outside the Guildhall School of Music before I had actually worn them! Admittedly I was now in receipt of £100 a year from a family trust, but by the beginning of 1935 my money was running out and I was still without a job.

Not surprisingly Hawtreys appeared a very promising prospect. Indeed, the £350 and all found offered during my apprenticeship at Beachborough seemed a fortune. The £600 a term 'draw' on my share of the Hawtreys' profits, with all found again, three years later, was not only, to me, magnanimous but I even considered it sufficient to justify the indulgence of a six-day-a-week hunting holiday.

My early love of hunting and that final fling shortly before the war was suddenly and unexpectedly recalled by an incident that occurred at the beginning of a course at Pendley in November 1948, probably the most important course that we had so far held. It had become increasingly obvious during the first year or two of Pendley that we could never exist on nothing more than our week-end courses and evening activities. If Pendley was to be viable we had to fill the mid-week periods with something more than the occasional usage by the local authorities who found Pendley an acceptable place for conferences or refresher courses. We decided that we should approach industry, though we appreciated that this was the greatest venture of faith of all. We were asking people to come to the week-end courses paying for themselves, which was reasonable. We were asking industry not only to pay for their employees to come to Pendley out of working time, but also to continue paying their wages while they were away from work: was this reasonable?

That our first courses connected with industry were a success is entirely due to Sir Charles Bartlett, Chairman and Managing Director of Vauxhall Motors, and R. R. Hopkins, his Personnel Officer, both men of exceptional vision. They were the first to appreciate what it was that we were attempting to do, and their promised support was of great encouragement. Accordingly we ran, as first effort in this new genre, a broadly non-vocational, non-technical course, entitled *The World We Live In*, in which we attempted only to broaden the minds of people who had left school at an early age before going straight into business. The course, limited to twenty-four people, the majority of whom came from Vauxhall Motors, as it had proved difficult to sell the idea very widely elsewhere, was put on once a month. The second course, aimed specifically at foremen and supervisors and, therefore, with a wider appeal (being more vocational), was run twice a month in winter and once a month in summer. We were fortunate in obtaining the services of Cyril Matheson to organize these courses. Like so many who have served Pendley, he came initially as an ordinary guest on a course. The ultimate success of the course was entirely due to him.

The pilot course held in November 1948 had a somewhat embarrassing start. Half way through my opening address a very tough looking man at the back of the room called out: 'Don't think you can pull any wool over our eyes. We know what the likes of you are up to.' Before I could attempt to reassure him he went on in a broad Scots accent: 'How on earth do you expect to get a working man to have any time for a place like this? Don't you know what Pendley

Manor and the like mean to a working man? Well, I'll tell you: "Kick him down the back stairs and set the dogs on him." That's you lot.'

I was shaken, and hurt. When his colleagues had persuaded him to sit down and keep quiet, I carried on. I asked him only to approach all that we were doing with an open mind. His attitude as it turned out, was understandable. He had come from Glasgow where he had been unemployed for seven years. Finally he had walked all the way to Luton where, eventually, he was offered a job, but for many years retained his bitterness – until, in fact, he came to Pendley, for the story has a happy ending. Gradually the chip on his shoulder disappeared. Indeed, he was to become a good friend of ours, frequently bringing his wife to weekend courses. Most satisfying of all, some twenty years later his son came on a course, having been advised by his father on no account to miss the opportunity.

Sir Charles Bartlett, speaking in the United States told a meeting of industrialists how he deliberately sent to Pendley those who were the least well-adjusted, most likely to be trouble-makers, because he had found that after a week at Pendley they were noticeably less antisocial. Equally satisfying was an article in *Personnel Management and Welfare* in which it was stated that workers who had attended courses at Pendley Manor were more responsive to reasoned argument, more alive, better adjusted to the group in which they worked, and generally improved their attitude to their job – a view to which our friend from Glasgow would, at that time, have been most unlikely to subscribe. Even less when, unbelievably, as I finished my session the sound of hounds could clearly be heard in the park.

'Set the dogs on them!' Sure enough, the 'dogs' were in full cry across the top of the park! They ran into the garden at the edge of the lawn, the whole field coming through the front gate and galloping down the drive. It was the Old Berkeley West, now a part of the Vale of Aylesbury, with their Master, Mrs Harold Morton, whose husband had recently resigned from the Mastership of the Whaddon Chase Hunt which he had taken on when Lord Rosebery had resigned at the beginning of the war. Throughout the war, and in the three years since I had started Pendley, I had scarcely given hunting a moment's thought. It was an entirely different world in which I was now involved. I had not been hunting for ten years, not since that last season before the war when we had indulged in our hunting holiday.

With the realization that being a headmaster and hunting were not wholly compatible, especially as the school was situated in isolated Thanet, we had decided to enjoy a fortnight's hunting in the Midlands. Originally it had been planned for December 1937, before I had actually gone to Hawtreys, but unusually severe weather had ruled it out. It was deferred, therefore, until the following year, by which time we had experienced two not very easy terms at Hawtreys, with diminishing numbers, financial strains and the crisis of Munich when there had been the disagreement as to whether or not we should remain on the east coast. Reluctantly we had agreed to do so. As usual, in those days, when under any sort of pressure my leg blew up, the dermatitis, or whatever in reality it was, being particularly virulent. Over Christmas, 1938, it was so bad that on Christmas Day we had to call in a doctor. My own doctor was on leave, so the locum came and did not at all like what he saw – it was swollen, purple and porous – advising me that on my arrival at my in-laws' home at Banbury, which we were making our base for our hunting holiday, I should immediately see a doctor, to whom he wrote a letter which I was to give him.

Having been cheated of our hunting holiday a year earlier we were anxious not to miss it again. My mother-in-law, a great believer in mind over matter, procured a new kind of shiny Wellington boot which had a top that folded over and clipped. She was convinced that it would be quite possible for me to ride in this as it was, though I doubt if I would have dared to say it was not. Although it was against the doctor's advice I went out hunting the very next day, and my leg was no worse afterwards. I went out five consecutive days, frost, sadly, preventing the sixth. It was the same the following week: five days with the Bicester, Warwickshire, Grafton and one day's frost. We then went on to my own parents' home in Somerset for two days with the Blackmore Vale. Sport was universally good with points of five miles (twice), six miles and eight miles. If the meet was too far away we took the horses by train, a common practice in those days as horse-boxes were still a rarity.

Long before the end of our hunting holiday my leg had completely recovered, and during the second week I was able to wear an ordinary top boot. Delighted at the relief from discomfort and inconvenience, back in the usual routine I never gave it another thought. It was nearly a year later when, once again wearing the coat in which I had travelled to Banbury, a coat that I only used in very cold weather, I found in the pocket an envelope. I examined it, but as, at first, it meant nothing to me I opened it. It was a letter from the Thanet doctor, which I had forgotten to deliver, to my in-laws' doctor at Banbury. In it he wrote that he was sure that his Banbury colleague would be equally disturbed at the state of my leg, and had little doubt that he too would feel that the only solution was to amputate below the knee! Reading it a year later gave me quite a shock. I could only thank my lucky stars – and my hunting holiday.

Seeing the hounds at Pendley that November morning inevitably brought back memories, a certain nostalgia even, but I knew that at the present there could be no thought of my taking up hunting again. I was wholly involved at Pendley, which because of the precarious financial situation was, not for the first time, experiencing financial embarrassment. The small grant that we had received from the Hertfordshire County Council had been suspended – at the time I believed it to be because of some outspoken comments I had made on the extravagance of local authority spending. More probably, as I now appreciate, it was due to one of the regular axes on public expenditure, education – especially adult education – invariably being the first to suffer. At a later date it was restored, but had to be used to enable Hertfordshire students to come at reduced fees. With no reserves, no capital, disaster can overtake a place like Pendley very quickly. So it did at the beginning of 1949 when, despite the additional income from the industrial courses, it became apparent that unless we could find £10,000 we would have to close down. From various sources we collected a limited amount of money and we put up the fees, but it was not enough to cover the deficit. It appeared that we had no option but to close.

I had always been disappointed at the lack of coverage that Pendley received in the national press, considering that we were pioneering in this particular field of education, but now that we were closing it hit the headlines. *The Times Educational Supplement* devoted the whole of its front page to the 'tragedy'. *The Times* itself carried a leader which was followed a week later by a letter at the head of the correspondence column from Sir Richard Livingstone. This sudden belated interest in Pendley produced immediate results. The required capital became available with remarkable celerity, even from the L.C.C. – now G.L.C. – which had always withheld any support. Before the summer was out we were able to announce that for the present at any rate we were able to carry on.

It had, however, been a very testing and worrying time. We had been to the very brink, and the anxiety had caused great concern, leaving all of us exhausted. Nor was I very well in myself. My wretched leg was giving me a certain amount of trouble again. While getting both enjoyment and satisfaction out of the Pendley venture I had during the last five years worked extremely hard, virtually without any time off at all, other than a short holiday in the South of France with my great friend John Wyld after the death of his first wife. With the Pendley problems at any rate temporarily solved it seemed as though some sort of reaction set in. I had another attack of jaundice, not as serious as the one during the war, but debilitating enough. This led to a really bad outbreak of my dermatitis, spreading this time in a most unattractive fashion to my face and neck so that when friends came to see me in the nursing home to which I was taken in Amersham they found me completely masked in white paste, resembling some sort of space-man or clown.

After a fortnight or so in the Home I went to recuperate at my father's new home at East Burnham Park, near Farnham Royal. He had recently married Brenda Hickman, and they were not only devoted to each other, but from an equestrian point of view they were entirely complementary. Under his guidance and instruction she not only became the leading British dressage rider of the fifties and sixties, but she did much to popularize dressage. They were extremely happy in their beautiful home which was open house to anyone interested in horses. They were looked after by a small but dedicated staff, inside and out, which made it always a luxurious play to stay. It was a long time since I had stayed with my father for more than the odd night or a few days. Naturally we reminisced a great deal, particularly about the old Greens Norton times which inevitably awakened some of my old enthusiasm for hunting, now so long neglected. That this was at least partially responsible for my taking up hunting again cannot be doubted. I found myself recollecting all the fun that I had had hunting with the Grafton before the war, getting on for twenty years earlier. I remembered, too, the almost miraculous cure that I had experienced for my bad leg the year before the war when we had had our hunting holiday. Almost by chance shortly after I had returned to Pendley I went over to see my old friend Paul Hoskin, now Rector of Wicken, a charming village on the borders of Buckinghamshire and Northamptonshire. He had just returned to his parish after a highly distinguished war service as a naval chaplain. Within weeks he was responsible for my taking up hunting again, a totally unexpected development.

In my book *Pendley and a Pack of Hounds* I have recounted how this unique eighteen-stone hunting parson had turned his beautiful Queen Anne rectory into a successful guest house, and how much more with faith and enthusiasm than money he had become the owner of show jumping ponies and point-to-pointers. Later he was to have race-horses, sponsor a lad from the village as a motor-racing driver and open a highly successful restaurant in the cellars of his rectory.

He had convinced me that although I might be doing a useful job at Pendley it was quite wrong that someone with my background should not be hunting – and in style. Paul may be unconventional, but he usually gets his way. In this case he had it all organized. A local dealer, a big farmer in his parish, would find me the right horse, and would keep it for me, taking it each day to the meet. He would keep a room for me at the rectory, which would be my base: it was all too simple. He certainly made it sound very easy, and logical. Before I left Wicken next morning I had more or less fallen in with his plans and arranged to go the next week to see Mr Will Ivens, the farmer dealer, whose sons were childhood friends of ours in the Pony Club. I had also more or less agreed that it ought not to be impossible to arrange my life so that I could manage at least one day's hunting a week. The best days with the Grafton in those days, as in the Greens Norton era, were Mondays and Fridays, the least busy days at Pendley, thus presenting no great problem.

For many years Will Ivens had had a good trade in hunters, mostly in the middle-priced range. He was a first-class judge of a horse, and a first-class salesman, which is to say that he could talk most people into buying anything. When in due course I visited him I looked round his yard, tried one or two, but did not see anything which entirely took my fancy. It was nearing the end of the season with the resultant falling off of trade. In all my hunting life I had been fortunate enough only to be associated with the highest-class horses. The ones he showed me appeared to be left-overs. Experienced as he was Will Ivens appreciated that I was looking for something with rather more quality than anything he had shown me so far.

'Well, sir,' he said, as be began to leave the yard, 'there is just one other horse here that I've not shown you, in fact, did not really want to show you, or anyone else, as he just suits me myself down to the ground. I'm not as young as I was and I like something that I can trust completely. This is the safest, boldest jumper I've ever known. I've never sat on a better; never in my whole life.'

'I'd like to have a look at him,' I said eagerly, never suspecting for a moment that I could be falling into a carefully prepared trap, if that is not too strong a word for what was no more than cunning dealer technique.

'Well, there's no harm in your looking at him, sir, but as I said, I don't really want to sell him; I really don't.'

Returning to the yard he brought out a big, strong, brown almost black horse with splendid limbs, a good shoulder and a fine, noble outlook. He stood about 16.3 h.h.

'Five years old,' he said, 'with just the right amount of experience and up to any weight.'

'What are you asking for him?'

'Well, I'm not that keen to sell him at all, as I've told you, but of course I'd like to help you out, if I possibly can, for the sake of your father – but I couldn't take a penny less than three hundred for him – guineas,' he added.

In those days three hundred guineas was the absolute top price for a hunter. It was just about double what I had meant to pay. For me even 200 gns would have been flying high; far, far higher, to tell the truth, than I had ever gone before, not having ridden since before the war.

'Have a ride on him, sir,' said Mr Ivens, 'you won't think him expensive then.'

I duly rode him, and he certainly gave me a grand feel.

'I must say you look great on him,' he said flatteringly as I came back to the lane. 'He really might have been made for you, I have to admit. The two of you made a proper picture. He's just the sort your father always liked and your father was as good a judge of a horse as I ever knew.'

'I'll have to think it over,' I said cautiously, though I was beginning to believe that it was he who was doing me a favour. 'I'll think it over and let you know.'

Paul Hoskin, with whom I discussed the matter, had already thought it over. 'Of course you must buy it,' he said. 'If you waste time thinking it over you'll miss it. Anyway,' he asked, 'what's £300?'

'Guineas,' I reminded him.

'A mere bagatelle,' he insisted. 'A man in your position – only the best is good enough: you can't go wrong.' He always thought big where money was concerned – others' as well as his own, nor would I have been surprised if he got a rake-off from his old parishioner. Without much difficulty I was persuaded and a few days later Duke, as he was called, became mine.

He gave me four great seasons, proving himself to be all and more than Ivens had claimed. There is, however, an interesting twist to the story. When I became Master of the Whaddon Chase in 1954 I let the official gate-shutter use him as the old horse's legs were not as good as they were and I was afraid I might break him down. Imagine my surprise when a Whaddon Chase farmer, Frank Spratley, told me one day how pleased he was to see that I still had his horse.

'Your horse?' I asked. 'I don't think I've ever had one of yours.'

'Oh, yes, you have,' he replied. 'Duke.'

'Duke?' I said. 'But I bought Duke about four years ago from Will Ivens, as a five-year-old.'

He then told me how he had bred the horse, but as it was rather too big for him had decided, when it was four, to sell it, asking Ivens if he knew of a customer. A week or so later Ivens had telephoned him back to say that I was going over to his yard to buy a horse, and as he did not think he had anything suitable himself could he send Duke over? It sounded just the horse, he imagined, that I was looking for. He duly sent over his horse, which Ivens then produced for me as his own particular favourite! As it turned out, thanks to my being so gullible, he did me a good turn, as I am sure he wanted to, if only for the sake of the rector and my father. Apparently, the horse was then four, not five, and had only once before been out hunting! However, had he not turned out to be such a good hunter I might never have become so involved in hunting again. I had enough on my plate already. I would never have persevered with a dud. As it was, old Ivens had started me on a path which was to bring me many years of pleasure – and cost me a lot of money! Duke, indirectly was also to lead to my first contact with someone with whom before very long I was not only to become closely associated but who was to become a life-long friend. When first I went out with the Grafton again Colonel Neil Foster had just been appointed Master. An outstanding horseman, brilliant across country, but a man of few words, he had a reputation for being somewhat taciturn as a Master of Hounds. Apart from acknowledging my 'Good morning, Master' he had little conversation with me for several weeks, although his wife, an old friend of Maurice's, always went out of her way to be friendly.

Late one afternoon we had a good hunt from Weedon Bushes. Neil Foster was riding an outstanding horse called Freematch while I was on Duke. Eventually, from the original quite small field there were only the two of us left. On the brilliant Freematch Neil led me a great gallop over some fearsome obstacles in the best part of the country, until finally we jumped into a lane, from which there seemed to be no way out. Finding a weak place in the bullfinch opposite I managed to force my sturdier Duke through, Neil following. Two or three fields further on hounds marked their fox to ground. Collecting them, with a certain amount of difficulty in the absence of their huntsman, we jogged back together to find the rest of the field, who with the huntsman had taken a wrong turn. Almost for the first time Neil spoke to me: 'Useful horse that,' he said. I agreed, pleased that he had noticed, but he then added, 'Ivens usually gets them rather common.'

I was somewhat taken aback. It was true that Duke lacked the quality of Freematch, but I felt that he had more than held his own on that occasion. So, I have no doubt, did Neil, but he always said what he thought, which was probably why we became such close friends. There was nothing mealy-mouthed about Neil; one always knew exactly where one was with him. He was as straight as the line he took across country, his apparently blunt manner being largely due to his reserve and his genuine abhorrence of unnecessary frills. His standards were very high in every respect, especially with horses and hounds, on both of which he was an authority, and on anything to do with the administration of a hunt. Not surprisingly as a Master he was greatly respected.

My first meet with the Grafton when I started hunting again was in the unfashionable Wednesday country, so it did not surprise me that there was only a small field with only one person wearing a top hat. But when I went out the following week on a so-called fashionable Friday I could scarcely believe my eyes. I still carried memories of the two or three hundred people out on pre-war Fridays, all superbly turned-out and mounted. Now there were only forty or, at the very most, fifty people with precisely three red coats. Having been away from hunting so long I had completely failed to appreciate how great the changes had been. After so long it was almost like going out with a ghost hunt, an impression enhanced by the presence of a bare handful of those who had been amongst the most elite in the Greens Norton era, now twenty years older. It made a strange impact. My one firm contact with the past was Will Pope, the huntsman my father had appointed in 1928, twenty-one years earlier. He had kept the hunt going almost single-handed through the war years, helped by Guné Atkinson as Secretary. He seemed hardly to have changed: as courteous, as cheerful as ever, and still, in his own way, a beautiful horseman. Any horse that he rode was improved, he never seemed in a hurry and was loved and respected by the whole countryside, especially the farmers, even more than in the old days – a fact which was before very long, perhaps predictably, to become a problem. Much less predictably it was to prove, for me, an opportunity.

Nor was it only the size and make up of the field that were different; there were other changes, even more significant. Whereas before the war the Grafton had been almost wholly grass country, now much had been ploughed up. Barbed wire, too, which a special committee had kept down to a minimum before the war, was now everywhere. One could never jump a fence without making sure that there was no wire on the other side. The most noticeable difference, however, was the appearance of the members of the field; half-clipped horses with manes unplaited, riders in mufti. In contrast to the pre-war display of style, self-confidence and prosperity there was now a muted, almost drab atmosphere; a sense of struggle to survive which, of course, had I known it, was probably the same with every hunt in Britain, for it *was* a struggle to survive. The sport itself, once hounds were running, was just as satisfying, creating the same sense of excitement and elation, but the overall effect brought home to me more clearly than anything else in my experience how greatly the war had affected the ordinary way of life in the countryside. One knew that cities and towns had been devastated until they were barely recognizable, but somehow one had imagined that the countryside had remained unscathed.

Attitudes, too, seemed to have changed, as was forcibly brought home to me at about this time. I was quite unprepared for it, but it made me examine my conscience very closely. I had hurried back to Pendley after hunting one Monday evening, arriving a few minutes late for the opening session of an industrial course. I apologized for keeping the course waiting and then, quite naturally but, as I soon realized, with a quite ingenuous naïvety, explained that I had finished hunting later than I had expected. At the end of the session a member of the course came up to me, stood before me in a somewhat menacing attitude and demanded how on earth I could justify hunting.

'Surely', he said, 'a man of your intelligence must realize how bestial and cruel hunting is. In this day and age it cannot be justified, on any count. It ought to be banned and you ought to be ashamed for being a part of it: a person of your intelligence!' He then added, 'I despise you; you're nothing but a barbarian,' which, apart from taking me completely by surprise, very much upset me.

I have to confess, with some shame, that until that moment I just had not given the subject a moment's thought. I had taken hunting for granted. It had, as far as I was concerned, always been an accepted part of the countryside. In all my life, apart from the occasional jibe from odd misfits at school, I had never heard anyone question or criticize it. Like most countrymen I was an animal lover and hated any form of cruelty. Yet, when I began to think about it there was, obviously, cruelty in the hunting and killing of foxes. It was unavoidable. How then could I, a so-called compassionate person, condone it?

For the next few days I indulged in some very hard thinking: indeed, I thought of little else as, just beginning to take up hunting again, it seemed to me of the greatest importance. It was essential, especially as an educationist, that I should get it absolutely straight in my own mind. A few days later I set down my findings in the journal I kept at that time. I quote them now in full:

> Hunting provides sport and enjoyment for more than a hundred thousand people who ride to hounds, follow in cars or on foot [the number today would be considerably higher]. Hunting provides employment for at least ten thousand people, grooms, hunt staff, maintenance men, drivers. Hunting creates its own trades: horse dealers, forage merchants, saddlers, farriers, tailors, bootmakers, and brings business to farmers. Hunting is a traditional countryside sport with a fascinating history of venery and country lore.
>
> All this is at the expense of the fox.
>
> But the fox is officially designated as vermin, which must be controlled: for instance, in parts of the country where there is no hunting thousands of lambs are killed by foxes annually. The alternatives to control by hunting, that is instantaneous killing by hounds, are

> trapping, snaring, gassing, shooting – and probably maiming, the fox being by nature a nocturnal animal and not, therefore, an easy target. All these must be more cruel than hunting.
>
> In addition, were it not for protection which, paradoxically, hunting provides, together with the knowledge of fox movements and behaviour inherent in country people, then the fox, prey to every hand, might soon become extinct.
>
> The evidence, therefore, is that foxhunting is justified. It is also legal.

I accepted then, as I accept today, that many sincere people – I do not mean militant cranks – will always be opposed to hunting on ethical grounds. But my own conscience, I decided, after very thorough soul searching, was clear. It is as clear today.

'A person of your intelligence!' my hunting opponent had said, the usual implication that only halfwits and numbskulls could ever enjoy hunting. That this is palpably untrue is almost too obvious to state. There are, of course, many very simple, unintelligent people hunting, as there are playing rugger or motor racing. But just as to be a successful Formula 4 driver or a brilliant stand-off half requires a very high level of intelligence, so to be able to hunt hounds requires someone of a higher than usual intellect, although it may well be the almost instinctive intellect of the naturalist. Obviously everyone who hunts cannot hunt hounds himself, but it is the work of the hounds in which the genuine foxhunter is most interested and as such it is likely that he is at least of average intelligence. There are, of course, many people of the highest intellect who enjoy hunting and have done so down the ages. A good example is the poet Siegfried Sassoon, whose *Memoirs of a Foxhunting Man* is an accepted classic. One could mention many, many more from all walks of life – dons, playwrights, tycoons, even ministers and millionaires.

The millionaire with whom I was best acquainted because he hunted with the Whaddon Chase was Nubar Gulbenkian, an extremely shrewd and very civilized person with an outstanding wit; a wit he often employed against himself. When still at University he took up point-to-point riding. Being a very indifferent horseman he had posted, at his own expense, an ambulance at each fence to make sure, as he used to explain, that there was an ambulance ready for him at whichever fence he fell off. He used to enjoy the story, often believed to be apocryphal but which he insisted was true, of his first day out with the Whaddon Chase. Resplendent in scarlet, he wore a large orchid in his button hole. At the meet the Master, Lord Dalmeny, later Rosebery, approached him and eyeing him disapprovingly told him coldly that it was not usual to wear an orchid with a red coat. To which Nubar replied courteously, 'No, my lord, but then it is not usual for an Armenian refugee to come out hunting.'

On one occasion he had just withdrawn from the hunt to enjoy the very substantial lunch that was packed in two leather cases either side of his saddle when he noticed a lady in a car a little farther down the road drinking coffee from a flask. Thinking that a cup of hot coffee would round off his lunch very pleasantly on this cold day he approached the lady and asked if he could have a cup. She agreed a little hesitantly and then proceeded to castigate him for indulging in so cruel a sport. He soon realized that it was the local 'anti', given on occasions to indulging in demonstrations at the meet. He continued to listen courteously, however, as was his wont, and then with great charm insisted that, in exchange for the coffee, she had a drink from his large flask. A little taken back she reluctantly agreed, after a few sips enquiring what it was that she was drinking. 'Foxes' blood, madam,' he replied, at which, glancing in horror at his upturned mephistophelean eyebrows and his splendid beard – and doubtless the great orchid in his buttonhole – she leapt into her car and drove off.

Only once did I know Nubar Gulbenkian to lose his sense of humour. Well towards the back of the field, an elderly gentleman fell into a ditch when there were not many people even further behind than he was to pick him up. Nubar was one of them and with two others he succeeded in rescuing the old gentleman from the ditch. To do so he had dismounted. The problem now was how to remount. Usually his groom provided a little set of steps, but on this occasion the groom was absent. 'How on earth am I to get on?' he asked, for he was a considerable weight, far too heavy to be given a leg up. It was then suggested that he put his horse in the ditch which would mean that he was above the horse and so would be able to get on quite easily. This he managed to do, finally, when the horse was more or less stationary, putting his foot in the stirrup and, with some effort, swinging his leg over the saddle, only to find that he was facing the tail! He was not amused, but despite this anecdote he was certainly not unintelligent.

It is easy enough to depict the hunting set as a lot of morons, 'the unspeakable in pursuit of the uneatable' as Oscar Wilde is so often quoted as saying, which indeed he did, though it is usually conveniently forgotten that he was speaking at a Melton Hunt dinner. His remark was intended as a joke, a joke at which I have little doubt his hunting audience roared with laughter, it being my experience that hunting people invariably enjoy a joke against themselves, which cannot always be said about intellectuals. Later the line went in a play.

Certainly when I started hunting again after the war two of the aspects that most appealed to me were the congenial company and the post-mortems, after a day's sport, with others such as Neil Foster and Will Pope, more knowledgeable than myself; to analyse all that had happened in the course of a hunt may be a simple exercise, but not necessarily one lacking in intelligence: indeed, it often demands a great knowledge and understanding of nature, as I was before long to learn. However simple an activity may appear to be there is, more often than not, much than can fully stretch one's intellectual faculties.

Chapter 7

Master of one

Once I had decided that I was justified in taking up hunting again, and had discovered that I could do so without any drastic interference with my work at Pendley, I soon reached the conclusion that I was also entitled, like other people, to take a holiday from time to time. I now had an excellent staff at Pendley, quite capable of running it in my absence, much as I might like to think that I was indispensable. I had always felt that as Pendley was my family home I should be there whenever people came to stay, especially on weekend courses. It was as host that I saw myself rather than Director or Principal or Warden. To be absent seemed to me as uncivil as inviting someone for the weekend and then going away. This was, I think, an understandable attitude, but it did not prove difficult for me to be persuaded that it was unrealistic, arguably arrogant. I even convinced myself that I might do my job better if I had an occasional holiday.

A very happy ten days in the South of France, therefore, when I found myself seriously considering marrying again – but it takes two to make that sort of decision – was followed a month or two later by an amusing weekend in Paris with a young friend, Caryll Cavendish, now Lord Waterpark. We drove down from Calais in an open car on a sweltering day in August and staying with his charming and fascinating aunt, delightfully named Mimi de Gielgud, one of the celebrated theatrical family. On our arrival she plied us with litres of cold white wine to quench our thirst. Having then dined us superbly – her table was famous, even in Paris – she took us, together with an attractive young opera singer, to the famous Bal Tabarin, where of course champagne was immediately served at our table on the edge of the floor. It was very hot and after the long drive and rather too much wine it was all that I could do to keep awake. The lights went down, the cabaret started, the floor in front of us opened and from the centre of the great cavity appeared a huge tinselled tree with no less than forty beautiful nudes dangling from the branches, some of them close enough to touch. It was all too much for me and I fell asleep. When I woke up – five, ten or twenty minutes later, I do not know – the tree had vanished, but not the nudes. They were all languishing around in various poses on my side of the stage, while a glaring white spotlight not only bathed them in its beam, but also included me as part of the show – 'the Englishman whom forty Paris nudes sent to sleep'. Madame de Gielgud did not seem too pleased, but the little break did me good.

My next holiday was the result of an unexpected invitation from a friend who worked for a bank in Barcelona – a holiday that I will always associate with an incident that was to have a great effect on my life. On my arrival at the airport I was greeted by a complete stranger who informed me, in a slightly inebriated manner, that he was a colleague of my friend, who with his wife had been called away to Paris to attend a funeral. He had been instructed, therefore, to install me in their flat two or three miles from the centre of the city, up on the hill. Here, he said, I would find all that I needed including some money, under the pillow (there were still strict currency regulations), and an attractive Spanish maid who on my arrival was on the sofa in the sitting-room with her boy-friend watching the television. She entirely ignored my presence until after the boy friend had departed, after which she looked after me extremely well. I was most comfortable and very happy, enjoying particularly the presence of some budgerigars in a cage – for me an entirely new experience, which I found most engaging and relaxing. I explored the city, went sight-seeing, and worked on a production of *The Tempest* which was to be produced later that year at Pendley. When my friend and his wife, a French girl, returned it appeared that the tiring journey had affected their relationship for they never stopped quarrelling. Few things are more embarrassing to an outsider than married couples quarrelling, so I decided, first, to forget any thought I might have been entertaining of marrying again, and then, after three days, to make an excuse to pay a visit to Majorca as I had not been there before. A travel agent soon fixed me up at a very pleasant hotel at Campo de Mar where, to my astonishment, though I did not at the time appreciate the significance of it, on either side of the reception desk hung large prints, heavily framed, of the famous Cecil Aldin pictures of the Grafton and the Whaddon Chase Hunts.

On my arrival back in Barcelona after a pleasant little interlude my friend informed me that there was a message for me at the bank – the only address that I had been able to leave – asking me to ring the B.B.C., at once. Surprised and impressed I did so immediately, eventually getting through to the right person in the right department. They were proposing to televise some show jumping from Richmond Royal Horse Show the following week. They would like me to do the commentary: could I manage it? Needless to say I could, although it meant finishing my holiday earlier than I had originally intended.

At The Horse of the Year Show the previous October Peter Dimmock, then Head of Sport, had asked me if I would be interested in doing a television commentary as he liked the way I handled the public address. 'You've got a good voice and you seem to know your stuff.' Over the last year or two I had built up something of a reputation for myself as an 'announcer', attempting to be interesting as well as factual. I made it my business to be as well-informed as possible about the horses and riders, aware that in those days few people had any knowledge of this little known sport of show jumping. Obviously, the idea of being used by the B.B.C. had appealed to me, but I was not over-hopeful. So often something that is mooted, even promised, does not materialize. Peter Dimmock, however, was as good as his word, perhaps because he had recently married Polly Elwes, who had performed once or twice in our productions at Pendley. Hurriedly packing my bags, I set off for home, confident that fame and fortune were within my grasp, if that was what I really wanted. But not for the first time, and certainly not for the last, I was quickly disillusioned.

Before going to Richmond I had taken the trouble to be even better briefed than I usually was for a public address job. I had satisfied myself that I was fully familiar with every relevant detail of both horses and riders, the rules and the dimensions of the fences as well. Unfortunately, however, the Show was running an hour late. When the time came for transmission the arena was occupied by the Metropolitan Mounted Police, who were presenting their musical ride, about which I could think of very little to say despite the fact that before the war I had been a member of the Mounted Specials which had given me the opportunity to enjoy at first hand various ceremonial occasions, in 1937 Coronation and some first-class football matches, but had taught me nothing of their musical ride. After a lengthy hiatus, which added to my embarrassment, a class of hackneys came into the ring to be judged. Here again I had little to say because of inadequate knowledge. I pointed out lamely that they picked up their feet very high, suggested that they wore heavy shoes in training, referred to the bearing rein similar to that worn by Ginger in *Black Beauty*, but apart from an unfortunate reference to a well-known lady driver while the screen was filled with a close-up of the hind-quarters of one of the hackneys I had remarkably little to contribute.

'I thought you were supposed to know something about horses,' hissed the producer down my earphones.

'I do, but . . .'

'Shut up!'

I had forgotten that anything I said went out to a million homes.

'This is hopeless,' I heard him mutter.

Much to my chagrin the jumping had not even started by the time we were off the air. I was mortified. Prior to the programme the producer had suggested that I went round to the 'scanner' after the transmission. It would all have been recorded which would enable me to see a playback for myself. But I could think of nothing more devastating than to go through it all again, so as soon as it was finished I slunk away to my car and drove back to Pendley. To my delighted surprise Peter Dimmock telephoned me a few days later to ask me to do another broadcast. This time it was from none other than the International at the White City. No mention whatever was made of the Royal Richmond, for which I was most appreciative.

At the White City the commentary was shared by three of us: Peter Dimmock, Bill Allenby and myself. We sat there, in the open, like three crows on a branch, each talking for ten or fifteen minutes, then handing over to the next. After two or three more small shows I was invited to commentate at the Horse of the Year Show at Harringay, on my own. Shortly afterwards commercial television came into being, whereupon the B.B.C. offered me a 'retaining' contract for my exclusive services, which meant that I could not work for the rival organization. I was guaranteed a minimum of £600 a year, which seemed to me very generous for a beginner.

Show jumping quickly became extremely popular on television – it is, in fact, a natural television sport – riders and horses such as Harry Llewellyn and Foxhunter, Pat Smythe and Tosca and Prince Hal, Wilf White and Nizefela, Peter Robeson and Craven A, soon becoming household words. Inevitably I gained a certain reflected glory, as did Pendley. People hearing of my association with Pendley seemed interested to meet the man behind the voice. Visiting speakers at that time ensured that our week-end courses were full. They included W. A. Darlington, Ivor Brown, Brian Vesey Fitzgerald, Clemence Dane, Stanford Robinson, Roger Bannister, Fitzroy Maclean, Sir David Kelly, the Ambassador to Moscow, Lord Boyd Orr, the nutrition expert, Chris Barber and Humphrey Lyttelton of jazz fame, and many others. Nevertheless, I felt more than ever that I should be present at Pendley when the house was full. I also believed that it was important that I should be present at our industrial courses on which we were so dependent financially. I was, too, personally involved in them. In the non-vocational 'The World We Live In' I played the part of the narrator in a special feature at Pendley known as 'Pages from the Past', which we presented as a means of depicting the cultural as opposed to the political development in different periods; it was the old Radio

Scrapbook technique. In the course for foremen and supervisors, I developed a talk on communications, convinced that many of the problems in industry were due to the lack of, or inaccurate, communication between one department and another, one level and another, between management and the floor, so many people finding it difficult to express themselves, especially at a meeting or on a public platform. This talk, which I called 'Putting It Across', was aimed at helping people to communicate more effectively. It was soon in considerable demand outside Pendley, with companies, societies, schools, and with various police forces, in particular the Police College at Bramshill where for twenty-five years I regularly contributed to their programme. Another reason why I felt that I should be at Pendley as much as possible was because I knew that it was alleged in certain quarters that I had only started Pendley in 1945 to save it from being sold out of the family, thus enabling me to continue to live there, at other people's expense. It was important that the cynics should not only know that I worked there, but that I worked hard and that I as well as Pendley was doing something worthwhile.

With hindsight I realize that I should have seen the conflict of interests looming up. Perhaps I did, but was so fully stretched that I did not have time to appreciate it, though looking back I have to admit that the facts spoke for themselves. Running Pendley, even allowing for the fact that I had an excellent staff, was really a full-time job. It must have been fairly obvious that my work for the B.B.C. would proliferate, as show jumping and, indeed, anything to do with horses, was becoming more and more popular. Already I had done two programmes from Pendley, one on the centre, one on my horses. I had been involved in programmes for children and programmes connected with the countryside, and I had also appeared on a number of panel games. Television could quite easily become a full-time occupation. Now I had taken up hunting again, finding it increasingly compelling. Should that also develop in such a way as to dominate my life, as seemed increasingly possible, then there could surely be a serious conflict of interests.

It came sooner and proved greater than I could possibly have anticipated. Once I had acquired Duke it did not take very long for me to become as enthusiastic about the sport as I had been in my childhood and before the war. Duke seemed to be a first-class hunter, only lacking, a little, a real turn of foot. In the 1950–51 season we had excellent sport, so much so that before long I was not only going out on Monday *or* Friday, but was making every effort to go out on Monday *and* Friday. The field at that time was small, but extremely friendly and as dedicated as I was. Most of them, living in the country, managed to hunt at least two days a week, often three and sometimes four, though they certainly could not be described as smart or wealthy. They just, for one reason or another had little else to do in the winter months.

Being able to hunt only one day a week, or at the most two, I began to feel out of it. It was frustrating when I went out on Monday to hear of the wonderful sport that they had enjoyed on the previous Friday or Saturday. In January Will Ivens, my wily dealer friend, told me that he had a nice young grey horse on which he would like me to have a day. We met at Wappenham village, right by the scene of the Cecil Aldin picture, had a brilliant hunt from Kingthorne, the covert just below Greens Norton, at the end of which only eight of the original field were still there. Needless to say I immediately bought this good five year old and called it Pied Piper.

Sport continued to be first class. January and February always being quiet months at Pendley I often managed, with my two horses – each as good as the other – to hunt three, even four days a week, dashing back to Pendley for the evening activities, and occasionally, even fitting in a talk before leaving for the meet. Being very much an outsider, in no way closely or personally involved in the Hunt, I had not appreciated that the Grafton Hunt was experiencing considerable problems, or if I had heard rumours I did not pay very much attention to them. All that mattered to me was the splendid sport that I was having, in the most congenial company on two outstandingly good horses.

A few weeks before Christmas, apparently, Neil Foster and his Joint-Master Claud Leetham had resigned. The reason for this was that the huntsman Will Pope, who had the full support of the farmers and most of the older subscribers, had threatened to resign himself unless there was a change of Mastership. When Dr Huggins, the Director of Music at Stowe School, who had so valiantly taken on the hounds after the war had had a bad fall and declared that it must inevitably put an end to his hunting, the Committee had invited Neil Foster and Claud Leetham to take over, but had never informed Will Pope who greatly resented it, and therefore them. It was well known that he wanted to complete his twenty-five years' service, the huntsman's equivalent to the 'ton' of a motor cyclist. To deprive him of this, therefore, was bound to lead to an unfortunate reaction amongst his farmer friends who were already talking of closing the country to the Hunt if their beloved Will Pope was allowed to resign before he had completed his twenty-five years in two years' time. By the end of January there was a serious impasse, a further complication being provided by the Hunt's critical financial position. Nor did it help when Lord Hillingdon, the so popular Master of my childhood, now Hunt Chairman, announced that he, too, intended to resign.

Not living in the country, but only dashing up to hunt from Pendley meant that I had few close social contacts and, therefore, knew little of what was going on, though obviously I was aware that all was not well. My chief contact in the Grafton country was Paul Hoskin who, despite his great weight and size, enjoyed his hunting to the full, riding a magnificent big heavyweight called Richard, which not only performed well in the hunting field but also won in the show ring. Paul Hoskin, like his father before him, always contrived to have a finger in the pie as, I have no doubt, he would be the first to admit. There was something of the kingmaker about Paul, something almost Machiavellian, yet invariably he had an instinct for doing the right thing, seldom with anything but indirect benefit to himself in mind. Having now made up his mind that some sort of action was necessary, of his own accord he went over one evening to see Will Pope who, he appreciated, was the key figure in the whole dispute. They had a long talk, during which, amazingly, Will Pope suggested that all the difficulties would be resolved if only 'Mr Dorian' were to take over the Mastership. He had been appointed by the father, he declared, so why shouldn't he be seen out by the son. Even Paul was at first taken aback, but he took the suggestion seriously.

When a day or two later Paul mentioned it to me I in turn assumed that he was joking, but by this time Paul had made up his mind, and once he has set his course he is not easily deflected. 'Think about it,' he said. 'We'll talk about it properly when you're here on Friday.' But as far as I was concerned there was nothing to talk about. During the next few days, however, he sounded out a few people in the Hunt. Ready at that moment to clutch at any straw, all were prepared to see it as an ideal solution, my father's brief era twenty years earlier still being remembered as a hey-day in the Grafton's fortunes. Thus fortified, Paul brought all possible pressure to bear on me. Reluctantly I had to agree that many of his arguments were persuasive: the chance to save the Grafton Hunt, the opportunity to fulfil an ambition – which he knew I had – the honour, the fun, the relaxation, the social advancement! How proud it would make my father, a return to the great days of the past, a still unique experience for a young man – an unparalleled privilege.

'But what of the cost?' I asked.

'A gentleman never considers the financial side of an undertaking,' said Paul grandly, airily waving away a possible, indeed probable, objection. 'Money is of the least importance.'

'Then what about the time?'

'No problem at all. You don't have to hunt every day. You will have a flat here. It only takes up five months in the year' – which, of course, he knew to be quite untrue. He said it need only be for a couple of seasons, just to see Will Pope out; everyone would be prepared to help; Ivens would find the horses and transport them to the meet for me. But I was still far from persuaded, especially when I thought of buying the Hunt horses. It was all that I could do to mount myself, as I began to explain. But Paul interrupted me:

'How would it be', he asked in an overpowering manner, 'if everyone were to shirk responsibility? You know perfectly well that as your father's son you are the right person. You know that it is your duty, and that if you really want to you can find both the time and the money. It is all a question of priorities. I am convinced that when you have thought about it sensibly you will not let me down. You know I would do the same for you, as my father would have done for yours.'

His devotion to the Grafton, if his efforts to solve their problems were anything to go by, was even greater than mine. But he was fantasizing, as I made clear to him when, confidently, I asked him: 'Who do you think you are? You are not even a member of the Committee. Even if I said yes – and I have no intention of doing so – it would mean nothing. It is the Committee that appoints the Master, not you.'

If I expected him to be nonplussed I was quickly disappointed. 'I represent the Committee,' he said confidently, then speaking deliberately added: 'I promise you that if you agree to accept the Mastership now, you will be officially invited within twenty-four hours. I'll give you until tomorrow morning to think it over. The Grafton needs you,' he concluded dramatically.

I had to admit to myself, as I drove back to Pendley that it was a great temptation; a dream unbelievably come true, but how could I possibly manage it? I went over that evening to see my father who after first remarking that they seemed to accept anyone nowadays as a Master of Hounds betrayed his real feeling of pleasure and pride when he said that he would give me £500 for two years if it helped. £500 would be a mere drop in the ocean, but it would certainly help; for some reason, moreover, the very fact that he had made the offer seemed to weaken my resolve.

I telephoned Paul in the morning and, hedging, told him that I could only consider it if I had a Joint-Master, preferably Neil Foster, as, in the first place, I was only too well aware that I had not the necessary knowledge. Secondly, I was certain that I would not have the time to run it all on my own. I also told him the absolute maximum that I would be able to find financially, which meant that someone else would have to find the bulk of the money. To my surprise, without any hesitation, he said: 'That's splendid; come over this evening and I'll take you to see Norman Gee.'

Norman Gee, a wealthy man who lived at Wakefield Lodge, where Lord Hillingdon had lived when I was a child, had been charged by the Committee with the responsibility of finding a solution. Obviously they had hoped that he would be prepared to take over the hounds himself, but with his very heavy business commitments this was impossible. Paul, at some time, had put his idea to him and he had been impressed. We went over, therefore, to Wakefield, in which I had not set foot since I was a child, but which Norman and Sheila his wife had made even more beautiful than I remembered. We had a long talk, during which I told him that I had really been bullied by Paul into going as far as I had, great honour though it would obviously be for me to become a Master of the Grafton. I explained to him that the only possible contribution I had to make was my name, which might enable Will Pope to carry on for two more seasons as huntsman, thus satisfying the farmers. I would need help, and even more important I would need money. I could only afford a sum which I realized was totally inadequate.

He told me at once to forget the financial side. He was prepared himself to buy the Hunt horses and would be responsible for the difference between the actual cost of running the establishment and the Committee's guarantee, in those days £3000 (the same as in 1922 and £1000 less than 1932!). As regards help, he believed that Neil Foster, for whom, like everyone else he had the greatest respect as a Master, could be persuaded to carry on contributing a similar sum to my own, but obviously we would have to see him and discuss the matter. This we did in Neil's tack room in his stable yard at Blakesley, on the way back home from hunting the following day. Neil and I did not then know each other very well, but neither of us anticipated any difficulty in our working in double harness. He could provide the expertise, while I would simply contribute on what one might call the public relations level, securing the services of Will Pope and the backing of the farmers. Norman Gee would, apart from our humble contributions, provide the money.

In view of Norman's great generosity and the service that he had done the Hunt in achieving a solution to their problems – thanks not a little to Paul Hoskin – we insisted that he should join us in the Mastership, should the solution be acceptable to the Committee. We assured him that between us we would relieve him of any administrative responsibility and see that his generosity was not abused. Somewhat reluctantly he agreed, but even at this late moment I still hesitated finally to commit myself, asking if I could be allowed just a little longer before making an irrevocable decision. Norman Gee reminded me that it was stipulated by the Masters of Foxhounds

Association that all new Hunt appointments should be settled by 1 February. It was now 12 February. The Hunt Committee was meeting in three days' time: I must make up my mind, without fail, within forty-eight hours. I had the impression that Neil, too, welcomed the breathing space.

On the way home I called in on Will Pope. It was obvious that he was sincere when he said that unless I came in as Master he intended, quite definitely, to resign. He also said something to the effect that at present it was the old 'uns who were keeping hunting going, as they had in the war and ever since. How was hunting going to survive unless some good young 'uns came in and helped? he asked. He then made a remark that I have never forgotten and which all the time that I have been a Master of Hounds I have found to be true:

'Sport is the priority,' he told me. 'If you provide good sport you'll never have to worry about finance. I'll see you have good sport, sir. We've the best pack of hounds and the best farmers in the country. You come in, sir, and we'll put the Grafton right back at the top of the tree.'

Before I left the Kennels I knew that I was committed. The simple philosophy of Will Pope had convinced me. That evening I telephoned Norman Gee to tell him that I would definitely accept the Mastership, with Neil and himself, if invited. Two evenings later, 15 February, he rang me back to say that the Committee were extremely grateful to the three of us for agreeing to take on the hounds. Next day out hunting at Stoke-Nine-Churches – what a lovely name – I was greeted as a hero, almost as a saviour, such was the relief that the future of the Hunt was settled, and I began fully to appreciate for the first time the enormous responsibility that I had taken on.

Looking back, I know that I should have considered the whole situation much more thoroughly, in much greater depth. In which direction did I really want to go? Was I completely dedicated to Pendley, the Adult Education Centre, with the Sports and Arts Centres that we had been contemplating? Or did I hope to make my name on the B.B.C.? Or had I, in my heart of hearts, always had an urge to return to my roots and live the life of a country gentleman? If I had taken the time and trouble to consider the whole problem seriously, weighing up all the factors, I would, I imagine, have accepted that the logical thing to do was to settle firmly for one, or possibly two of the options. But impetuous, over confident perhaps, I was carried away and greedily settled for all three, which was a challenge, but hardly practical. I had already been referred to on more than one occasion as a jack of all trades. At least I could now say that I was Master of one.

Chapter 8

Green swards and pastures new

Jack of all trades. In the early fifties it was certainly hard to refute the accusation that I seemed to have enough 'trades' to occupy two or three people: Director of an Adult Centre, broadcaster, lecturer, writer, producer, Local Councillor, County Councillor, Rotarian, Master of Foxhounds. By rights some of these interests should have suffered – most of them, perhaps. But it was as though I had the luck of the devil, and the devil well and truly looked after his own. I was fortunate, too, in that I was possessed of boundless energy. No day was too long for me, no distance too great. I had always enjoyed being busy of course and now, as long as I knew the direction in which I was going the amount of work involved never worried me. I was happier than at any time since the Greens Norton days, more confident than at any time since I left school.

Admittedly I managed to shed much of the load. I gave up my Council work and Rotary. In the latter I had reached the level of Chairman of the District International Committee, which had greatly interested me, especially the clubs I founded for people from overseas, which I believe still flourish. I limited my broadcasting to commentating on equestrian events, and I delegated much of my responsibility at Pendley to the excellent staff I then employed. Nevertheless, there was still more than enough to occupy me fully. But of all the 'trades' it was the one of which I was Master – in the titular sense only – that not only for the next year or two involved me most, but which gave me the most pleasure and satisfaction.

Yet within weeks of becoming a Master of Foxhounds something happened which could easily have proved a total setback. A Master of Foxhounds is officially appointed as from 1 May. Before the month was out I was in my study at Pendley one evening working on the draft programme for the following year, helped by a charming Swedish au pair girl, Anna Greta, when the telephone rang. As I walked across the room to answer it I turned to her and said, 'This will be bad news.' It was one of the hunches that one occasionally has, and unfortunately I was right.

Neil Foster was on the telephone. I could tell from his voice that it was serious.

'Norman Gee is dead,' he said.

I was staggered. I had spoken to Norman on the telephone only the evening before, discussing affairs connected with the Hunt. Now he was dead, apparently as a result of a shooting accident at his home at Wakefield Lawn – an unbelievable tragedy. The wider implication of it all was not lost on me, but being human it was almost impossible not to react, after the first awareness of the immensity of the loss, to its implication for oneself. Before long I realized that Norman's death automatically ended the Mastership. Neil confirmed that this was so. The Committee had appointed us as a triumvirate. We were under no obligation to carry on, just the two of us. Nor was the Committee in any way committed to retaining just us two as Masters. I was appalled. It was unbelievable, it was cruel, it was – words, thoughts, simple common sense failed me. I told Neil that I would be over the first thing in the morning and put the telephone down.

For hours next day Neil and I talked, discussing the situation from every angle. The one point on which we were in complete agreement was that neither of us could put up the money that Norman had so generously guaranteed. Yet I felt sure that for us to back out now would be to let the Grafton down just at a time when it seemed that we had helped to save it. Nor, obviously, did I relish retiring from the Mastership after precisely three weeks. Eventually, impulsive as ever, I told Neil that if the Committee wanted the two of us to carry on, as I believed they would, then I would undertake somehow to find the money: I did not know how or where, as there were few wealthy people in the Grafton Hunt, but I was convinced that it could somehow be raised. We duly informed the Chairman that we were prepared to carry on if it was their wish. Our appointment was immediately confirmed and Neil Foster and I carried on as Joint-Masters.

Within a few weeks of his death Norman Gee's widow, Sheila, who as a child had been in the Pony Club with me and loved her hunting, wrote to me on behalf of Norman's executors to say that all his commitments would be honoured in full for two seasons. This very generous gesture understandably took a great weight off our minds, especially mine. Fortunately for me, too, work connected with the Hunt in the summer months fell much more heavily on Neil than on me, it being in the summer that I was most involved with my commentating on show jumping, which was still becoming more and more popular. The onus of responsibility for the Kennels fell on Neil, the horses, of which I was in charge, being happily out at grass in the park at Pendley. Nevertheless, I spent as much time as I could visiting farmers in the Grafton country, both those who were old friends of more than twenty years earlier and new ones. I also concerned myself fully with the administration, having agreed to look after the wages, insurances and all that side, with the help, of course, of the office staff at Pendley and my father's old Greens Norton secretary, Arthur Hornsby.

The figures involved speak for themselves. Even though they refer to nearly thirty years ago it is difficult to believe them. The wages of Will Pope, in his twenty-third season as huntsman of one of the best-known Hunts in Britain, were £6 16*s* per week. (When he had started as 'covert lad' at the age of twelve he had been paid 2*s* 6*d* per week!) In addition he received a coal allowance of £17 p.a. and a light and heat allowance of £1 5*s* p.a. He had his cottage, of course; a delightful old place, in the middle of Paulerspury village, adjoining the fine stable yard and across the road from the Kennels. Even allowing for his rent-free accommodation his real salary was less than £500 p.a. yet he was not only huntsman, he was also stud groom – someone, in fact, who carried a great responsibility. He received, as do all huntsmen, his 'perks' – the money made from skins, grease, manure and so on, worth in a good year, he once told me, £1000 p.a. The whipper-in, Joe Miller, who had been with the Hunt nearly twenty years, received £6 per week, the grooms and kennelmen £5 per week, with their cottages, of course, and coal and light allowances, but nothing else. 'Perks' were exclusively the huntsman's. When Joe Miller succeeded Will Pope as huntsman in 1953 I suggested that he should share the 'perks' with the other kennel staff, but he would not hear of it. He would not have waited twenty years for the job, he said, unless he had been sure that he would receive the 'perks', the huntsman's one realistic reward. If he were not to get them in full he would not accept the job.

New kit for the Hunt staff in 1951 amount to £50 approximately, plus £7 tax: 18 gns for a red coat, £20 for two pairs of twill breeches, £10 for one pair of boots. Caps, overalls and hunting whips came to another £12. Huntsman, whippers-in, grooms and kennel staff were expected to provide their own stocks or hunting ties and stable or kennel clothes. The tack, saddles, bridles, leathers, irons, etc. which we had to buy for the Hunt cost us £150.

We reduced the number of hounds from sixty couple to fifty couple and decided that we could manage with eight horses instead of twelve as had been considered necessary in the seasons since the war – compared with Lord Cadogan's forty-two horses in 1939. But the cost of keeping these in our first season amounted to £1160, to which had to be added veterinary stores, veterinary surgeons' fees, the blacksmith, stud fees and transport – another £700. With wages – a little over £2000 for both stable and kennel staff – fuel, various items of equipment, postage and telephone, licences and insurances, the total cost to the Master was £5200. Of this the Hunt guaranteed £3000, exactly the same amount as they had guaranteed my father in 1928, over twenty years earlier. The Masters, therefore, were considerably out of pocket, entirely apart from their own hunting expenses.

The Hunt itself, in addition to paying the Masters, was responsible for the upkeep of the Kennels, stables and cottages, repairs and damage in the country and the Secretary's expenses – in those days £500. All this amounted to a little over £2000, making a total, with the guarantee, of £5000. Subscriptions, the Point-to-Point and various fund-raising activities, just about covered this.

The following season the figures, both for the Master and for the Hunt, remained more or less the same. It may be of interest to compare the figures of my first season, in 1951, with the figures for my father's first season in 1928, and my Whaddon Chase figures for the season 1976–77, remembering that both in 1929 and 1951 the Grafton was a four-day-a-week pack, whereas the Whaddon Chase in 1977 was a two-day-a-week pack.

The guarantee in 1928 was £3000; in 1951 £3000; in 1977 the Whaddon Chase Masters' account was met entirely by the Committee with a contribution from the Masters. Subscriptions in 1928 were £6400; in 1951 £3400; in 1977 £16,000. Maintenance of country in 1928 was £2000; in 1951 £1500; in 1977 £4400. 'Caps' and field money amounted in 1928 to £250; in 1951 to £605; in 1977 to £4500; cost of Kennels rates, rent, repairs, was in 1928 £725; in 1951 £1200; in 1977 £2500. Profits from Point-to-Points in 1928 £300; in 1951 £255; in 1977 £2000. Postage came, in 1928 to £25; in 1951 to £200; in 1977 £500.

To summarize, one can say that the cost of running a four-day-a-week pack in 1928–29 was £6000; a four-day-a-week pack in 1951–52 was £5000; a two-day-a-week pack in 1976 was £20,000, which reflects first the comparatively extravagant way in which a Hunt was run in the 1920s, the shoe-string methods necessarily employed immediately after the war and the ravaging effects of inflation in the late seventies. As a matter of interest the cost of running a five-day-a-fortnight pack when I first became Master of the Whaddon Chase in 1954 was £6000. These figures will be of only academic interest to many, but they do, I believe, shed valuable light on Hunt finances over the years.

Remembering my father's insistence on organization I did my best to emulate him. With Neil's agreement I divided the country into areas, each one to be organized by someone experienced, respected, enthusiastic, who would make every effort to make the country more rideable by persuading farmers to take down barbed wire and by putting in hunt jumps. The area organizer was also asked to do all that he or she could to stabilize, and improve where necessary, the relations between the Hunt and the farmers. Originally a member of the Hunt had been invited to be responsible for his or her own parish, but after the war many who had previously looked after a parish had given up hunting, left the district or died. It was considered preferable, with many fewer people now hunting, to have much larger areas. Even with twelve areas it was not easy to find people to take charge of them. Before the beginning of the season, however, we had collected twelve volunteers who immediately set to work with enthusiasm. It was quickly appreciated that the operation was going to cost money. Officially the organization of the country is the responsibility of the Committee, but as was quickly made clear to us, the Committee just did not have the money to do anything. We decided, therefore, to formulate a Social Committee which would be responsible for raising the necessary money. The target, which seems modest enough today, was £500. The response was most gratifying, by the end of the summer the Committee having all but achieved its target. There was a feeling that something was being done, that the inertia of the post-war years was now being replaced by a determination to provide once again sport of the highest order. At all levels there was wonderful co-operation, which as the opening meet approached created an atmosphere of excited anticipation throughout the country.

Going round the farms in the Grafton country that summer I soon appreciated how much I owed to my father and the reputation that he had created more than twenty years earlier, not only during his brief spell as Master, but even more during his eight years as Secretary during which he had earned such affection and respect. Again and again visiting a farmer I would be told that I could count on his whole-hearted support, just because I was the son of my father. Again and again both by farmers and subscribers I was made to feel that as my father's son I was the harbinger of a return to the good old days. The end of my father's Mastership in 1931 had been followed by the critical thirties with its economic problems and looming war. The war itself had been followed by a period of re-adjustment when there were still great shortages, when the country was still committed to a war-time agricultural policy, when the younger generation was only gradually doffing its uniform and re-establishing itself in civilian life.

When the fifties came, life in the English countryside was almost back to the pre-war normal. It was the exact psychological moment for a renaissance in foxhunting in Britain. It was my fortune to be part of that moment – even more to appear, though unproven, to have the required qualifications. In the autumn of 1951 there was a growing belief that at last, after some twelve twilight years, we were nearing the dawn, we were on the threshold of expansion when once again hunting would come into its own. The privations, restrictions, frustrations of war-time were at last behind us. In our Hunt, a microcosm of what was happening all over the country, this feeling was infectious, inspired by the fact that there were two young Masters, both with foxhunting in their blood, with a veteran huntsman, the doyen of his profession, thus combining the best of the new and the old. Many were reminded of a famous era of the Warwickshire Hunt when in 1935 Dickie Samuel (now Lord Bearsted) and John Lakin, two youthful enthusiasts, took over the hounds, appointing George Gilson, himself a young man at the beginning of his career, as huntsman. In the history of foxhunting there are many instances of the fortune of a Hunt being revived by the appointment of a young Master, often at the end of a difficult period. Invariably such an appointment is accompanied by a wave of optimism and enthusiasm.

Shortly before the opening meet Neil and I attended a Farmers' Dinner. When we entered the room the whole company rose, giving us a most gratifying ovation. In the minds of those keen hunting farmers we were associated with a hopeful new era, with the restoration of the great days of the past which would eclipse the difficulties and disappointments of the last decade. It was, of course, fortuitous that I should be the one to benefit from this current state of euphoria in the Grafton Hunt. Sir Hereward Wake, who had succeeded Lord Hillingdon as Chairman of the Hunt Committee, wrote to me: 'I hear such good accounts of what is going on from every side. It all reminds me of those grand days when your dear father was Master with Arthur Guinness and you were still on a pony, and hunting meant so much to all of us.'

What a great privilege I had inherited, what a responsibility, what a challenge I had accepted. I was thirty-seven, but I felt and perhaps behaved as though I were ten, fifteen years younger. Indeed, it was as though I had lost altogether those post Greens Norton, post Harrow years, which in retrospect seemed so unreal, so blurred, so indeterminate. Being relieved, too, of the almost total involvement with Pendley, much as I had enjoyed it during the past five years, made me feel as though I had shed years. I was young again rather than middle-aged, or so it seemed to me. Apart from the contacts connected with my job I mostly associated with people much younger than myself, especially of the opposite sex. My attitude to situations was far more that of someone in his early twenties than in his late thirties. I reacted to any given situation enthusiastically, or in despair. I loved or I loathed. I succeeded or I failed. For many with similar youthful characteristics there are no half-measures.

It was probably true to say that while, in the early fifties, I was on the brink of maturity, I still retained much of the blind enthusiasm associated with immaturity. It was this, perhaps, that gave me such confidence – a confidence that enabled me to surmount many mistakes, but also to take many risks. In the autumn of 1951 as my first opening meet approached, though increasingly aware of the problems and pitfalls, I was confident that I could succeed as a Master of Foxhounds. Indeed, I was taking it so seriously that failure seemed out of the question. How could I fail when everything was going so right for me? Nevertheless, as I drove from Pendley to Blakesley on Monday 9 November 1951, I was as nervous, taut, excited as a bridegroom, or a Member of Parliament about to make his maiden speech.

I met the hounds at Bradden cross-roads two miles from the meet and rode with them to Blakesley. The huntsman and both whippers-in were mounted on greys, two of which Norman Gee had bought before his death. By chance I, also, was on a grey. It had been my intention to ride a brilliant thoroughbred chestnut that at the end of the previous season I had bought from Phil Oliver, Alan's father. He was a hard puller, no longer in his first youth, which was why I only had to pay £200 for him, but an outstanding hunter. Unfortunately a week earlier he knocked himself, developing a big leg, so had to be left behind. No doubt we looked a very gallant sight, all on greys, as we rode into Blakesley where Neil was waiting for us – but how I was to rue it before the day was out.

There was a splendid turnout. I had persuaded as many as possible to wear red coats even at the risk of the reek of mothballs distracting hounds from the fox's scent. Out of a field of more than eighty there were some eighteen riders in scarlet. It was the best and most impressive turnout since the war. As a faithful foot-follower remarked, it was just like old times. Not quite, to be truthful, but it was much nearer to the hunting that I remembered with the Grafton twenty years earlier. Neil, despite his seniority, insisted on my acting as Field Master. We had arranged at the beginning of cubhunting that each would take charge on alternate Mondays and Fridays, the other being responsible for the Wednesdays and Saturdays. It worked out that it was my turn the week of the opening meet. I had suggested that the rota should start again with hunting proper, Neil starting off as Field

Master on the important day, but he would not hear of it. In his eyes we were *Joint*-Masters in a new régime; the fact that he had already been in office for one and a half seasons was, to him, immaterial. Greatly honoured, I was at the same time very apprehensive. Indeed, I nearly had the whole field left when after killing a fox locally we drew Greens Park. I had no link between myself and the whipper-in at the top of the covert. It was at Greens Park, too, that I suffered my first major embarrassment as a Master of Hounds. After a thoroughly enjoyable hunt in a big circle over the best of our country, lasting more than an hour, the fox returned to Greens Park, which is not so much a covert as a strip of woodland either side of a brook. Only a hundred yards or so long, and very narrow, it was likely that our fox would go straight through. Obviously, therefore, Will Pope, the huntsman, wanted someone at the end of the strip. To my surprise he called out to me to 'get up to the top' in a somewhat peremptory tone. But I was holding the field at the bottom of the strip to make sure that the fox could leave it in any direction.

When I did not move he shouted at me, from the other side of the brook, even more sharply. This, I admit, annoyed me. After all I was Master. To be shouted at by the huntsman in front of the whole field, even if he had known me as a boy, was an indignity that I did not appreciate. When he shouted again, to save my face I asked one of the field to go to the top of the strip. It was then that Will realized at whom he was shouting. He had mistaken me for his first whipper-in, also on a grey. He was, of course, mortified. Later I laughed at the incident as much as anyone, but at the time I was not amused. It had punctured my new found glory as an M.F.H.

That night Paul Hoskin held a dinner party at Wicken for Neil and Rose Foster, Toler Aylward, the very popular Hunt Secretary and his wife, and myself. He insisted on our wearing our red evening coats, but I firmly refused, remembering an experience of my father's. When he and Arthur Guinness were Masters the local G.P., Doctor Murray of Blakesley, invited them and their wives to dinner as the executors of one of his patients had given him a bottle of priceless brandy from her cellar. He begged Arthur Guinness and my father to come in their red coats as he wanted it to be a festive occasion. When the great moment came to drink the brandy it was discovered that the bottle did not contain brandy at all – it was furniture polish! The old lady, a teetotaller, unbeknown to her executors, had poured all the brandy down the drain. Poor Dr Murray was wretched, his guests in their red coats unable in any way to compensate him and Mrs Murray for their disappointment.

No furniture polish was in evidence at Wicken that night. It was champagne, a vintage claret and an unimpeachable brandy. Paul was determined to make it an evening of celebration. The sport enjoyed at the opening meet had not in any way let down the high hopes shared by every section of the local countryside community, the farmers, those who rode to hounds, those who followed on foot or in their cars. This was, Paul insisted in his flamboyant style, the beginning of a great era.

It must be difficult for many today to understand such an intensity of feeling, such exuberant optimism about something so irrelevant as foxhunting. But at that time, in the countryside, there was something almost symbolic about foxhunting which in almost every county of Britain dominated the social scene. It was not only in Europe that on the outbreak of the war the lights had gone out: in the English countryside it was as though a curtain had been drawn. Six years later the war was over, but the countryside was deprived. It took many years to recover – to some it seemed that it might never recover, thanks to the continuing privations and a growing socialist ideology. The first hint of dawn, therefore, at the beginning of the fifties was heralded all over the country as a return to Utopia, the less attractive features of the pre-war years being conveniently forgotten. It was a return at last to the good old days and as such was welcomed almost with hysteria, but also, in the countryside, with an endearing optimism. Before long the fact that times had changed, even in the hunting field, would have to be accepted, but in 1951 the new dawn was greeted with an unshakeable confidence. One was only too ready to identify oneself with it.

I had no less than sixty days' hunting with the Grafton between the beginning of November and the end of March, my first season as Master. With typical beginners' luck sport could not have been better. Day after day, except for a brief and welcome respite when frost prevented hunting in February, sport was as good as one could hope for. But although good organization, experience and skill are essential in providing or improving sport, it is nevertheless indisputable that good sport is dependent upon good scenting conditions. In 1951 from the very start of the season scent was exceptional; indeed, I can remember few periods in my hunting experience when scent was better. My hunting diary at that time makes evocative reading: 'brilliant forty-five minutes with a six-mile point from Brackley Gorse'; 'finding in kale by Sulgrave they ran at top speed towards Allithorne, which was missed by half a field as they swung for Stuchbury, which they also missed, racing for Greatworth where they checked for the first time after thirty-five minutes.' (James Hanbury and Tony

Murray-Smith, Masters of the Belvoir and Quorn respectively, were out on this day.) 'Lovely evening hunt from Bairstows: they flew to within a field of Ascote Thorns, left-handed to Grubbs Copse and to ground in the earths beyond: fifteen minutes of the best, the bitches almost impossible to live with.

Thanks to the efforts of the entertainments committee the money that had been raised had been well spent in making the country more rideable, taking down barbed wire and putting in hunt jumps. There was a wonderful feeling amongst all sections of the community; everything was going better than one could ever have hoped. Will Pope, in his twenty-fourth season, was at his best. It was obvious that he was determined to finish in a blaze of glory. In the opinion of many he was back in the form that had made his fame in the thirties. It was as though he was determined to ensure the success of the new régime, wanted to justify the stand that he had taken, which had, of course, resulted in my becoming Joint-Master. He was well into his sixties, but to see him ride across country was still an inspiration. He was never in a hurry, seemed almost instinctively to know the quickest way out of any field, often jogged into a really big fence which his horse then jumped better than many who attacked it with much greater speed and determination. His hounds, particularly his bitches, which were the joy of his life, were never in better form than that 1951–52 season. If there was any scent at all they could be guaranteed to provide sport with Will seldom having to touch them: 'The wire-free fences, thanks to Henry Brook, enabled a large field to see the bitches hunting quite beautifully across the grass', from my diary. Hunting four days a week two separate packs were employed – a bitch pack and a mixed pack. In earlier days, as is still the case in a few countries, a pack entirely of dog hounds was hunted in the woodlands on Wednesdays and Saturdays, Bitches, of course, are faster than dog hounds, which is ideal in a grass country, but it is reckoned that the presence of a few dog hounds in a bitch pack has a steadying influence – the reverse, some might say, of human society!

There was still the odd occasion when Will Pope would have a lapse. It was unfortunate that one of these days was a day when Neil Foster could not be out due to the start of his duodenal ulcer trouble. This meant that I was in sole charge. Hounds met at Silverstone where, in pouring rain, the Hunt staff and others were entertained at the village pub. I myself arrived late, not in the best of humour. Hacking up towards Silverstone from Whittlebury I had dropped my whip. As I dismounted to pick it up something frightened my horse, which shied away, then tried to bolt. As there was no one with me I had to hang on, and was dragged about fifty yards down the muddy road. I was not quite as elegant as I would have wished, therefore, as I rode up to the pub. I gratefully accepted a drink, realizing that Will Pope had already equally gratefully accepted more than one. Due to a fall on his head during the war a little alcohol went a long way with Will. For the most part he was aware of this, being careful not to take more than was wise. It was, perhaps the cold, ceaseless rain falling that day, that made him throw caution to the winds on this occasion.

We went straight to Bucknells, a huge woodland which was also a reservoir of foxes. Hounds finding immediately we listened to them as they hunted round the wood for half an hour or so, while we waited by the entrance hoping that a holloa from Joe Miller's usual corner on the Wappenham side would tell us of a fox's departure. We were in need of a warming gallop. There was then complete silence which, after an hour, I realized had been abnormally long. Had hounds slipped away without my knowing? Had Joe's holloa not been heard in the ceaseless rain? I asked one of the small field to go round the side of the wood and find out if Joe was still there. Ten minutes later he returned, accompanied by Joe, who, like us, had heard nothing. I asked him to go into the wood and see what was happening. It was a quarter of an hour before he returned. He then beckoned me to join him some yards down the ride, away from the field. He had 'found Mr Pope, sir' – his horse tied up to a tree, Mr Pope sitting in a ditch, sound asleep. 'Perhaps you'd better speak to him, sir.' I could not see how that would help, but, thinking quickly, I said, 'Tell Pope that I've given the order for home, that I would like to see him at Colonel Foster's at Whittlebury at seven this evening.' I then suggested to the field that as it was so wet and that as it seemed unlikely that any fox would ever leave the wood, we should all go home, although it was only one o'clock.

At Neil's that evening – I thought it better that he, too, as senior Master should be involved, though it cannot have helped his ulcer – Will, by this time completely sober, was abject in his apologies, assuring us that it would never happen again, an assurance that proved to be very nearly true. At all events sport continued to be first class until the end of the season.

Neil Foster and I from the very beginning worked together in complete harmony, our efforts and responsibilities being complementary, though it was Neil, living in the country, and running the Kennels, who bore the lion's share. Officially in charge of the stables I left this side almost entirely to Will Pope who had for so long been responsible for the stables, 'without interference' as he put it. My main contribution was on the social and public relations side which, with everyone so friendly, co-operative, enthusiastic, I could not fail to enjoy, though often it meant getting back to Pendley later than I intended. Having called in at a farm on the way home from hunting it was not easy to hurry away, nor had one any desire to do so. There are few more satisfying experiences than relaxing in a cosy farmhouse with the family over a cup of tea or with a large whisky in one's hand, yarning over the day's sport. I enjoyed every minute of it.

If I were likely to be very late, or if as on a Friday or Saturday I were hunting two days running, then there was always my room at Wicken. Paul revelled in the fact that he had the Master under his roof. Close friends of long standing as we were, it was the fact that I was a Master of Hounds that gave him so much pleasure. He had been brought up to believe that the Master was the most important person in the countryside. He would, doubtless, have agreed with Trollope that a Master of Hounds is second only in importance to the Lord Lieutenant, superior even to the local Member of Parliament. With Paul nothing was too good for the Master, nothing too much trouble. Only the best food and drink were suitable, Paul being able to provide both at the rectory which was becoming increasingly successful as a guest house for elderly gentlefolk. On any pretext he would insist on giving a dinner party; always a hilarious affair. It was sufficiently hilarious on one occasion for a guest to bear no resentment when he found that my terrier had eaten away one leg of his new dinner suit under the table. On another occasion he invited a wealthy tycoon to dinner, ostensibly to introduce him to the Master, as his daughter was thinking of taking up hunting, but before the evening was out he had collected a cheque for £500 made out to the Grafton Hunt. Two of the inmates of his rectory were octogenarians, both widows of famous Masters of Hounds. One was Mrs Clayton, whose first husband, Anstruther Thomson, had been a distinguished Master of both the Bicester and the Pytchley. The other was Mrs Selby Lowndes, whose husband was the legendary Master of the East Kent, and whose father was none other than Parson Milne himself, for so long Master of the Cattistock. They fought constantly, each using a barbed invective: 'My dear Mrs . . . – I can never remember your name.' Rosie Clayton would say, 'I have more foxhunting in my little finger than in your poor little body.'

'Maybe,' the brave little Mrs Selby Lowndes, crippled with arthritis, would reply, 'but I think you will find that more people today have heard of my husband than yours,' which was true enough – and then, rubbing it in, 'either of them', with a final deflating, 'or your father.'

'Why?' the imperious Rosie would ask witheringly. 'Was your father anyone special?'

It was like something out of Somerville and Ross, the best tonic that one could possibly wish for at the end of a day's hunting, which had probably finished at about 4.30 pm with only a handful left out. The handful usually included Anne Holt (now a Joint-Master of the Grafton herself and married to Dick Hawkins, another Joint-Master), Billy Beale (now Master of the Tedworth), Sheila Gee, Norman's widow, Henry Russell, a popular farmer who had the privilege of piloting the Prince of Wales when he hunted with the Grafton in 1977, and Paul Hoskin. There were seldom more than eight or ten left out for these evening hunts when so often the sport is best and, therefore, with such a small field, the most enjoyable – a regrettably selfish attitude, one has to admit. Naturally it was those who were keenest who stayed out until the end, and as such were probably better mounted. There were no second horses in those days. For Paul so often to be amongst this 'happy few, this band of brothers' was both a tribute to his pluck and a liability to the rest of us. Paul Hoskin rode all of twenty stone, and his great horse, Richard, was well over 17 h.h. He never hesitated to jump anything that anybody else jumped, though there were occasions when he tackled an obstacle for which he was not ideally suited, such as a wide brook or a post and rails under a tree. Nothing, however, deterred him, nor did he ever resent his tumbles. When, usually on a Monday, there was only this handful left out we used to take it in turns to assume responsibility for Paul. This involved keeping an eye on him and picking him up if he fell off. Our fear was that if anything happened to him, with no one following, he might find himself lost and abandoned as night fell. Yet, resourceful as he is, I have little doubt that he would somehow have turned it to good account. Certainly he made the most of any incident that he had experienced when he regaled his guests at dinner in the evening.

'Champagne, Derek! This is an occasion for celebration! Only the best is good enough for the Master! Bring up a bottle of brandy and fetch the cigars. We must live like gentlemen, my dear D, as befits those who enjoy the sport of Kings! Eat, drink and be merry, for tomorrow – ! Where's the meet tomorrow?'

His enthusiasm was boundless, and infectious. No one staying in his guest house could be anything but a supporter of foxhunting. Except on Sundays, and only briefly then, was the conversation on anything but foxhunting, other than racing. The village accepted his eccentricities, and filled his church when on more than one occasion he gave them a racing tip from the pulpit, or told them he expected them to support the meet in the village the following Saturday.

Hunting at this time may have absorbed much of my time, but not quite all of it. I was still running Pendley, though I could never have done so without the help I had from my staff. Ronnie Ogden and David Hicks were successively most reliable Number Twos, the latter marrying the charming housekeeper of that time, Katherine Messenger. Patrick Stevenson, an Irishman, who looked after the Art and Music, was most gifted and slightly unconventional, something that always goes down well in a place like Pendley. Perhaps the most talented, certainly the greatest character, was Murray Fieldhouse, who ran the Pottery, earning the admiration of the great Bernard Leach himself. It is probably true to say, however, that the member of the staff who made the greatest contribution at Pendley – and stayed the longest – was Margaretta Bennett, principally responsible for the weekend courses. Despite the fact that she had one paralysed arm there was nothing that she would not tackle from cooking in a crisis to gardening. She could lecture on almost any subject and was an extremely clever writer, being responsible for our 'Pages of the Past' mentioned earlier. She could also be very forgetful in an engaging way, once forgetting to confirm a weekend course, with the result that fifty people (trade unionists, unfortunately) turned up totally without any warning. When she left she departed without her leaving present! She and I were completely opposed politically, but the greatest of friends, largely due to her enthusiasm and marvellous sense of humour, an essential quality in any member of the staff at Pendley at that time. Only the heads of departments were English. The domestic work at Pendley was undertaken by girls from overseas who came to us for a year at a time. We had many particularly charming and capable girls: Mireille from Switzerland stayed on to become for a short time my secretary, Francina from Holland became housekeeper and returned to England to be matron at a Greater London Council residential school, Marejka, another Dutch girl, was one of the nicest girls we ever had, but one could have forgiven her if she had never come at all. Due to a misunderstanding she missed her train, arrived in the middle of the night, walked two miles into Tring with her cases in the pitch dark, actually passing Pendley, finally knocking up complete strangers who most kindly brought her to the house. Anna Greta was a most attractive Swede who adored England and never wanted to leave. She came back after a year to marry an English doctor.

Finally in this era there was Liliane, from France. She was very shapely, very excitable, generally very Gallic, and not very good at her job. She was engaged in a constant feud with Murray Fieldhouse, whom she would refuse to serve when she was on dining-room duty. He usually accepted her behaviour with exemplary composure, but on one occasion he exploded, as only he could, tipping the coffee urn all over her. With a shriek she swooned, collapsing at the foot of the stairs, to be surrounded immediately by a number of attentive police sergeants who were on a course at Pendley. As can be imagined the sergeants handled her with the greatest care, loosening her belt, undoing various buttons, all but giving her the kiss of life. Hearing the commotion I came down from my room upstairs, picked my way over her prostrate body, knelt down and asked her if she was all right. Letting out a weary sigh she then opened one eye very wide and winked. She loved being the centre of attention, and knew when she was well off !

On another occasion a foreman from Burslem gave Liliane a playful pat on the bottom as she passed him in the hall. Turning, her eyes blazing, in her most haughty tones she informed him that in France they did not do things like that, to which the foreman replied cheerfully, 'And in Burslem they do not have bottoms like that' – which could well be true.

Liliane was succeeded a year or two later by Arya from Finland, who loved Murray as dearly as Liliane had hated him, and so remained at Pendley for several years. She was very lovely in character as well as physically – and was known as the Marilyn Monroe of Pendley. One evening when she was in her room changing my two-year-old son walked in to find her standing there completely nude. For several moments he surveyed her, then solemnly pointing at her feet, he said, 'You've got no shoes on, Arya.' Such tact.

Old Springham, the Pendley butler, had retired, but in those years I could never have survived without the maintenance man, who cleaned my hunting clothes, looked after my car, kept the chickens, did a hundred and one other things for me, all on top of his routine work at Pendley. His real name was Silvanus Cheeseman, but having once misheard his wife calling him, as I thought, Cyril – instead of Sil – he has at Pendley been Cyril ever since, and I am glad to say after thirty years still is. In the early days of the Shakespeare productions he played a vital and prominent part, not as an actor, except for one brief appearance as Peter in *Romeo and Juliet*, with all but one of his lines cut, but with the scenery, the lighting, the awning erected over the seats when there were no stands; on more than one occasion he even acted as prompter. He was a real man of all work, and a great friend.

It was at about this time that the Festival came to assume, through unusual circumstance, a rather more important role in the Pendley curriculum. *Henry VIII* and 'Falstaff' had been followed by *Twelfth Night* which was performed in the rose garden round the sundial (a professional producer, Juanita Hayes, was kind enough to write that it was most pleasing on eye and ear and the most imaginative production of the play that she had seen) and *The Tempest* was performed in the rockery. In 1953 we decided to produce *Romeo and Juliet* against the west side of the house, using the library balcony and the balcony above it, the glass conservatory becoming the ball-room. It was a setting to give a producer most challenging and exciting opportunities. The cast that year was, too, the most talented that we had as yet had, led by a very young Romeo and Juliet, both of whom were to make names for themselves professionally. Antoinette Galetti featured in several films before she married, and Anthony Page became the leading producer at the Royal Court Theatre, Sloane Square. The first performance earned universal approval, the second performance was somewhat spoiled by intermittent rain, the third was wrecked by a thunderstorm. After so much hard work, lasting several months, it was frustrating in the extreme. Since 1949 less than half-a-dozen performances have been seriously affected by rain, but, understandably, knowing the vagaries of English weather, one was anxious in those early days with only three performances, lest at least one, possibly all three, might be rained off. I decided, therefore, that if the Festival were to run for a week one might be unlucky enough to lose one or two performances, but never all of them, thus the work put into a production could never be wholly wasted. In extending the Festival we naturally had doubts as to whether there was a big enough potential audience to support six performances of one play. The obvious answer was to put on two plays, which might be a gamble, but in those days we were confidently in the mood to take a gamble. A bigger problem was casting. To find enough people to take the thirty or forty speaking parts in two Shakespeare plays was not going to be easy; to find enough local people would be impossible. The solution seemed to be to recruit people from further afield, though this would create problems with rehearsals. One could hardly expect people to come twenty-five miles or more to rehearse so many evenings a week and at weekends. The problem was resolved by adopting a pattern which has been followed at all Festivals ever since. One of the plays – later it was to be both – was entirely cast with people from further afield who would be accommodated at Pendley for a week before the performances, rehearsing all day and every evening. We were confident that it would be just as possible for a team of dedicated amateurs to produce a play in a week, as for a professional repertory company.

We advertised in the *Amateur Stage* and *The Times Educational Supplement*, both of which produced promising results; auditions were held and the casts assembled. The plays selected for this first Festival proper were *A Midsummer Night's Dream* and *Julius Caesar*. For the most part the former cast from locals, the latter from the 'residents'. The atmosphere was that of the old country house cricket week. Everyone involved had the same interest and, therefore, whatever their background, or age, mixed well. With everyone so fully occupied an infectious urgency was generated, with everybody ready to turn their hand to anything that might be demanded.

It proved to be a strong company, with real talent, and the weather could not have been better. In the wonderful open-air setting there was a kind of magic – especially in *A Midsummer Night's Dream* – seldom experienced in the indoor theatre. There was, too, one particularly dramatic effect in *Julius Caesar* when at the end of Mark Antony's famous 'Friends, Romans, countrymen' speech, as the crowd rushed off shouting: 'We'll burn his body in the holy place: and with brands fire the traitors' houses! Go fetch fire!' a huge bonfire a hundred yards out in the park, screened by the ten-foot-high yew hedge at the back of the stage, was lighted, throwing up a great sheet of flame which lit up the whole sky. From the first performance the Festival was sold out. The status that it has reached today undoubtedly stems from that year or, more accurately perhaps, from the preceding year when the thunderstorm had wrecked *Romeo and Juliet*.

By coincidence the B.B.C. was that year running a series entitled 'Out of Doors' transmitted live on Sunday afternoons. Godfrey Bazeley, of 'The Archers' fame, who was the producer, asked me if I would care to contribute one Sunday talking for a few minutes about the breeding of hounds. When he came down to Pendley to discuss the programme he learnt something of the various Pendley activities, including the Shakespeare, a rehearsal of *A Midsummer Night's Dream* actually being in progress. The result of this was that he decided to devote the whole programme to Pendley that Sunday, a rehearsal of *The Dream* thus being televised. One could scarcely have asked for better publicity.

It was comparatively unusual for me to be doing an 'in vision' broadcast as when taking on the hounds I had decided to limit myself to commentating, persuading the B.B.C. to agree to my never working on a Saturday between 1 November and 31 March. I had given up being chairman of a programme about dogs called 'The Smokey Club' which was recorded in Glasgow each Friday when it was decided to transmit it live on Saturdays. I had enjoyed it, although coming down from Glasgow by sleeper each Friday night in time for hunting was tiring. Nor was I very happy with my own performance in the programme. For any but the most professional it is not easy to relax in a studio, the exact timing that is essential making concentration difficult. If every sentence is learnt by heart it lacks spontaneity, and if it is left to chance one is worrying all the time about the clock, when one has enough to worry about already. It was once pointed out to me by Peter Dimmock, the head of Outside Broadcasts, that in interviewing I had fallen into the habit of repeating the answers: 'Which is your next show?' 'Next week I go to Geneva.' 'Oh, you go to Geneva?' 'How long for?' 'I am going for a week or ten days.' 'A week or ten days. Which horses are you taking?' 'I'm taking Happy Days and Chronicle.' 'Oh, you're taking Happy Days and Chronicle. Do you think they'll win?' – and so on. It is an easy habit into which to fall, a habit not altogether unknown amongst interviewers today.

To succeed 'in vision' necessitated, I felt, being involved full time. I was not prepared for this. I was content to be a commentator, believing that my voice had more to contribute than my face. Fortunately for me I found myself quite sufficiently occupied as a commentator, show jumping now being firmly established as one of the most popular sports programmes on television due, ironically, to the only post-war Olympic Games in which I was neither directly nor indirectly involved, and which were not televised.

Chapter 9

The horseworld beckons

In the 1948 Olympics at Wembley my public address commentary on the show jumping on the final day had been fed into the television which was covering show jumping for the very first time. The Helsinki Olympics in 1952 were not televised. This was a great disappointment to me as my father had been responsible for the training of the Three Day Event team. There can be no doubt that they would have won a medal had Major Lawrence Rook not had a most unfortunate fall at the end of the course when his horse, Starlight, put its foot in a gutter and turned over. Lawrence remounted, but having been concussed he went the wrong side of a direction post and was disqualified, thus eliminating the whole team. Everything, therefore, depended on the British Show Jumping team which, unbeaten in two years, started as hot favourites. As no British performer had won a medal of any sort in any sport at Helsinki it was more than ever important that the British riders should succeed. The first round, however, was disastrous, Britain standing only sixth after an uncharacteristically bad round by Foxhunter and Harry Llewellyn: but the second round was a very different story. Both Nizefela ridden by Wilf White and Aherlow ridden by Colonel Duggie Stewart achieved good rounds, Foxhunter finally clinching it with a brilliant clear round, the only clear in the whole event.

As traditionally the team show jumping is always the last event before the closing ceremony this was a medal for Britain literally at the fifty-ninth minute of the eleventh hour. Not surprisingly the British team came home to a hero's welcome. For the first time show jumping received full coverage from the press. The British riders had saved the day. Show jumping was a sport at which the British could succeed and Foxhunter was a superman, or, more accurately, a superhorse. This was just the tonic that was needed both by the public, frustrated by the failure of our athletes, and by show jumping. The Horse of the Year Show a few weeks later was completely sold out. Two competitions were televised each evening, the last event often over-running by anything up to an hour, the B.B.C. knowing that the viewers would be infuriated if it were cut off before the end. In those days timing was not so important. Nowadays the show and television co-operate to ensure that the events finish on time; only very rarely does a major over-run occur. The sudden enormous popularity of this new sport was greatly to my advantage, and at that time I had the field more or less to myself. More than that, as the producers, although technically brilliant, then knew very little about show jumping I also had a considerable influence on the production. As I have described in my book *The Horse of the Year* (David and Charles, 1976) I was responsible at that time for both the public address and the television commentaries, using two microphones. No one seemed to think this particularly strange, although people often imagined it must be very difficult when it was, in fact, easier. Doing both, the two commentaries could be made complementary, and one could not be interrupted or contradicted in the middle of saying something. Occasionally one picked up the wrong microphone or forgot to switch off the public address. Once at the Royal International Horse Show at White City I announced that Her Royal Highness Princess Alice, the Countess of Athlone, was coming into the ring to present the rosettes, then turning to Raymond Brooks-Ward, who at that time was my assistant, remarked 'And my god! what a hat!' which observant comment echoed round the arena to a roar of laughter. As the public address was difficult to hear in the centre of the arena I tried to persuade myself that Her Royal Highness never heard what I had said, but I was firmly given to understand later that other members of the Royal Box party heard it well enough!

For technical reasons it would today be almost impossible for a commentator to do both commentaries, but in those days I used to enjoy it and, obviously, it made my voice well known to a large public. Frequently I was referred to as Mr Show Jumping. There was another aspect of my commentaries which was unusual. Partly because I was doing the public address which was always done from 'control' so that one had access to immediate information, and partly because from the very beginning I felt that it was impossible to communicate atmosphere successfully if one was enclosed in a sound-proof box. I always did my commentaries from the ringside or, as at the White City, from the centre of the Arena. In this way I felt that I could involve the viewing audience in the atmosphere of the show. I have always believed that, although the first responsibility of the commentator is to inform and identify, it is equally important to communicate the atmosphere.

One of the advantages of being involved from the beginning was that it enabled me to evolve a style of my own. In *Clear Round* (Hodder and Stoughton, 1957) I wrote, 'It is the duty of the commentator, by the whisper over the viewer's shoulder, as it were, to keep stimulating interest, answering the instinctive question before it is asked.' I still see it that way: 'the whisper over the viewer's shoulder'. I learnt very quickly that although statistically one might be talking to five or ten million people one had to remember that one was also just talking to two or three people in their own sitting-room at home. They did not want to be shouted at, or addressed as at a public meeting. They wanted only to be informed, but they liked, too, to identify themselves with the 'live' audience at the show, sharing their excitement. I have sometimes been criticized for being partisan, a criticism that I cannot honestly deny. But while I appreciate the danger of overdoing it, I believe, nevertheless, that it is the duty of the commentator to convey to the viewing audience the emotions of the 'live' audience. If everyone is rooting for Britain then so am I, if everyone is in an agony of suspense as David Broome sets off against the clock to beat Alwyn Schockemohle, then so am I. In other words I am communicating, which seems to me more the commentator's job than merely being coldly factual. Obviously one can say too much, but if one has built up the competition effectively, then an 'ooh' or an 'ah', or an intake of breath is sufficient to communicate the atmosphere. Nor should it be thought that a British audience is supporting only British riders. Fair and knowledgeable, it often shows its enthusiasm for a rider from overseas, a d'Inzeo, Winkler, Schockemohle, Eddie Macken. One tries to communicate this, too.

Within two or three years of my first broadcast I had been lucky enough to televise shows from Paris, Brussels, Rome, Aachen, Rotterdam, Dublin, Vienna, Stockholm, all of which added to the variety in my life in those years. Paris in 1953 was the most exciting show that I had, up till then, been to, being the forerunner of the Horse of the Year Show. Called, simply, Le Jumping it had an atmosphere all of its own; an atmosphere created by the uninhibited enthusiasm of the Parisian audience for their favourites d'Oriola, d'Orgeix, and, of course, the exquisite little Michèle Cancre. It is Brussels, however, that I remember best. To begin with it was the very first overseas show to which the B.B.C. had sent me. To discover that I was considered sufficiently important to be sent to a foreign country at someone else's expense was extremely gratifying. Even better, I was accommodated, much to my surprise, at a first-class hotel, the Belgian television service providing a car to take me to and from the show, executives of the Belgian television service looking after me and entertaining me most handsomely. Unfortunately the show itself was not quite such a happy experience. Timekeeping has never, in my experience, been considered very important at a Continental show. On the occasion of the broadcast from Brussels, which was live, the show was running at least one and a half hours late. It soon became obvious to me that far from getting the end of the competition in the forty minutes transmission time it was unlikely that we would even get the start. I explained the problem, on the telephone, to 'presentation' back in London. Not very helpfully they informed me that it was up to me to fix it with the organizers.

Fortunately I had met the Director of the Show when earlier in the year he had come over to the White City. Seeing him in the centre of the ring directing the building of the course, I approached him and told him of my difficulty, but he was quite unmoved. I explained that we were televising the show live to Britain from 9.20 to 10.00. He was not impressed. 'I cannot bother about television,' he said. 'They pay me nothing.' (This was true. The huge viewing audience for show jumping in Britain, and the consequent huge fees, are unique. I remember being told in Rome that R.A.I. paid only £300 for transmission of their whole international show; that figure could be multiplied by a hundred in Britain. No Continental show is likely, therefore, to bend over backwards to accommodate television.) I pleaded with Monsieur le Directeur, but to no avail. His only concession was to allow Pat Smythe to jump out of order, with the result that she was one of precisely three riders British viewers were fortunate enough to see after I had filled in on nothing for nearly half an hour. 'Presentation' was in near hysteria. It was not exactly a push-over for me either!

On one occasion the international show at Rotterdam coincided with a production of *Henry V* in the Shakespeare Festival at Pendley, but this did not appear to present any problems as the transmission was from 3 pm to 4 pm and there was a plane back from Amsterdam at 6 pm arriving at Heathrow at 6.45 pm. To my dismay, however, halfway through the broadcast I was informed that as the England versus Russia athletics match at the White City had been cancelled the transmission of the show jumping would continue until 5 pm. Apparently a female Russian athlete had been caught shoplifting in C & A stores in Oxford Street, three rather exotic hats having taken her fancy. The Russian manager objected to her being accused of stealing, but the police refused to withdraw their summons so, at the very last moment, the Russian team walked out. Continuing with the broadcast, I managed to organize a car to collect me and convey me to Amsterdam where the authorities had been alerted to hurry me straight through passport control and customs to the plane. All fortunately went according to plan, although I caught my plane with only two minutes to spare after a drive resembling a Hollywood chase. When we touched down at Heathrow, however, it was raining heavily and I realized that the performance at Pendley would have to be cancelled, so did not drive back to Pendley in too much of a hurry. When I arrived at five minutes to eight I was greeted by Ronnie Evers, Chairman of the Committee responsible for the Festival, who told me that despite the weather – at Pendley there was a steady Scottish mist – the stands were more than half full, the audience apparently quite ready to sit through the performance. As I was taking the part of Chorus, which opens the play, I had to don my costume in seconds rather than minutes and dash for the stage at the top of the lawn. We started on time to the astonishment of the audience, many of whom had been listening to me in Rotterdam only a couple of hours earlier. That we started at all under such unpleasant conditions was greatly appreciated by the audience, which was, of course, under cover. As it turned out the inclement conditions were responsible for one of the most effective productions ever staged at Pendley. Flags and cloaks drifted in the wind, glistening as the lights picked up the moisture, horses squelched through the mud on their way to Agincourt and smoke from braziers spiralled in contorting patterns across the stage. Neville Barber, a heroic young Henry V, was later to have a successful professional career, but I doubt if he ever encountered more remarkable conditions.

Vienna was memorable for a wonderful four days with the Spanish Riding School, as a guest of the great Colonel Podhajsky. This was for a very interesting joint production by the British and Austrian television services. Equally memorable, though less pleasant, was a near disastrous landing at the airport in a snowstorm, necessitating three attempts, since when I have always tried to avoid flying in winter. Undoubtedly the most enjoyable assignment of all was Stockholm in 1956. Because the quarantine regulations prevented the equestrian Olympic events being held in Austria, they were held separately in Stockholm. Although the most effective transmission was, as is generally the case in the Olympics, the show jumping, with a bronze medal for Britain, whose team included Pat Smythe, the first lady to ride in the Olympics, it is for the Three Day Event that I will best remember the Stockholm Olympics. My father had heard that the Queen would like to be represented in the Olympics, and had bought a horse called Countryman III from a young West Country farmer, Bertie Hill, who had ridden in the 1952 Olympic Games. It was decided that the horse should be owned jointly by the Queen, the Queen Mother, the Duke of Beaufort and my father, but should be registered in the Queen's name and remain the mount of Bertie Hill.

Their performance soon led to their being selected to join Colonel Frank Weldon with Kilbarry and Major Lawrence Rook with Ted Marsh's Dublin Champion, Wild Venture.

As is invariably the case overseas, even in the Olympics, the arrangements for televising the cross country were virtually non-existent. The only way that we could cover the event was to take a camera round on a Land Rover while I simultaneously recorded commentary or 'dubbed' it on during transmission. The weather in Stockholm had been fine until the evening before the cross country when, as in Canada, it rained all night, making the going on the course very treacherous. The first to go for Britain was Lawrence Rook with Wild Venture. Their round was the best of all those who went first for their teams, many having problems at the twenty-second fence, a trakena – a rail standing in a very wide ditch. By the time Bertie Hill and Countryman's turn came almost every horse, thanks to the treacherous approach, was faulting at this fence. By luck, our B.B.C. Land Rover was at Number 22 when Bertie Hill arrived, obviously making a very fast time. He met the fence perfectly but as he took off the whole bank gave way, leaving Countryman straddled across the pole with Bertie catapulting over his shoulder. Helped by many hands, including my own – to get him going again seemed far more important than to carry on with my commentary – Bertie tried to pull him over. All to no avail. Fortunately Colonel Gorden Cox-Cox, the Director of the Badminton Horse Trials, saw what was happening from where he was watching a little distance away, rushed down and insisted that a horse straddled across a pole could only be pushed backwards, never pulled forward, as he had learnt from personal experience. He was right, and in seconds Countryman was back on the take-off bank and Bertie remounted. With unbelievable calm – and courage – he took him back no more than six or eight strides, turned him at the fence again, jumping it effortlessly. But in addition to the wasted time it had cost him sixty penalties for a fall and twenty for a refusal. Ironically, immediately after Bertie Hill's fall that side of the fence was railed off. (At the Geneva International Show in 1977 a German horse got straddled across a wall. He too was only released by being pushed backwards.)

In our Land Rover we raced across the course to the last fence but one, a wide pile of logs, arriving shortly before Countryman reached it. The Queen and other members of the Royal Family were there with the Duke of Beaufort. The Duke beckoned me across to ask if there was any news. I told him of Countryman's fall, but the Queen could not believe it. By her timing her horse had reached the log pile quicker than any other horse. He could not possibly have had a fall, she said. I assured her that regrettably he had, but had not wasted too much time. In fact, despite the fall he still achieved one of the fastest rounds.

For Frank Weldon's round on Kilbarry we waited by the great electric scoreboard on which we could plot his progress. A different coloured bulb lit up at each fence as a horse came to it: yellow for over, green for a refusal, red for a fall. Standing with Frank's wife, Diana, and my father, the suspense was unbearable as we followed Kilbarry round the course – yellow, yellow; Fence Number 19, yellow, Fence Number 20, yellow, Fence Number 21, yellow, then an agonizing pause. This seemed to last for several minutes. Had Kilbarry, too, fallen at Number 22? Had he refused? The seconds ticked by. Suddenly, inexplicably, we noticed that the yellow light had not only gone up for Number 22, but it was also up for Numbers 23 and 24. Whether this was due to some arresting of our mental processes, whether it was some sort of optical illusion, or whether it was just a fault on the scoreboard I shall never know. What I do know is that when the yellow light went up for the last fence, and we saw Frank thundering past the finish below us, many of us were in tears with relief and excitement.

Despite Countryman's fall Britain was in a commanding position at the start of the third phase, the show jumping. Three good rounds clinched the matter, with an individual bronze for Frank Weldon – but for his unlucky fall Bertie Hill would undoubtedly have won the gold for the Queen as, twenty years later, but for an unlucky fall, there could so easily have been a medal in Montreal for Princess Anne. For the first time I had the unspeakable thrill of bringing to millions of viewers at home news of a gold medal. The lap of honour by those three magnificent quality horses, at full gallop, is a sight that I shall never forget, any more than I shall forget the Queen's cocktail party on board *Britannia* during that magic week in Stockholm. I will always remember, too, the dinner, a month later, that my father gave at Quaglino's for the owners and connections of the winning team, the Queen, Queen Mother, Princess Margaret and the Duke of Edinburgh all being present. The menu was most appropriate. On the front were sketches by Joan Wanklyn of the three members of the team. Inside there was a reproduction of Chrys's cartoon from the *Daily Mail* depicting a yokel shouting at a carthorse pulling a hay wagon crashing through a gate, with the caption 'And just what gave 'ee the idea that anything Countryman III could do you could do better?' Opposite was the menu itself, the first course, Ryltarolympiadens Smorgasbord, reminding us of Sweden. There followed A Countryman's sole, A Wild Duck's Venture, A Kilbarry Kooler (Soufflé grand success) and A Copperplate Trident (Trident had been the reserve horse at Stockholm). After this magnificent meal the forty or so guests danced until the early hours, a wonderful climax to an unforgettable event.

Indeed, for me it had been a wonderful decade: Pendley a success against all the odds, the happiest involvement once again with hunting, and now something of a name in television, thanks to my association with show jumping. It was, of course, an era dominated, as far as show jumping was concerned, by a remarkable man and a remarkable horse: Colonel Harry Llewellyn and Foxhunter. It is not easy today to remember the tremendous force they were in show jumping, the incredible adulation in which the public held them. Llewellyn and Foxhunter were names of no less magnetism than Stanley Matthews, Geoff Duke, Stirling Moss, in their own respective sports at that time. My own wife as a teenager, like a thousand others, sneaked into the collecting ring at the White City to steal a few hairs from poor Foxhunter's tail. Entwined round a horseshoe they survive to this day, in our bedroom. Huge crowds flocked to the Royal International Horse Show at the White City, the Horse of the Year Show at Harringay and many other shows just to see the legendary Foxhunter and Harry Llewellyn. When, in 1953, they won the King George V Cup for the third time they became national heroes.

It was wonderful for me to find myself on intimate speaking terms with Harry. He had been something of a hero of my youth, not, of course, for show jumping, but as an amateur National Hunt jockey. I had seen him win the Cheltenham Foxhunters and, the year before the war, come second in the Grand National on Ego. Now he was an Olympic Gold Medallist, the greatest name in international show jumping and we were moving in the same circle. I was both surprised and impressed when on one occasion, almost before we were on speaking terms, I had a post-card from him telling me that something I had said on television about Foxhunter was, in fact, inaccurate. How he knew I did not know, but he was right, as he was on another occasion when at the time of Foxhunter's retirement, in 1956, he told me that I had got the number of international events in which he had competed wrong – which I had – by one! In other words he missed nothing. His capacity for absorbing, and being generally involved in, a wide variety of interests is remarkable, as is now regularly evidenced in his capacity as President of the British Equestrian Federation and Chairman of the Sports Council in Wales, to say nothing of his interests in Kenya, the Algarve and, of course, his Welsh ponies.

It would not be true to say that his rise and fall was meteoric because with Foxhunter he totally dominated the scene from 1948 to 1953, but there is little doubt that he was subjected to and suffered the usual pressures of fame. There came a time when so great was Foxhunter's notoriety that he was expected to win on every occasion that he appeared in public. This put an almost intolerable strain on Harry and he began to falter. People said that he was losing his nerve, that he was having trouble with his eyes – which was, perhaps, partly true. But, as I see it, the real problem was that knowing that so much was expected of him he began to tense up; deprived of that relaxation which produces spontaneous judgement, so essential in the relationship between rider and horse, he was finding it difficult to see his stride, with the result that Foxhunter was making mistakes. Harry Llewellyn might not agree with this, but as a very constant observer I am convinced that this was the real cause of the great partnership's loss of form and eventual retirement, in 1953, mercifully still at the top of the tree.

Nor was the press always kind: 'Foxhunter fails again'; 'Another fall for Llewellyn'. Again it was largely a question of so much being expected of him. The press had run out of superlatives, and the natural reaction was to find fault. I once had the temerity to remonstrate with a well-known journalist who had written unkindly of Llewellyn and Foxhunter. He told me a strange story. Apparently Llewellyn had been flying to the continent to participate in the European Championships. At the airport a young reporter, who had been told to get an interview with him, asked him why he was going to Geneva or wherever it was. Harry promptly replied, 'to play ping-pong, of course', doubtless intended as a joke, though he might well, quite understandably, have felt that it was rather a stupid question in view of the fact that he was now a household name. According to my journalist friend this temporarily alienated the press who decided, as undeniably they can, to 'crucify' him, reporting only the bad things. The journalist's divulgence made a deep impression on me, and ever since I have tried myself to co-operate with journalists. After all, they are only doing their job, and to be snubbed or frustrated must be galling. Not that I am suggesting in this particular case that Harry Llewellyn had any intention of being awkward, but he suffered nevertheless.

If Harry was the hero of the fifties, Pat Smythe was certainly the heroine. With a modest background and little in the way of private means she reached the top while still in her teens, entirely unaided, on horses each of which had cost her a mere pittance: Finality, Tosca, Prince Hal. Until she partnered Bob Hanson's Flanagan, her mount in the 1956 and 1960 Olympics, she seldom rode other people's horses, yet she was National and European Ladies Champion on innumerable occasions, without any doubt the greatest lady show jumper of all times. Success never spoiled her; she remained as simple and dedicated as when she started. Indeed, the fact that to the end of her career she kept every rosette that she ever won, even if it was only a humble yellow for fifth, seems to suggest that she never entirely lost her sense of insecurity. It was as though she wanted constantly to remind herself of her success. From time to time her name was linked with various well-known riders, but it was not until nearing the end of her career that she married her childhood sweetheart, Sam Koechlin, who had been a student at the hostel her mother ran in Gloucestershire. He had returned to Switzerland, married the daughter of his employer, but after his divorce met up again with Pat and married her. They now live happily in Switzerland with their family.

Music was her great love and, I suspect, her safety valve. I once collected her from the little bedsitter she kept in Brompton Road for when she had to spend a night in London. When she opened the door she immediately asked me if I had a radio in my car – she was listening to an opera and did not want to miss any of it. We were going to the Horse and Hound Ball and finished up sitting in the car outside Grosvenor House waiting for the third act to finish.

Pat was also amazingly strong. She could never be described as big, but for a normal sized girl in her early twenties she possessed unusual strength. We watched the Coronation together from David Satow's flat in Pall Mall. Later, after dinner, we went along to cheer outside Buckingham Palace and watch the fireworks on the Embankment. Down there the crowd was of enormous proportions and after we had been there half an hour or so a quite frightening sway developed. It was not a pleasant experience at all. Suddenly Pat said, 'Let's get out of here,' and to my astonishment she shoved through the vast crowd with no difficulty at all while I was fighting to keep up with her. With her horses, of course, she was quiet and wholly sympathetic, having that rare ability to coax every horse she rode to give of its very best for her. In 1952 she lent Prince Hal as a possible for the Olympic team. Nobody could get on with him at all. At one show at which both she and members of the team were competing they handed back Prince Hal. Despite the fact that she had not ridden him for six weeks she proceeded to win the competition, beating all the Olympic riders.

Harry Llewellyn and Pat Smythe, backed up by others such as Wilf White, Peter Robeson, Dawn Palethorpe and Ted Williams, certainly made the public show jumping conscious in the fifties. I do not think that I am being too biased when I suggest that it was the hey-day of British show jumping. Inevitably I gained a certain reflected glory, but if I can claim that any success that I achieved in television at that time – I was twice nominated, unsuccessfully, for Guild of Television Producers and Directors Award – was mostly due to my own effort, the same cannot be said for the other equestrian activities that increasingly involved me during the fifties: the judging at horse shows of hacks and hunters, and election to the Council of the British Horse Society.

I was first invited to judge at a show for no other reason than that I was a Master of Foxhounds. It appeared to be assumed that if one had a pack of hounds one automatically had an eye for a horse. Mrs Gregson, for many years Master of the Crawley and Horsham Hunt and a great authority on hounds, was connected as Chairman or President with a big one-day show in Sussex. It was at this show that she invited me to judge. I told her on the telephone that I had never judged before, that I was totally inexperienced and considered myself quite unworthy to judge other people's horses, but she insisted that as the son of my father I obviously knew a good horse from a bad one, that as a Master of Hounds I had to buy hunters for myself and the Hunt staff and that it was only hunters that she was asking me to judge. It was obvious, therefore, that I would be capable of judging. She then told me that she was also inviting Neil Foster. Although at that time he, too, had done very little judging, I knew that he was as good a judge of a horse as he was of a hound, so felt justified in accepting. We drove down to Sussex together to commence with a class of heavyweight hunters at 9 am. Some eight came forward, each of which we both rode and, together, inspected. Having asked them to walk round we called them in, the best first and so on down the line. We were just having a last look when a man at the ringside called out in a most aggressive voice: 'Do you realize that the horse you've only pulled in fourth belongs to me? It's never been beaten.'

Without a moment's hesitation Neil said: 'Let's send them out again. We'll teach him a lesson.'

I was somewhat diffident but Neil, with his strong character, was adamant. They walked round again. We called them in again, but this time the big grey horse that had stood fourth was only called in sixth, which meant that it did not even get a rosette. Its owner walked away in disgust, fuming and promising all sorts of dire consequences for the judges, but others at the ringside applauded. Spectators, exhibitors and judges alike were tired of the bullying behaviour of this wealthy but unsporting patron. The constant flow of invitations to judge that followed this incident was doubtless due to the fact that, thanks to Neil, we had shown ourselves to be judges of integrity, not easily intimidated.

There is a great deal of enjoyment to be had from judging, but it is also hard work. Most show classes begin at 9 am, or even earlier, which means a very early start from home unless one can find the time to stay overnight. During the course of a day's judging one can ride as many as forty horses – on occasions more – and one therefore has to be very fit. There are rewards, of course. First, looking at and riding high-class horses, though by no means all the horses one judges today are high class. So many of the best three-quarter bred horses which constitute the majority of show horses are now creamed off for the more lucrative pastimes of show jumping and Combined Training, and a judge can have some appallingly bad rides, as well as good ones, especially at the smaller shows. Secondly, there are the very pleasant people one meets in the showing world. Most of those who organize shows do it in an entirely voluntary capacity despite the enormous amount of work involved. They tend, therefore, to be generous, selfless people, ready to do anything to help. The same can be said for the Stewards who spend hours in the ring with no reward other than a coloured badge on their lapel, and a free lunch if they are lucky enough to find time to have it. Exhibitors, too, and those who ride the horses, either as amateurs or professionals, are for the most part genuine people. Few grow rich from showing horses; most do it for love. Inevitably there is a certain amount of backbiting and criticism, but it is kept to a minimum. Were this not so, showing could never be so popular. Inevitably, too, there are a few sharp operators in the game, but as a judge one is far more likely to encounter two categories which are better described as opportunist rather than sharp.

First there is the flatterer: 'I've never seen the horse go better than it did for you, sir'; 'Most of them go better for you, sir, than for their own riders'; 'You really looked the part on him, if I may say so, sir'; 'No need to warn *you* that he only wants the lightest of contacts'. Such remarks are always very friendly and encouraging, but few judges are really influenced by them, nor do the riders expect them to be. It is just that they believe that a friendly relationship might be to their advantage, and that anything that can influence the judge in their favour is justified, and therefore worth a try.

Secondly there is the crafty one who, by chance, manages to let one know the horse's breeding – 'The image of old Game Rights, isn't it, sir?' – or its previous successes: 'It's come on well, don't you think, since it won at Newark, sir?' or 'I hope it gives you as good a ride as when you judged it at Leicester'; or 'It's only four, sir, but having won five in a row it has just about settled down'. Again the remarks are harmless, never really resented and, by most judges, totally ignored. Nor is it always flattery that a judge encounters. When I arrived at 8 am a few years ago to judge at Windsor the show ground was almost totally deserted except for one lady sitting at the ringside in front of the members' enclosure: 'Good heavens, are you still judging?' she greeted me.

There can, too, be anxious, even dangerous moments, as I was to discover early in my career. To my delight, in 1955, I had been invited to judge at Dublin for the first time. This was really due to the great affection and respect old Judge Wylie, that unique personality who for so long ran Dublin, had for my father. When after judging at Dublin for twenty-five consecutive years my father retired, to maintain the continuity the Judge invited me. I was asked to judge the lightweight classes. The system of judging at Dublin in those days is too complex to describe in detail but it amounted to seeing all the classes in the morning, discarding those horses that one did not think too highly of; then in the afternoon those which had not been rejected came back to be ridden and placed. Having called in the first class in an approximate order, I went to the bottom of the line to start riding, while the senior judge began at the top. As I approached my first ride its owner greeted me with a friendly 'good day, sa'ar', then hissed out of the side of his mouth, 'I should throw that away, sa'ar. He won't have that.' He indicated my riding stick, which I accordingly handed to my Steward. I took hold of the reins and, about to mount, lifted my left leg to the stirrup, when urgently he expostulated, 'No! no! sa'ar: he won't have that. He's never in his loife been mounted loike that, sa'ar. Let me throw you up', which I did with considerable misgivings. As I moved out of the line the horse went straight into top gear, circling the little ring about three times before I managed to get it under control. All was well, however, but I had quickly learnt that in Dublin as well as riding some of the best horses in the world one is likely to have some rather less reliable ones which can result in some tricky or embarrassing situations. But when it comes to judging the Championship, the privilege of the senior judge in each of the weight classes, in the most famous arena in the world, then one feels that any little discomfort or inconvenience is more than worthwhile. It is an unforgettable experience.

Belfast, too, is a wonderful show, but on one occasion it proved something of an ordeal. The first class of the day was for four year olds in which one horse stood out above all the rest. Having called it in first I went to ride it and was given a leg up by the Steward. As I landed in the saddle, and because of the unexpected weight, perhaps, his own rider being a lightweight, the horse reared and came over backwards, landing on top of me. No harm being done, fortunately, I was put up again, this time rather more carefully, and the horse duly won his class. There was, however, an amusing and unexpected sequel. Many years later, when I was judging at Dublin, an Ulsterman stopped me as I was walking through the arcade. 'Excuse me', he said, 'but I promised my next-door neighbour that I would speak to you if I saw you.' He then asked me if I remembered a horse coming over backwards with me in Belfast. When I assured him that I remembered the incident very clearly he told me that his neighbour had been in the stands on that occasion, in a fairly advanced state of pregnancy. Such was the shock of the accident that she immediately gave birth to twins, on the show ground. 'She thought you'd like to know', he concluded, 'that as a result of that she called one of her twins Dorian, and the other William', adding, 'and, sure, they're fine big boys now.'

If to be invited overseas to broadcast was an exciting experience, to be invited to fly out to South Africa and judge at the Rand Show, Johannesburg, was even more exciting; satisfying, too, in that the show kindly also invited Jennifer, whom I had married a year earlier. This first visit to the Rand was a wonderful experience, introducing us to many new friends. There was only one anxious moment. Judging a riding-horse class with well over sixty entries I carefully selected a front line of horses which I thought was worth riding, leaving the remainder in the back row. I had just started riding when the Senior Steward asked me if I would mind riding one particular horse in the back row as it belonged to an Afrikaaner and no Afrikaaner had ever exhibited before. I agreed, with some hesitation, as not only was his animal little more than 14.2 h.h. with a long flowing mane and tail, but it was quite obvious that the way in which this horse was ridden was very different to my own – more like the American saddle-horse style of riding. Sure enough I was all too soon at sea. Away it went with me at a pace more like a run than a trot, getting faster and faster. The harder I pulled on the reins to stop it the faster it went. After five or six circuits of the arena at top speed I decided the best way to bring it to a halt was to ride it into the lines of horses, which I did, as somewhat unceremoniously and not entirely voluntarily I dismounted. Fortunately none of the horses kicked out at us, and as I returned the horse to the Afrikaaner he thanked me most courteously.

Return visits to South Africa have been equally enjoyable, as have visits to other countries, indeed, to all shows, big and small, including of course those at Wembley. Curiously enough, I had never judged at either the Royal International or the Horse of the Year Show, being on the Committee and later Chairman of the Judges' Selection Committee, until recently when one of the Societies invited under a new scheme to nominate their own judges suggested, in 1976, that I might like to judge the Cobs. It was one of the wettest days of the year, the outside arena getting very deep. Nevertheless I was thoroughly enjoying the different rides until one, hitting a boggy patch, turned head over heels with me, for which unfortunate experience it seemed hardly worth waiting twenty-five years. There was, however, a happy ending to the story. Despite the fall (which was in no way his fault) I placed the cob fourth. Later that day the rider informed me that he had bought this cob two years earlier as something safe on which to start riding again, having earlier broken his spine in a riding accident. He was persuaded to enter the Horse of the Year just for fun, never in his wildest dreams expecting to qualify for the final judging at the evening performance under all the lights in the indoor stadium with its magnetic atmosphere, and to receive his rosette from a V.I.P.: a magical moment for him, and rewarding for me.

Although a judge can give complete pleasure to only one exhibitor in a class – the winner – yet often he can give pleasure to those less successful, just by telling them that he likes their horse, or that theirs is the sort of horse on which one would like to go hunting, or how well their horse is turned out. Despite the necessary detachment it is possible for a judge to establish a sympathy, a mutual respect, an understanding with exhibitors. It is not possible for every horse to win, but it is always possible for an exhibitor to catch a judge's eye just by taking sufficient trouble over its presentation. It may not be entirely ethical, but a judge is inevitably impressed by a rider whose turn out and presentation suggests a professional approach. Frank Weldon used to say, as usual with his tongue in his cheek, that when judging a hack class he awarded 50 per cent to the horse and 50 per cent to the girl riding it! Not surprisingly when once we were judging together we put up a smart little bay horse with an attractive girl on top. The horse had the delightful name of Reynali Arabesque, the girl was called Jennifer Neale. Two years later I married her.

It was Frank Weldon, too, who made a very true remark about elections to the British Horse Society, the premier equestrian organization in the country. In 1952 I had been asked if I would agree to be nominated for the British Horse Society Council. I suspect that I was only considered eligible because I was a Master of Foxhounds, as when first invited to judge, or because my father had been both Chairman and President. I accepted with some diffidence as although my father had been one of those who by amalgamating the two pre-war Societies, the Institute of the Horse and the National Horse Association, had brought the British Horse Society into being, my own involvement with the Society had so far been slender. It was limited, more or less, to the International Horse Show and the Badminton Horse Trials, the two B.H.S. promotions. I was fully occupied with Pendley, with television and with the Grafton Hunt, yet I was not unduly disturbed at the thought of a little additional responsibility as it did not seem likely to be very heavy. Everything seemed to be going so well for me at present; everything that I did was giving me such enjoyment: the thought of now being in close proximity to the seat of power in the horse world attracted and intrigued me. In any event I hardly anticipated being elected. There were only eight vacancies and the sixteen nominations included three Olympic riders, Alec Scott (1936), Arthur Carr (1948), Reg Hindley (1952), the international show jumper Ruby Holland-Martin, the first Director of Badminton Horse Trials, Trevor Horn, that great character and patron of show jumping, Bob Hanson, two doyens of the Riding School world, Jack Hance and Sybil Smith, and my stepmother, Brenda, who with my father was the driving force in dressage, had helped to train the Helsinki Three Day Event Team and was considered almost certain to be the first British rider to represent Great Britain in Dressage in the next Olympics. The redoubtable Glenda Spooner was also a candidate.

Greatly to my surprise and, I imagine, to the surprise of everyone else on the Council, I was duly elected. It was at my first Council meeting that Frank Weldon made his wise comment, which was not in any way intended maliciously. In a Society with a nationwide membership the votes inevitably go to the best known people, whatever the worth of their contribution to the Society might be. His name was a household word as an Olympic Gold Medallist; I was on television fifty or sixty times a year. To the ordinary membership our names were more familiar than those of others who probably had a much greater contribution to make. This statement by Frank was so palpably true that I resolved to do all that I could to be worthy of election. Within a very short time I had become fully aware of the value of the Society's work of which previously I had been almost totally ignorant. Not only was it responsible for Combined Training, Dressage, the Pony Club, the various B.H.S. examinations, an involvement in breeding, the International Horse Show (it did not become Royal until 1957) and the Badminton Horse Trials, but it was beginning to extend the area of its responsibilities, looking after the interests of ordinary riders. It was at this time that the Riding Club movement came into being. As in 1952 the Society had less than five thousand members, I was fortunate enough to become part of the administration when it was still at ground-floor level. The membership today is twenty-five thousand, plus another hundred thousand Pony Club and Riding Club members. The staff at the old Sloane Street office barely reached double figures. At Stoneleigh today it approaches seventy. The turn-over in 1952 was about £25,000; today it is £1¼ million. It has been fascinating and rewarding to be a part of its development, though as future chapters will show it has not always been plain sailing.

Certainly when first elected I never envisaged the total commitment that it was to become. For me, at that time, it was just another absorbing and satisfying interest which seemed in no way to conflict with my other activities – rather it appeared to add to my stature, giving me increasing self-confidence which enabled me better to enjoy my busy life. For the present I was on the crest of a wave. Obviously it could not last for ever, but I could see nothing to interfere with it in the foreseeable future.

Chapter 10

Life begins at forty

It was still hunting, despite all my other activities in the early fifties, that gave me most pleasure and satisfaction, and probably absorbed most of my time, particularly in the winter. The end of my first season with the Grafton was as good as the beginning: 'The last days of the season produced days typical of the whole season', it was reported in *Horse and Hound*; 'Hounds flew again', according to my diary; 'another racing thirty minutes', 'A superb gallop from Kingthorne to Weedon Bushes, flat out all the way', 'hounds hunted superbly', 'for the first time I had two horses out: both brilliant.' But my real memory of that first season is the wonderfully happy atmosphere. Everyone seemed determined to help. We had co-operation on all sides: landowners, subscribers, farmers, those who followed hounds in the cars. This latter was something quite new and, therefore, a little suspect; even now there is a certain controversy. It cannot be denied that the over-zealous car follower can spoil sport, by heading foxes, and cars can also cause congestion on roads, to the annoyance and inconvenience of other road users. But this basically is a matter for education, certainly more needed today when car followers are much more numerous than thirty years ago. On balance, even then – and certainly now – I was in favour of car followers, though I suspect that I was in a minority. It always seemed to me that they not only supported the hunt, demonstrably, but they also acted as ambassadors for the hunt. As others enjoyed their football or their racing on a Saturday afternoon, so they enjoyed their hunting, carrying back on Monday their genuine enjoyment of hunting to the different backgrounds from which they came. It was a case, too, of those who are not against us are for us, and in the changed post-war conditions we could not have too many for us, or so it seemed to me.

The leader of the car followers in the Grafton country was a great enthusiast called Ernie Griffith, for whom nothing was too much trouble. At the end of the day his delight was to give those still left out a cup of coffee, or something stronger, and a sandwich, and to organize their transport, the horse-boxes probably being several miles away. He and his friends formed a loose organization of car followers which they called the Car-ites. I tried to persuade the Hunt Committee to recognize this little group officially, but they could not then agree to do so, feeling that it was too unconventional, and the hunting world is very conventional. This was a pity as they could probably have claimed to be the original Supporters' Club. Today over 70 per cent of the Hunts in Britain have their Supporters' Clubs, most of which play a vital role and are considered invaluable.

At the first dinner that the Car-ites organized at the end of the season at Blisworth, where Ernie Griffith lived, to contrast the existing happy situation with that of a hundred years ago, I quoted from *Vanity Fair*, a publication which specialized in salacious gossip a hundred years earlier:

> There have been terrible and mighty doings in the Duke of Grafton's country last week; such a breeze, in fact, that unless something gives way, hunting will have to come to an end for the rest of the season. In the Duke's absence Lord Charles Fitzroy, as is known, has been acting as master of the hounds, and naturally also as squire to the ex-Queen of Naples who habitually graces the meets. Now a few days since Lord Charles in stern language rebuked one John Elliot, a local farmer of substance – and a good rider to boot – for holloaing the fox away, John Elliot respectively but firmly denied that he had done any such thing, upon which Lord Charles asked if he meant to call him a romancer, and some awkward explanations ensued, which resulted in a third person avowing that it was he who had holloaed. Lord Charles thereupon telegraphed to the Duke, who replied from Hyères with a general order that whenever Mr Elliot came out the hounds were to be taken home. At the next week this telegram was read officially to Mr Elliot who, instead of returning the way he came, replied to it, 'I shall come out as often as these hounds come out.' There is a fearful deadlock, which I should say ought to have been provided for in the Queen's Speech.

I cannot help wondering whether this John Elliot was not also the J. M. K. Elliot whose book published in 1899 entitled *Fifty Years of Foxhunting with the Grafton and other packs*, is a marvellous chronicle of the period. It includes the huntsman Frank Beers' diaries which make the most absorbing reading for anyone who has hunted in the Midlands. If John and J.M.K. are the same, then it would appear that they resolved their differences, for it was Lord Charles Fitzroy who invited Elliot, then Secretary of the Grafton, to pilot the Prince of Wales when he hunted with the Grafton in 1871. In his book he gives the following delightful description of the occasion:

> Having long before made up my mind that, when a man is upon a 'hunter', the safest place in the hunting-field is close to the hounds, I asked the Prince to gallop fast to get to the front; and this, the pace not being great, we accomplished in a few fields.
>
> The hounds then began to run over the large pastures near to Bradden. A real good stake-and-bound fence presented itself to us, with the ditch on the taking-off side. Over the Prince went! and I never saw a fence better jumped. On reaching the top of the hill there was a very nasty double fence which had to be jumped, so I gave the lead over, and the Prince landed well into a large grass field where there was every sign of a run. Hounds had settled down and matters were going very nicely when the hounds turned right-handed and set their heads straight for a brook. Having made up my mind I raced down, jumping a fence into the meadow and charged the brook, and was no sooner over than I turned round and called out: 'Send him at it!' The Prince rode readily at it and jumped the brook in gallant style. The pack ran up to Blakesley Village and did not do much afterwards. His Royal Highness was charmed; he declared that he had never jumped such a good piece of water in his life. Lord Royston and another gentleman in attendance got into trouble over the same place. The Prince informed me that Lord Royston was not content with fewer than two falls a day! The weather was very hot, and no sport of any account followed.
>
> In addition to being pilot I was timekeeper, and the time came for the Prince to leave for the station, when he expressed himself very kindly and left for the train.
>
> The honour of being within speaking distance of the Prince did not again fall to my lot for twenty years after that day, when His Royal Highness came to stay with Sir Francis Hesketh at Easton Neston, and hunted from there, on which occasion he came and shook hands with me and spoke most cordially.

If the Car-ites dinner in April gave me special pleasure, the Master of Foxhounds lunch in June gave me no less. This lunch was run annually by Colonel Jack Lowther, Master of the Pytchley, but, unfairly in my opinion, it was accompanied by a certain controversy. When it was first held I do not know, but at some time in the late forties Jack Lowther conceived the idea of inviting a few of what one might describe the traditional Masters, men from a similar background whose families had had long associations with foxhunting, probably as Master of Hounds, to lunch together before the Master of Foxhounds Annual General Meeting. The accusation, of course, was one of snobbery, but it always seemed to me reasonable that a group of people who all spoke the same language, with identical interests, were as entitled to lunch together before the A.G.M. as were, for instance, a group of farmers or a group of people who worked in the City, generously devoting a part of their wealth to hunting. There is nothing worse than inverted snobbery. I will not deny that I was very flattered when, again on the reputation of my father, I was invited to the lunch, even though I was given to understand that I would receive a bill for about £4. (It is now about £14!) I will not deny either that the list of those attending resembled a countryman's *Debrett*: The Dukes of Beaufort and Northumberland, the Marquess of Exeter, the Earls of Dalkeith, Halifax, Yarborough, Fitzwilliam and Feversham, Viscounts Knutsford and de Ramsay, all of whom had, of course, been most closely associated with foxhunting and its history for generations – indeed, were the pillars of the sport. With them were those who had made the most significant contribution before and since the war either through old family connections, or because of their modern expertise: Sir Peter Farquhar and 'Ikey' Bell, who had been pioneers in the introduction of Welsh blood into English foxhounds; Murray-Smith and Hanbury, Charlie Barclay, Heber Percy, Marcus Kimball, now Chairman of the British Field Sports Society, and Ronnie Wallace, now Chairman of the Master of Foxhounds Association, and regarded as the outstanding Master of Foxhounds of modern times.

This was not just the establishment, it was the élite, a group of people who represented the whole spectrum of foxhunting. Few other Masters resented this private lunch party prior to the A.G.M., though it was, perhaps, unfortunate that due to the M.F.H. Association Committee meeting over-running on the one occasion lunch started very late and therefore, despite the tradition of no speeches – apart from the annual funny story from Jack Lowther – finished very late. When some ten minutes after the time appointed, those who had attended the lunch went down to the meeting looking, understandably, well dined and wined, their cigars between their fingers, the reaction in the crowded room was somewhat, if mistakenly, cynical. The lateness, far from being due to the leisurely lunch, was because of the excess of work tackled by the Committee, but not all those patiently waiting appreciated this. It has not happened again, nor is likely to. Indeed, I anticipate the lunch one day being open to any who care to pay for it, though I suspect that a few survivors will regret the exclusivity that it once enjoyed.

One who is not likely to forget it is a young Master who some years ago was, because of his 'good connections', invited to the lunch, 12.30 pm for 1 pm. Anxious not to err in any way he arrived on the stroke of 12.30 pm to find that there were, at that time, only two people in the room, one of whom was his host, Jack Lowther, whom he knew well. Jack greeted him warmly and then in his quiet, rather mumbling voice, with its hint of a stammer, introduced him to the tall, upright gentleman with him.

As they shook hands the young Master said, 'I'm sorry, sir, I didn't quite catch your name.'

'Beaufort's the name,' was the reply, at which the young Master would, I have no doubt, gladly have welcomed the floor to swallow him up, instead of which he had to attempt to carry on an amiable conversation for some ten minutes before the next guest arrived. Needless to say, both his seniors were charming and friendly, attempting to put the young man at his ease after his almost Bateman-esque brick. The Duke of Beaufort – 'Master', as he is known to the whole hunting world – is, of course, the doyen of Masters, having been Master of his own hounds since 1924. For many years his car number has been MFH 1. His contribution to foxhunting is far too well known to be enlarged upon here, but understandably his presiding annually over the M.F.H. lunch has always been greatly appreciated. Kinsman to the Queen, Courtier, Master of the Horse, Master of Foxhounds – who better to preside at our lunch than 'Master'? All part of a bygone era, perhaps, though in the opinion of one more usually labelled a radical than a reactionary in this particular field, not necessarily any the worse for that.

The two occasions, the Car-ites dinner and the M.F.H. lunch at the Dorchester, could not have been more different. The menu at the former at 9*s* 6*d* per head, including a bottle of beer, consisted, according to the menu still in my possession, of Oxtail Soup with rolls; Roast leg of Lamb with roast potatoes, green peas and gravy; Sherry trifle and cheese and biscuits; while the latter's menu at £4 10*s* read as follows: 'Canteloupe Glace, Saumon froid Parisienne, Poulet de Printemps May Fair with petits pois and pommes noisettes; pêche fraiche melba with friandises; café.' At the one the attendance comprised the highest in the land, wealthy landlords, eminent county personalities, representative at that time of the world of Masters of Foxhounds. Today there would be a strong leavening of business men and farmers. At the other dinner the company was far more cosmopolitan: a smattering of gentry, but for the most part farmers, farmhands, grooms, railway workers, roadmen, factory workers from Northampton, retired people, pensioners. These two gatherings seemed to symbolize for me the breadth of support for foxhunting in the countryside. Is there another sport where all from dukes to dustmen can not only enjoy it, but actively participate? Nowadays, of course, Hunt Clubs' and Supporters Clubs' dinners, reflecting a complete cross section of those who hunt, mounted, on foot or in cars, are gratifyingly commonplace; but, generally speaking, the 1952 countryside, despite its overall support for hunting, was not quite ready for such get-togethers. Thus the Car-ites dinner was almost unique. It was the atmosphere, inherent in that dinner and all that it implied, that made my first season with the Grafton so happy, so stimulating and, I like to think, so successful.

The following season was no less successful, and if anything sport was even better. Again it was a wonderfully open season with scarcely a day lost because of frost, but despite everything going so right for us, it was, inevitably, tinged with sadness. After twenty-five years Will Pope was in his last season as huntsman. He had been born in the Grafton country where his father had worked at the kennels, his grandfather having been stud groom at Biddlesden, also in the Grafton country. At the age of twelve he had been employed by the then Master of the Grafton Hunt as Covert Lad, leaving in 1912 to work for the trainer Captain Paynter. In 1920 he had returned to the Grafton as second Whipper-in, becoming first Whipper-in three seasons later. It was at this time that my father had formed such a high opinion of him, in 1928 bringing him back as huntsman after his highly successful association with Clarence Johnson in the Bicester country. Perhaps his greatest contribution had been his single-handed management during the war. Now his innings was coming to an end. Not surprisingly, as one of the most popular personalities in the country his pending departure filled all with genuine sorrow. As the end of the season approached fields were larger and larger, everyone, from near and far, wanting to have a last day with Will. The season was extended to the latest possible date, 8 April. Hounds met at the farm of one of his greatest friends, Leslie Lester, at Leckhampstead. There were followers from the Old Berkley, Oakley, Whaddon Chase, Warwickshire, Bicester and Pytchley Hunts as well as from the Grafton. In addition there was a great concourse of cars and foot-followers.

Will was riding his favourite mare – on the only occasion on which I rode her I found her unbelievably uncomfortable, but she went superbly for Will and he adored her – and he was hunting his favourite bitches. The weather was warm, not ideally suitable for hunting, but balmy and pleasant. In the afternoon hounds found a fox in Hyde Lane and hunted prettily across Foscote – now my home – round the back of Leckhampstead, all on grass, up to Wicken Wood, through which they hunted with characteristic perseverance until Joe Miller's holloa brought them out on the Lillingstone side. A few more fields, a few more fences, and it was all over. For the last time Will Pope blew for home. When, taking their time, everyone had said good night, I rode on with Will towards Paulerspury, in silence.

In *Pendley and a Pack of Hounds* I quoted from that night's entry in the diary I then kept. I cannot do better than quote from it again:

> We reached Paulerspury turn where our ways diverged. Shooting buds in the hedgerows and the gay, evening chatter of birds told of spring, but it was the sweet melancholy of autumn that dominated the atmosphere: and I wished intensely that it was autumn now and that the season was just beginning.
>
> For a moment we stood by the signpost, as I tried to pluck up the courage to say something. He gathered up his reins.
>
> 'Just a minute, Will,' I blurted out, 'I want to ask you something.'
>
> As though divining my request he pulled out his bent and battered old horn from its case and handed it to me.
>
> 'I would like you to have this, sir,' he said. 'It's the one I always use, always have. Lord Hillingdon gave it to me when he retired the first time, when I came here as huntsman. He had it from Lord Chesham, who was Master of the Bicester, and who gave it to his Lordship when he first took on a pack of hounds. Lord Chesham, you see, was given it by Lord Valentia, who was Master of the Bicester in the seventies. He first used it at Cambridge, I believe. Must be nearly a hundred years old now, sir. But I'd like you to have it. You ought to have it, sir.'
>
> I would have liked to explain that I had been going to ask for it, but would never have entertained the idea had I known its history. I only muttered that I could not take it before he reached home, because I knew that he always blew it as he entered the village to warn the stables and the kennelmen that hounds were coming in.
>
> 'That's all right, sir. We'll manage all right without it, tonight, sir.'
>
> Perhaps, unwittingly, he was sparing both himself and his staff, by denying them that final call on his horn as he rode into his kennels for the last time.
>
> 'Better get on then, sir. Goodnight, sir. Come on, little bitches. Come along on,' and they moved down the road before the sun.
>
> 'Goodnight, Will,' I called after him, clutching his little horn, as a bewildered child clutches a toy, 'and thank you.'

It was the end of an era, for the whole country; not least for me: an era that spanned from my childhood to middle age.

Will Pope retired to Dorset with his devoted wife, Trudi, and there lived happily, going racing whenever possible, visited by old Grafton friends, until his death in 1970.

It is not always appreciated what a unique character a huntsman has to be. The likelihood is that he has left school at an early age – the majority of huntservants in the nineteenth and the first half of the twentieth centuries had all left school at the age of twelve – and has, therefore, been denied much in the way of 'learning' in the accepted sense. Yet a huntsman in a fashionable country, and indeed not only in fashionable countries, is a person of great standing, the focal being of the whole countryside. If successful he is idolized – admired, respected, almost worshipped. To be seen to be on friendly terms with him, to be speaking to him at the meet is, for many, socially advantageous. If sport is good his name is on everybody's lips. He is quoted, copied, effusively thanked. Yet he must never forget that he is a servant; walking with kings he must never lose the common touch, lest he is accused of being big-headed. He carries enormous responsibility: not only is it he, and very largely he alone, who can provide sport, but he must manage an establishment of considerable size. There is not only the kennels – and, perhaps, stables – staff, and all those other 'fringe' helpers – earthstoppers, terrier handlers, drivers, maintenance men – but there are anything up to a hundred valuable animals. As a horseman he must have courage and ability, for it is he who has to go in front, not always on the best horses; though any Master worthy of his position realizes that to mount his Hunt staff inadequately is not only unkind, almost criminal, but is a certain way of ensuring poor sport.

A huntsman has to be someone of great patience and tact. By nature he may not suffer fools gladly, but in practice he often has to tolerate incompetent employers and well-intentioned interferers. Frequently his Masters or other officers will be in disagreement, but he must not take sides. Without giving offence he must repel undue familiarity from members of the field. It is not uncommon for a huntsman to be embarrassed by the unwelcome attentions of female members of the field. I remember as Master of the Grafton having to remind a lady, as tactfully as I could, that the huntsman was the Master's servant and I did not think it right that she should frequently be visiting him at the kennels. Yet despite a simple background and a humble upbringing he is expected to manipulate such problems, adapt himself to difficult situations, in short to behave like an experienced diplomat. Miraculously, and greatly to the benefit of hunting, a good huntsman has invariably proved to be one of nature's gentlemen, offending few, pleasing many; hard-working, long suffering, modest, courageous; yet accepting philosophically that at any time in his career, through no fault of his own, he can at the whim of a Hunt Committee, resulting in a change of Mastership, face dismissal. Courteous, smiling, above intrigue, anxious only to get on with his job at which he is an artist, a great huntsman has, down the years, proved himself to be a paragon of all the virtues. Indeed, it is only because he possesses outstanding qualities that he is great.

The South Midlands, with which part of the country I am most familiar, has been uniquely fortunate in having three famous neighbouring packs of hounds, each able to boast a huntsman who achieved twenty-five years' outstanding service. In the Pytchley Frank Freeman was appointed by the great Lord Annaly in 1906, retiring under his distinguished son-in-law, Colonel Jack Lowther in 1931. In the Grafton Will Pope was appointed by my father in 1928, retiring under myself and Colonel Neil Foster, nephew of one of the most eminent Yorkshire Masters, Gordon Foster, in 1953. In the Whaddon Chase Albert Buckle was appointed by me in 1954, and we are now in our twenty-fifth season together. It is almost impossible to exaggerate the value of continuity in foxhunting, something that year by year is increasingly difficult to achieve. I count myself fortunate in that the whole of my hunting experience has been associated with two outstanding huntsmen who between them spanned half a century of foxhunting; and in doing so provided wonderful sport for literally thousands of people, including myself. To have seen two great masters of their profession achieve twenty-five seasons, and to have been closely associated with both of them, is indeed a privilege.

Towards the end of my second season with the Grafton considerable financial problems loomed ahead. The Trustees of Norman Gee had generously agreed to paying what would have been his liability, but understandably did not feel that their liability extended to purchasing extra horses. Worse, our Kennels Account had developed a considerable overdraft to which the bank manager at Towcester was somewhat insistently drawing our attention. There was nothing for it but to go round with the begging bowl once again. This is never a desirable task, but on this occasion it was made easier for two reasons. In the first place sport had been exceptionally good, and as Will Pope had said, sport is always the priority. Secondly, the country as a whole was very anxious that the present régime should be enabled to carry on: not only because of 'the devil you know', but even more because with the retirement of Will Pope after so long it was felt that it would be wrong to have a change in Mastership as well.

Our request to the Committee to increase our guarantee to £4000 was, however, firmly turned down although they did agree to raise it from £3000 to £3500. In addition they suggested that a considerable amount of forage might be produced by the farmers, and that the number of days hunted per week might be reduced from four to three. Neither of these latter two suggestions had been properly discussed let alone resolved when, early in the new year, we agreed that we would somehow carry on for another season. My conscience was not too clear: both Pendley and the B.B.C. were now demanding more rather

20. The Prince of Wales, the Duke of Gloucester and the Duke of Kent, out hunting in 1929

An historic régime

21. Colonel V. D. S. Williams (right) with his Joint-Master Mr Arthur Guinness, who took over the Grafton in 1928

22. Will Pope, Grafton Huntsman from 1928 to 1953, riding his famous Cocktail

Following in father's footsteps

23. The Grafton in 1928. My father followed by Mike Ansell, 'Tiddly' Lucas, the Reverend Harold Vinning and my sister Barbara, side-saddle

24. The Grafton in 1951. Myself with Colonel Neil Foster, Master of the Grafton from 1950 to 1978, and the Reverend Paul Hoskin

A long partnership

25. Master of the Whaddon Chase since 1954, on Kingsway

26. Albert Buckle, huntsman of the Whaddon Chase since 1954

In the field

27. On Monty, with Joint-Masters 'Puggy' Wyatt (left) and Peter Stoddart

28. Away from Aston Abbots!

Shakespeare at Pendley

29. As Bolingbroke in *Richard II*

30. *Hamlet* – with Osric and Horatio

31. *Love's Labour's Lost*: departure of the Princess of France

32. *A Midsummer Night's Dream*: Pyramus and Thisbe

Television at Foscote

33. During the 'Year of the Horse' recorded at Foscote: Princess Anne, Captain Mark Phillips, Marion Mould, Barbara Hammond, Colonel Sir Michael Ansell, Raymond Brooks-Ward, Eddie Macken and Graham Fletcher
34. Relaxing with Princess Anne and Captain Mark Phillips after the programme

than less of my time, and I had only undertaken, originally, to do two seasons, and those two seasons were up. But I was enjoying it – not only the hunting itself, but also being part of a successful régime. I appreciated, of course, that it made sense that the Mastership should be continued with Pope retiring, but just where we were going to find the money I had little or no idea. Micawber-like, however, I was confident that something would turn up, which in part, it did with timely compensation for bomb damage to the old Hawtreys buildings at Westgate-on-Sea. This enabled me to pay off the overdraft at the bank and buy a new horse for Joe Miller who was to take on as Huntsman. My anxiety thus partially relieved, as a further distraction I now turned happily to point-to-pointing. On the day of the presentation to Will Pope at the Point-to-Point at Pattishall in April 1952 I rode in three races for the first time. It was an exhilarating experience, especially for one who had only ridden in his first point-to-point at the age of thirty-seven, the war and pre-war circumstances previously described having denied me an earlier opportunity.

Being a Master of Hounds qualified one, it seemed, to be a point-to-point rider, as it had qualified one to be a judge. During my first season I had been asked by a number of people to ride their horses. Without hesitation, despite my lack of experience I agreed, it never occurring to me, apparently, that I would not be able to perform quite adequately. My initiation to the sport, however, was not an altogether happy one. I had been asked to ride a horse called Cross Belts in a Maiden Race at Tweesledown. He was scarcely big enough for me and riding, in my inexperience, with almost hunting-length leathers, I must have looked too big for him. He was game enough, however, and, in a big field, we jumped off in front, it being all I could do to steady him as we bowled down the hill the far side of the course. By the bottom of the hill, having managed to pull him back to about fourth place, all seemed to be going splendidly. I felt quite professional.

In those days the fence at the bottom of the course at Tweesledown was very upright. Several strides out I could see that we were going to meet it wrong, but there was nothing that I could do about it. Sure enough we did. Cross Belts put in a short one but was right underneath it and, just to help matters, another horse barged into us as we took off. The result was a complete somersault with another horse and rider landing on top of us. As I was on my feet before the horse I put my leg across the saddle and he lifted me up. With cheers from the crowd – presumably of derision – we set off in pursuit (visions of Right Royal!), the rest of the field now being more than a fence ahead.

Riding around a strange course on an unfamiliar horse, entirely unaccompanied, is not, for a beginner, the most inspiring experience, as doubtless Charlotte Brew would have agreed after the 1977 Grand National. By the time I reached the open ditch at the top of the hill the crowd was all over the course, unaware of this lone tail-ender. We had no option but to jump it out of a trot which was also somewhat unnerving. By the time we reached the fence at which we had fallen poor Cross Belts had run out of puff and we were all but on the floor again. However, gallantly, we completed the course only to be asked by an indignant owner why we were so far behind. Until I pointed out the horse's mud-covered face and my dirty breeches she was reluctant to believe that we had been on the floor. Had she seen me in my bath that evening she would also have been able to see the perfect imprint of a horse's hoof on my ribs. Forgivingly, later in the season, she let me ride a better horse, Bay Prince, on which I had my first ever really exciting ride, in the Open Race at the Cottesmore. At the end of the first lap we were going so well that I had moved up into the lead hoping to give Salvage, the very hot favourite, the slip. I was still hopeful, though I could hear him breathing down our necks, at the one but last (penultimate in racing parlance!), then quite suddenly it was as though the petrol had been switched off. My horse stopped dead as Salvage swept past. We struggled on into fourth place to discover as we pulled up that Bay Prince had broken a blood vessel. It was only in my last race of the season that I managed to get into a place, finishing third behind Alan Oliver, who was as good a point-to-point rider as he is show jumper, on Perfect Night.

I was third again in my first race the following season, but in unusual circumstances. I was riding a horse of my father's called Masterpiece. He had been bought as a show horse, did moderately well, but had a difficult temperament. Out hunting he proved to be chicken-hearted which decided us to give him a race, hoping that it might sharpen him up, improve his courage. It was his first outing, a maiden race at Great Horwood in a field of twenty-one. Going up the hill on the second circuit, in appalling going, he blew up. Across the top, however, it felt as if he were getting his second wind, but by this time we were about two fences behind the leaders. Suddenly, however, those in front started falling about like ninepins. From three out I could see that the favourite, Linkstone, which my father was later to buy as a dressage horse, had come down, bringing down the second. Two more fell at the last but one, while another refused at the same fence, leaving me in front. As I approached the last a Steward waved me away from the fence, signalling me to avoid Linkstone, still on the ground. As I galloped past the wing I saw out of the corner of my eye the horse behind me jump the fence by the far wing. Realizing that I would be disqualified if other horses had jumped the fence while I had missed it, I turned quickly inside the wing, jumping the fence from a stand, by which time another horse had passed me, relegating me to third.

I went at once to complain to the Clerk of the Course, intending, perhaps, to lodge an objection, but taking me by the arm in a most friendly manner he said, 'Don't let's bother; we've had a good day, but it's horribly wet now and we all want to get home. Come and have a drink – which I did, starting a long friendship with a great Whaddon Chase personality, 'Spen' Johnson. Waiting in the horse-box at the Bicester Point-to-Point a week later, while the Stewards made up their minds whether or not to cancel the meeting because of snow, Masterpiece contracted pneumonia. Within a week he was dead. Despite his potential he had always been disappointing, though he had an endearing personality which made his loss a great blow.

At the Grafton Point-to-Point in 1952, having come second in the Members' Race on a good horse of Jack Bickerton's, Star Queen, I was approached in the paddock by a Hertfordshire farmer to ride one of his horses, a five year old which had never run before. It was very green, but we managed to complete the course, coming fifth the following week at Kimble from seventeen starters. Paradoxically, having the mount on one of the best point-to-pointers in Britain at the time proved a much greater challenge. This was a horse called Wiseacre, who had won at least a dozen open races, when ridden by a brilliant amateur Vivian Street. The previous season, however, with various jockeys, he appeared to have lost his nerve, either falling or refusing. His owner George Thomson, therefore, thought there could be no harm in inviting me to ride the old horse at the Grafton, of which he was Clerk of the Course. A preliminary gallop at Bob Day's training grounds near Northampton was almost a disaster. The horse started refusing a hundred yards before each fence. 'You'll have to drive him harder than that,' George said, obviously wondering whether it was worth running him at all, or whether he would not do better to replace the jockey. Oddly enough I felt instinctively that driving was not what Wiseacre wanted. With not too much difficulty I persuaded him to run him, and let me ride him. There was a field of about twelve, at the rear of which I set off at little more than a steady canter. He jumped the first two or three porkily. Going up the hill superior speed brought him into closer contention (racing parlance again) and he jumped the two downhill fences rather more generously. As we passed the winning post the first time we were lying about third and he was beginning to feel more like a racehorse. Suddenly as we approached the first fence on the second circuit there was a complete transformation. He was really racing, obviously wanting to devour each fence as he came to it. I steadied him up the hill, then slipped him into top gear, stealing a quick lead on Jack Bickerton, one of the most experienced point-to-point riders at that time, and Alec Cubitt. The third last fence at Pattishall used to produce more falls than any other point-to-point fence that I know. Approached down-hill one landed a foot or so higher than one took off – always dangerous. I therefore took a slight pull at Wiseacre as we approached it, to make sure that he was properly balanced. At once the other two were upsides with me, and we raced neck and neck down the hill, safely over the penultimate and on to the last.

This fence was at an angle. Knowing how often Wiseacre had fallen at the last, and being on the outside, I pulled a few yards right to make sure that I met it absolutely straight, giving him the best possible chance. In so doing I probably lost the best part of a length, but we cleared it safely. I caught the other two within half a dozen strides and, locked together, we finished in a line past the post after, to quote *Sporting Life*, 'a rousing triple dash over the last half-mile in the best race of the week'. I had no idea who had won but suspected that the race would go to the most experienced of the trio, the brilliant Jack Bickerton as, in fact, it did, Wiseacre finally being placed third. As I returned to the paddock flushed with excitement, elated at having got the great old horse back to his best, I was, to my surprise, booed in no uncertain manner. Wiseacre's reputation had resulted in his starting favourite and those whose money he carried obviously thought that I had thrown the race away by swerving right before the last. Perhaps I had, having erroneously, it could be argued, decided that to jump the fence at an angle might result in his falling again. The old horse won by a distance the following week, with a different jockey – the reason for the change being, I was assured, due to my being occupied that day at Badminton.

During that summer, 1953, the Hunt finances were gradually sorted out, but the future was obviously fraught with problems. The beginning of my third season was not auspicious. During cubhunting my leg blew up again, the result as usual of pressure of work and anxiety. This time the cause was Pendley, which was going through one of its difficult patches. Blood poisoning set in, with the result that I was out of action for five weeks, two of which were spent in hospital. I managed to make the opening meet, but could not wear a boot. Naturally, after whipping-in to Will Pope for eighteen seasons it was impossible for Joe Miller in his first season as huntsman to show the sport that we had come to expect from Will. Good days were few and far between. In addition Neil Foster was unwell, his painful ulcers frequently preventing him hunting, which inevitably put more weight on my shoulders. I was, too, experiencing problems with my own horses. My grey broke down, a new one proved unsuitable; my best, Gay Galliard, met with an accident which put him out of action until Christmas. More than once I had to ride a horse from the Hunt stables or borrow one from Neil. Knowing of my shortage of horses, a charming American who lived in the next village to Wicken insisted on giving me a fine thoroughbred chestnut called Carol, which he found too much for him. Even better was to follow. At a cocktail party one Saturday evening I happened to mention to the daughter of Bernard Sunley, a very rich property tycoon who lived in the country, that I would have to miss Monday as I had no horse. She immediately volunteered to lend me one – a show jumper that she had bought in Ireland, but which had proved too strong for her to hunt. She kindly volunteered to send it out to the meet.

I have to admit that I was not impressed at my first sight of Blaze. Unclipped and hairy-heeled he was hardly the sort of horse upon which a Master would expect to be mounted with a fashionable pack of hounds. It did not take me long to modify my opinion. Blaze might appear a little rough, but he soon proved himself a brilliant performer and a magnificent ride. Moreover, clipped out and trimmed, he looked the splendid strong animal that he was. Joan kindly lent him to me on a number of occasions, and each time his performance was more spectacular. I knew that I had to own him for myself. I also knew that I could not possibly afford the £450 that Joan was asking for him – a top price in those days. Apologetically I offered her £200, the very most that at that moment I could afford; more than I could afford, in fact. She replied that she could not accept a penny less than £450 as that was what her father had paid for the horse and she knew that he would not accept less. The horse, she told me, had come from Ireland, from the legendary Colonel Joe Dudgeon who had bought him on the advice of someone who had seen him performing brilliantly out hunting, having arrived at the meet between shafts. Joe had quickly appreciated that it was a potential show jumper and sold it as such to the Sunleys. My offer having understandably been turned down I assumed that that would be the end of the matter, and was surprised when a few evenings later Joan's mother telephoned me. Was it true that I had offered Joan £200 for Blaze? she asked. Was that the very most that I could offer? I assured her that it was, absolutely. To my astonishment she then said that if I would send her husband a cheque for £450, she would put in the post to me next day a cheque for £250. She was determined that Blaze was not a safe ride for Joan, then a beginner. She wanted him out of the yard as soon as possible. Needless to say I accepted her generous suggestion with alacrity, terrified lest she might change her mind. Fortunately she was not that sort of person.

In my riding career I have had many first-class horses, dozens perhaps, but Blaze was far and away the most brilliant. In addition he was a lovely character. I had seven great seasons on him, during which he was responsible indirectly for a most important development in my life. One day, early in the season, we were visited by Laurie Stoddart, Chairman of the Whaddon Chase Hunt, with his wife Gwendy, my old friend Dick Russell's sister. In the evening, with only a few left out, we found a fox in a little covert called Burntfold. There was always a friendly rivalry between Neil and myself. As it was impossible to out-ride him I often used to deliberately take a different line. Some of the field, the bravest, would follow him; others would follow me. On this occasion I took a wrong turn, followed by the Stoddarts and two or three others. As we headed towards Adstone I could hear hounds hunting to our left by Maidford. It was obvious that they were swinging farther away from us and at the first opportunity, therefore, I jumped off the road and headed in the direction from which came the cry of hounds. It was obvious that if we were not to be left behind there was not a moment to lose, which meant that there was no time to stop and open gates. Blaze being at his very best, we therefore sailed effortlessly over five gates in a line. Landing over the last I could hear hounds marking their fox at a drain in the corner of the field. We joined the others who, having come straight down a track from Maidford, could not understand why our little party appeared so exhilarated. Laurie Stoddart said that in his whole life he never remembered anything like it. Nor did he forget it.

As the season continued it became increasingly obvious to me that I could not possibly carry on as a Master of the Grafton. Not only was it costing me too much money, but it was taking up too much of my time. Weakly I could never resist going out each of the four days hounds were out, even if I knew that there were jobs waiting to be done at Pendley. By the beginning of December I had reluctantly reached the conclusion that I must resign: for me it had always been all or nothing. Unfortunately I was prevented from discussing the matter with Neil immediately as on 12 December he had been taken seriously ill and for the next few weeks was fighting for his life. With his usual toughness he pulled through, even hunted again before the end of the season, but it had not been possible to tell him of my decision until after Christmas, although I had earlier spoken informally to the Hunt Chairman, and had more or less persuaded my great friend Dick Hawkins, from Everdon, to take my place. Rumours were soon circulating, however, as they usually do in hunting countries, and it did not take them long to reach the Whaddon Chase. At the beginning of January I was approached by Laurie Stoddart and asked if I would be prepared to become Master in place of Major Cecil Drabble, who had just handed in his resignation. I could not give him an answer as my own resignation had not been communicated to the Grafton Committee. Whether this was fortunate or unfortunate depends upon which way one looks at it, but had I had to give an immediate answer then I would have turned it down out of hand. I had not even remotely considered such an idea. If I had my first reaction would have been that to go straight from the frying-pan into the fire would be ludicrous. I would never have dreamed of accepting that suggestion but in the New Year, having given the matter a great deal of thought, the idea began to appeal to me. The Whaddon Chase hunted only two, occasionally three days a week; the country was right on my doorstep; the Committee's guarantee was the same, indeed slightly larger than the Grafton's; there were the old family connections. I did not in the end need a great deal of persuasion. To leave the Grafton was a wrench, but to hunt with the Whaddon, if one was going to hunt at all, made much more sense. Two very generous subscribers offered me £1000 a year to stay on with the Grafton, fearing that because of his health the Hunt might also be losing Neil, but by then my mind was made up.

Ironically the week after my resignation was announced, Joe Miller, now showing excellent sport, had a bad fall. With Neil ill this meant that for three weeks I had to hunt hounds myself, an unforgettable experience, since which I have often said that for a Master to hunt his own hounds must surely be the only real compensation for all the headaches associated with the job. Such was my enjoyment – good scent enabled me to show quite good sport – that I asked Laurie Stoddart whether the Whaddon Chase would consider allowing me to hunt hounds myself. 'Under no circumstances whatever' was his uncompromising reply, which again turned out to be fortuitous for the Whaddon Chase. A week later I engaged Albert Buckle as huntsman. He proved not only to be remarkably talented, but over the years has proved himself to be an exceptional ambassador for foxhunting, and a very great friend.

To take on a pack of hounds on my own was a challenge – it was also, naturally, somewhat intimidating. Yet still in a buoyant mood, still intoxicated with the sheer enjoyment of the life that I had experienced over the last few years, it was a challenge which I accepted with confidence. At the same time I looked forward to the opportunity I would have to give more time to Pendley, and to my career with the B.B.C., which that year occupied me on no less than ninety days.

'Life begins at forty' seemed, for me, no less than the truth.

Chapter 11

On top of the world

It is both gratifying and stimulating when everything seems to go right. For the next few years I was extremely fortunate in that everything in which I was involved seemed to be successful. Pendley, out of its bad patch, suddenly forged ahead, and was constantly being held up as an example of what such a centre should be. The course for foremen and supervisors, in particular, became nationally accepted, firms tumbling over each other to send representatives. With only two from any one firm being allowed to come at the same time the intention of the course was that foremen should meet and exchange views with people from other firms. The Shakespeare Festival, with an almost chance development, suddenly found itself famous far beyond its own environment. After the inevitable transitional period following the war, with Cecil Drabble acting as Master for the Committee, the start of a new régime was heralded in the Whaddon Chase country with the same sort of enthusiasm and sense of anticipation as had been the case when I became a Master of the Grafton. In Albert Buckle I had found a companion spirit who was as determined as I was to make a success of the new régime. He quickly met the farmers by exercising the hounds all over the country, while I asked five or six farmers who had regularly visited the Grafton to introduce me to their neighbours. We had soon forged many new friendships. When cubhunting started at the end of August we made an auspicious start, the hounds immediately showing good sport. We nevertheless experienced considerable anxiety as the Opening Meet approached, because we knew that so much was expected of us. Thanks to Laurie Stoddart – and to Blaze, to Neil Foster and Will Pope, from whose experience I had so benefited, and thanks again to the reputation of my father, I myself had assumed a reputation which was going to take some living up to.

The Opening Meet was at Cublington on 2 November. Unexpectedly we did not find in the good Creslow coverts, probably because after heavy rain they were very wet. Fortunately there was a fox in a field of kale by Whitchurch which gave us a good gallop round the vale, but nothing very special. Although it was some way off I decided to go to High Havens, one of the best and most beautifully named coverts in the Whaddon Chase country. Hoping that we might run into the best of our vale I suggested to Albert that we draw it from the Stewkley end. For nearly ten minutes no hound spoke, then we heard the deep voice of a black and tan bitch called Vigil, which had come from the famous Dumfriesshire pack. Almost immediately from the far side came the bell-like holloa of Lord Knutsford, one of the greatest personalities of twentieth-century foxhunting: he had first hunted with the Whaddon Chase in 1911, returning after the war when he inherited Munden. His help to me in the early days was inestimable, his holloa the most welcome sound in North Bucks. It came across now, a clear, thrilling falsetto. We galloped down the side of the covert, and there they were, the whole pack flying down the slope to our left. There was obviously a screaming scent, and to keep anywhere near them we would have to ride for our lives – over the lane and across to Shorndown, over the Swanbourne road and down to a stiff set of rails on a narrow bridge. I knew that Albert would manage them all right, as for this very special occasion I had mounted him on Gay Galliard. I had no doubts, of course, about Blaze, but the horse belonging to Tony Dale, the whipper-in was an unknown quality. I looked back as he sailed safely over: then a crash. Cecil Drabble, my predecessor, on his great hog-maned bay, Tiny, had slipped as he took off and turned head over heels, fortunately not damaging the Major, but unhappily losing his bridle. This necessarily delayed the whole field, but hounds were in no mood for waiting and flew on, with just the three newcomers in pursuit. Right-handed over the Mursley road they raced, past the water tower and down to Salden Wood, where the vanguard of the pursuing field caught up with us, thundering down the lane; on across the bottom, up to the railway, with hounds now only a chorus chiming away in the distance ahead of us; on, up to the back of Newton Longville, where with relief we found them wandering around on their own, waiting. Whether they had killed their fox or run it to ground we had no way of telling. All we knew was that it had been a marvellous forty minutes. Again I had been blessed with beginner's luck. Jogging home in the dusk, members of the field left us in no doubt that we had, that afternoon, won our spurs. But as good if not better was to follow. Apart from the usual moderate conditions in November the 1954–55 season was another marvellous scenting season. Albert quickly had the hounds working beautifully – to such an extent that in January they scored six consecutive five-mile points. When at the end of February we had snow, which lasted well into March, such was the enthusiasm that huge numbers came out to join us hunting on foot: a most enjoyable experience, except when from Mentmore one day they scored a four-mile point! With Blaze, Gay Galliard and an exaggeratedly brilliant thoroughbred called Dilly, originally bought by my father for Dressage, I was outstandingly mounted. Albert, too, had an exceptional horse, an ex-show jumper called Lantic and a little chestnut mare, Princess, purchased from our old friend Will Ivens, that was as clever as a cat.

To provide such good sport was, of course, most satisfying, but no less satisfying was the wonderful feeling in the whole country, in particular the co-operation of the farmers who seemed as anxious as we were that the new régime should succeed. Nor did it end there. Soon after I had become Master, Jack Ivester Lloyd, that great countryman and writer, who followed hounds regularly on foot, approached me about forming a Supporters' Club. Knowing of the success and the popularity of the Car-ites in the Grafton country, he was of the opinion that something more official could be organized in the Whaddon Chase country. It is probable that some form of Supporters' Clubs had existed earlier, reputedly with the Cleveland in Yorkshire for instance, but in most hunting countries a Supporters' Club was entirely novel. It was an idea which very much appealed to me, always believing hunting to be a sport that should be enjoyed by the whole countryside. A committee was formed, therefore, and before the end of the season the 'Whaddon Chasers' came into being. It achieved immediate popularity, with a membership approaching five hundred. From the beginning their contribution to the Hunt was magnificent. Not only did they raise money, but they acted as valuable ambassadors for foxhunting, coming as they did from such a wide background. Over the years through my association with the Whaddon Chasers, I have been fortunate enough to make many close, lasting and greatly valued friendships. It is a wonderful feeling for a Master of Hounds to know that he has friends in every village, on every farm, at the roadside, wherever hounds go. It is very largely the Supporters' Clubs that provide these friends.

After one season with the Whaddon Chase I felt that I had found my niche, as surely as ten years earlier I knew that I had found myself again when launching Pendley. The 'this is where I belong' feeling is always very reassuring, and encourages one to achieve more than one might normally expect to. It is a matter of self-confidence. The Whaddon Chase and Pendley now seemed wholly complementary; thanks to a dedicated staff at the latter, a unique atmosphere had been created which people seemed to feel the moment they arrived. They felt at home, and before long Pendley 'belonged' to them, with the result that many returned again and again. Between three thousand and four thousand were now coming to Pendley each year, attending nearly a hundred different courses. Many were at first confused by my involvement with Pendley. What was a B.B.C. sports commentator doing at Pendley? Someone attending an industrial course asked if the Dorian Williams at Pendley was the same Dorian Williams who commentated on show jumping. When told that it was he asked, 'What the devil is he doing in a place like this?' On another occasion someone to whom I was talking remarked that it was extraordinary that I should have the same name as the B.B.C. commentator, Dorian Williams, Dorian being such an unusual name. He was astonished to find that I was one and the same person. In those days, to keep myself fit in the summer, I used to do all the mowing (to cover all the lawns at Pendley was a five-and-a-half hour stint: approximately eighteen miles of walking). As I was coming in to tea in a pair of dirty old trousers and shirt after an afternoon's mowing one of the guests told me how much he liked the informality of Pendley. It was particularly nice, he thought, that the gardener should be permitted to come into the house and take tea with the guests, in the baronial front hall. 'But why not?' he added, 'you've been working as hard as we have, though your work is physical, whereas ours is mental'; whereupon he gave me half-a-crown, assuming, of course, that I was the gardener. I accepted it gratefully.

The plays chosen for the 1955 Shakespeare Festival were *As You Like It* and *Macbeth*. As both were ideally suited to open-air performances it was not easy to decide which play should be performed on the final night. Because of the nature of *Macbeth*, weird, haunting, macabre, it occurred to me that a midnight performance might be unusually effective – certainly unique. Accordingly we decided to produce both plays on the last night: *As You Like It* at 7 pm instead of 8 pm, the earlier hour attracting, we hoped, a younger audience, and *Macbeth* at 10 pm, finishing at about 12.15 pm, to be billed as the Midnight Matinée. The idea caught on immediately, attracting a huge audience, far more than we could accommodate in the five-hundred-seater stand which for the first time we had had erected. The overflow sat on the lawn all round, even at the foot of the bank that formed the natural stage, which in itself created a tremendous atmosphere. Unbelievably, to add to the effects, the hooting of the Pendley owls contributed eerily, back in the wood the rooks cawed menacingly from time to time, bats flitted sinisterly to and fro across the stage and as midnight approached a great full moon rose above the trees to the audience's left. It was a magic that no producer could design. It is scarcely an exaggeration to say that the audience was overwhelmed by the whole effect. According to a *Times Educational Supplement* critic, 'It was the perfect setting for *Macbeth*. One could feel the shudders running through the large audience as the witches writhed and bubbled their necromancies round the steaming cauldron, the wild grasses of the glade behind them dripping blood, so real did it seem. This was superb theatre, surpassing anything previously produced at Pendley.' Certainly Birnham Wood came to Dunsinane more convincingly than in any other production that I have ever seen, with some fifty extras advancing from the wood at the back of the stage screened by the greenery of shrubs and bushes. The success of the Midnight Matinée resulted in its becoming a feature of the Festival. Today the best part of three thousand people attend the two performances on the last night, about 50 per cent of them sitting through both plays. An inclusive ticket enables something like two hundred people to see both plays and have dinner in between.

Strangely that first midnight matinée was to prove something of a turning-point in my life, not only because it had established the Pendley Shakespeare Festival as a cultural event of national importance, but more because it had succeeded in making me appreciate at last that there was a limit to my own energy. On that last Saturday of the Festival I had been up at 6 am to go cubhunting with my hounds. I had then driven to Northampton, first to judge three classes of hunters, then to commentate on the major jumping event for the B.B.C.'s Grandstand. Arriving back at Pendley at 6.30 pm I took the part of Jaques in *As You Like It*, being also responsible for the production. Finally I played *Macbeth*. Although, as is usual on such occasions, I was borne along for several days on the sheer exhilaration of it all, I was, in fact, exhausted. I decided that henceforth I should firmly control the tempo of my life. In other words, I decided that it was time, now that I was forty, to settle down.

That November I became engaged to Jennifer Neale, whom I had first met showing. Jennifer did not come from a horsey background, but from an early age she had been obsessed with horses and ponies. This, of course, is not uncommon with girls, but with many the obsession evaporates in their later teens as they find that two-legged animals have a greater fascination than those with four legs. With Jennifer, however, the obsession had persisted, it becoming obvious that she did, in fact, possess a very real knowledge of horses. This could have been due in part to her dedicated application: she has the determination to succeed – as with her tennis, which took her to the schools tournament at Wimbledon. With horses, however, it was, I believe, something instinctive. When she grew out of ponies her father bought her a little horse, not quite fifteen hands high, barely more than a pony in fact, with the delightful name of Reynali Arabesque. This was intended as an all-purpose horse, to help her through the transition from horse to pony and on which she could hunt, ride in cross country events, and show. Being Jennifer she worked very hard on it, achieving success in various fields. One day she took it to a small local show and produced it in the Riding Horse Class. The judge was a very eminent horseman and judge of horses, Colonel 'Handy' Hurrell. He was sufficiently impressed with the way that this little horse rode that he advised Jennifer to show it in a proper Hack Class. Before the end of that first season she had taken it to the top, winning the Small Hack Class at the Royal International Horse Show at the White City, and becoming Reserve Champion. Later she was to do the same at the Horse of the Year Show at Wembley.

It was at the White City that I first noticed Jennifer. The combination of elegant little horse and youthful rider was most attractive, and I found myself looking out for her at shows. Before long a mutual friend invited me to her house before a dance and I met her charming parents for the first time. It did not take me long to make up my mind that I wanted to marry her, although she took rather longer to make up her mind, but she has always been cautious where I have been impetuous. Her shyness appealed to me – I have never liked brash or over-confident women – and I respected her enormously for achieving so much from so little. There is a certain superficiality about my own approach to anything; but I have always admired dedication in others, envious perhaps of their temperament which enables them to be thorough and conscientious.

During the spring of 1955 Jennifer worked at the Ideal Home Exhibition (with the money she earned she bought her first horse and called it Ideal Home, though its official name was Rivulet). I took her out most evenings, which probably rather disconcerted her as I was nineteen years older, but at the end of the summer we became engaged. Naturally there were many who expressed doubts, because I was so much older, but on 4 April 1956, a grey, somewhat bleak day unfortunately, we were married, holding the reception at Pendley. This was attended by some four hundred of our friends, and finished with a dramatic send-off. The hounds were waiting for us when we came out of the front door, and for a few moments we mingled with them, chatting to Albert, then as we drove slowly away through the throng of waving guests there was a ringing halloa from the top of the park at the gate on to the London road. Away went the hounds, with Albert blowing 'gone away' on his silver horn, as he galloped after them, accompanied by the whippers-in and our speeding car. There was plenty of halloaing and hornblowing in support as we disappeared up the park.

Holding the gate open into the park to give us our final wave was Will Puddephat, the old Pendley gamekeeper. Now well over eighty years old, he had been born on the estate, married a local Miss Honeybone and spent the whole of his working life at Pendley. At the reception he had said to my uncle, the Bishop of Bedford, in his broad Hertfordshire accent, 'Yer grandfather christened me, yer faather married me. I 'opes y'll burry me.' Two days later the old man died. It was as though he had just lived long enough to see Master Dorian happily settled. His father had been one of the two Pendley keepers murdered in the woods between Pendley and Aldbury, a drama brilliantly described in one of her books by the Victorian novelist Mrs Humphry Ward, who lived in the beautiful Queen Anne house, Stocks, in Aldbury. It is now the home of that enthusiastic follower of the Whaddon Chase, Victor Lowndes, Director of the Playboy Club.

Until I married Jennifer I had never, literally, lived in a home of my own since Greens Norton. Always I had been living in an institution, except for the few months when I lived in a bed-sit in Warwick Road. Perhaps the greatest significance of marriage for me was having a home of my own. When we came back from our honeymoon we moved into the gardener's cottage at Pendley, later, with the arrival of the children, adding on to it. We spent seven very happy years there, using again the magnificent Pendley stables which had been empty for so many years. We even brought back into use the old indoor riding school which had originally been built as an indoor tennis court.

It was not only Jennifer's great expertise in anything to do with horses that was of such benefit to me after my marriage; she was also blessed with exceptional taste, with the result that, first at the cottage at Pendley, later at Foscote, we have always been fortunate enough to live surrounded by beauty and elegance. Most of her energy is directed towards horses and ponies, but she could equally well have succeeded in the world of art, interior décor – or cooking.

Towards the end of the autumn I had a telephone call from someone whose name at that time meant nothing to me, a literary agent George Greenfield. He invited me to meet him for lunch at Quaglino's, the following week, on 26 October. Hodder and Stoughton, the publishers, had asked him to persuade me to write a book about show jumping, something that, at that time, had never been done before. This very much appealed to me, as I had always enjoyed writing, gladly accepting any invitation to write an article or a report. It will be recalled that I had, before the war, produced one or two humble literary efforts. As is so often the way with publishers, the book was wanted in a hurry, the manuscript to be delivered by the end of the year, so that it could be published the following September in time for the Horse of the Year Show. It was proposed that the book should contain some sixty thousand words; it all required considerable research; could I possibly manage it in a little over two months? Needless to say I decided that I could. It may be that the discipline imposed upon me by the timetable for that first book, eventually entitled *Clear Round*, resulted in the method of working that I have practised ever since. The first draft is scribbled down at top speed, written whenever and wherever the opportunity arises, often at six o'clock in the morning. If a word does not come to mind immediately then a blank is left. However faulty the grammar, whatever inaccuracies there might be, I press on. Only by working at speed can I maintain the continuity of thought, the inspiration if you like, words and sentences coming to me as I write. In this way I can achieve as many as two thousand words an hour, even more. When I have got some five thousand words down on paper, the first draft is typed in double or even treble spacing. Having completed anything between twelve and twenty thousand words, I return to the original, virtually re-writing it. How much has to be re-written varies: occasionally it comes very nearly right first time: more often the second version is barely recognizable from the first. In this re-writing I hope to get the grammar, the syntax and the vocabulary right. I try, too, to eliminate repetitions, incongruencies, contradictions: generally to get it into something approaching its final shape. This second draft is then re-typed, beginning with luck to look something like the final product. Time permitting, I then lay it aside for a week or two, even a month, so that I can come back to it in a more detached frame of mind. Eventually I read through it again, polishing and pruning, taking out every unnecessary word – influenced by Simenon, I favour an economic style – satisfying myself on the punctuation; correcting any misprints. The final copy is then typed, and although it is read again for any minor corrections, I try, for the publishers' sake, to make the minimum alterations. One could go on revising for ever, never being entirely satisfied.

To produce a book of eighty thousand words has probably entailed a total of some two hundred and fifty hours' work, which in terms of a regular eight-hour day and a five-day week – something that is obviously, at least for me, quite impractical – means the best part of two months of unbroken work. It is a lot of work for a book that a reader throws aside after two or three days – or hours! Nor is it only hard work for the author. If the author, as in my case, writes in a longhand which, when written at speed, is virtually unreadable, then it can be something of a headache for whoever has to type it. Fortunately for me Wendy Anglis, who first came to work for us when she left school, starting in the stables, then taking over as receptionist at Pendley, finally becoming my secretary about twelve years ago, manages to cope both quickly and accurately. I owe her an enormous debt of gratitude. Had she had to leave my employment when she married recently, this would probably have been my last book.

Clear Round, the Story of Show Jumping duly came out in September 1957. It had excellent notices, but more gratifying than the notices was the 'now being reprinted' in the literary pages of the Sunday papers the following week. *Clear Round, the Story of Show Jumping*, was first of some twenty-five books that I have been fortunate enough to have had published, most of them directly or indirectly connected with horses. Writing, together with lecturing and broadcasting, has probably earned me about £200,000, which sounds a lot of money; but spread over the years, and with increasingly generous donations to the tax-man, an author and broadcaster does not earn all that much unless he is very lucky, and achieves best-sellerdom or becomes a television star. The real rewards are in the creation. Writing has over the years given me much satisfaction, enabling me to achieve an early ambition. But publication of my first book, gave me the most satisfaction of all, something similar, perhaps, to the satisfaction one experiences at the birth of one's first child.

By the happiest coincidence two days after *Clear Round* was published Jennifer produced Piers. Such is the vanity of man that to father a son is an achievement with which no other can compare. When one is in one's forties this achievement is the cause of even greater joy. The birth of my son and heir, Piers Dorian, crowned a wonderful decade: Pendley, Shakespeare, Master of Foxhounds, broadcasting, writing, lecturing, speaking – and marriage. I had much to be grateful for in the fifties. Not surprisingly I felt on top of the world.

Chapter 12

Losing a little of the shine

Just as in a heatwave it is impossible to imagine the fine weather ever coming to an end, so when everything is going well it is difficult to imagine it ever being otherwise. Certainly in the late 1950s, in my mid-forties, I felt provocatively secure.

I felt that I had, at least for the present, achieved just about all of which I was capable. Obviously there were higher peaks to be attacked if one had the energy, if one was prepared to take the risks, but the plateau on which I now found myself seemed adequate for one who had always lacked the ambition to scale the ultimate heights. In a word I was content and, arguably, a little complacent though, I like to think, never afraid of the hard work demanded if I were to maintain my position in the various aspects of my life, let alone go further. Having apparently been regarded as a successful Master of Foxhounds, I was little prepared for the sudden criticism which I encountered in my hunting activities. In the light of experience I now realize that a new Master can expect to enjoy a season or two when everyone is co-operative, when most people are prepared to give him the benefit of the doubt, hoping that he is going to be the solution to all the Hunt's problems. This is equivalent to the honeymoon period allowed a new Prime Minister. In one's third or fourth season criticism begins to raise its ugly head and the Hunt tends to divide into factions, those for you and those against. As it is virtually impossible for a Master of Hounds to give anything approaching universal satisfaction – I have always believed that even the greatest Master is only capable of fulfilling about 70 per cent of the duties required of him – the likelihood is that in the next season or two the criticisms will snowball. This frequently leads, in the fourth or fifth season, to resignation or dismissal, with little in the way of thanks for all the effort, and, in all probability, the money put into the attempt to provide sport. If, however, a Master can weather this early storm then gradually he becomes accepted by every section of the community – including the Committee – and can remain as Master for the rest of his life, or for as long as he wishes to, so relieved is the Hunt to be free of uncertainty about the future.

That certainly was my experience. After the first two or three seasons when no one appeared to be able to find fault with anything I did, suddenly I became conscious of grumbling. At first, it all seeming rather petty, I did not take it very seriously, buoyed up as I was by the sport that, thanks to good luck and Albert Buckle, I was then showing, and the popularity that I enjoyed thanks to the reputation I had made in the Grafton country. Inevitably some people complained of changes: 'it never used to be done like this'; 'why do they have so many white hounds now?'; 'it's ridiculous meeting in adjoining villages two weeks running'; 'they're always in the same country': 'the fields are much too big nowadays'. It was true, of course, that fields were big and that we often covered the same country, but with good sport that we were showing this was bound to be the case. I realize now, however, that I was somewhat insensitive to these criticisms.

With hindsight I am inclined to think, in particular, that the famous cancelled meet was tactless. We had met at Aston Abbots on a very foggy morning. Major Harold Morton, who had been war-time Master, with his wife, Bea, dispensed lavish hospitality to a large field. After more than an hour, though the fog had scarcely lifted, I gave the order to move off, embarrassed by our so imposing on our hosts. I instructed Albert to put hounds into the delightful little circular Aston Abbots cover, made famous by the Cecil Aldin picture, but after less than half an hour conditions were obviously impossible and Albert stopped hounds. Unfortunately a small group had earlier withdrawn to the village pub where they happily regaled themselves until news reached them that hounds had moved off. In the fog, of course, they were unable to find us and after a somewhat cursory search they finished up careering all over Major Morton's farm, jumping his fences, leaving his gates open, even attacking from both sides his point-to-point schooling fences. Not surprisingly he was extremely annoyed, as indeed was I, especially as only the previous week I had been given a great deal of trouble because of unnecessary damage and stupid behaviour by a small section of the field. It so happened that later that week there was a Hunt Committee meeting at which there was much adverse comment. Deciding, on the spur of the moment, to take the bull by the horns, I informed the Committee that I proposed to cancel a day's hunting the following week, in order to establish my authority once and for all. My proposal was generally welcomed, the meet at Oving the following Tuesday duly being cancelled. This inevitably resulted in considerable publicity which, although it was on the whole sympathetic to my action, was widely resented.

Still failing to appreciate the feeling in the country – 'Who is this bloody schoolmaster?' – I decided at the end of the season to circularize a short leaflet on proper behaviour in the hunting field. It was aimed at those who, because of our proximity to London, came out with us, had never hunted before, and therefore were understandably ignorant of hunting etiquette, but whose enthusiasm one whole-heartedly welcomed. Obviously it was invidious to send such a leaflet only to newcomers and it went, therefore, to all members of the Hunt, and to all hunting farmers.

Within a couple of days I had had a blistering letter from the redoubtable Christabel Ampthill, for whom incidentally I had the greatest admiration. Only a few weeks earlier I had watched her, well into her sixties, mount, side-saddle, a green four year old which she had never seen before, and ride it at the top of the hunt. Her letter combined a don't-teach-your-grandmother-to-suck-eggs accusation with a one-who-is-deeply-offended-not-to-say-insulted attitude. 'Your letter would make an admirable first letter to the Pony Club' was the withering start of her letter. 'To those of us who have had more than fifty seasons hunting it causes much offence.' At first we were amused, but in her response to my letter of explanation she insisted that 'a lot of people are furious and very much resent your lecture'. This worried me. When a few days later I received a letter from one of the most respected farmers in the country, one who had been a great help to me when first I became Master, in which he told me that my pamphlet had done a lot of harm, I was really worried. 'No one,' he wrote, 'least of all a Master, should instruct farmers what they should or should not do.'

My pamphlet had been divided into three parts: for mounted followers, for car followers and for farmers. It had never occurred to me that the latter section might cause offence. I had prefaced it by saying: 'Conscious of the fact that without the co-operation of farmers there would be no hunting at all, the Hunt is anxious to cause as little trouble as possible to the farmers who allow the Hunt over their land.' There followed four paragraphs: a request that farmers should let me know where on their farms their stock was; a request that they should report any damage to the Secretary so that it could immediately be repaired; a request that farmers should inform the huntsman when they knew the whereabouts of foxes; a request that the Hunt should be allowed to take down barbed wire or, if permitted, build a hunt jump. I concluded, 'The Hunt is only anxious to co-operate with the farmers to the best of its ability and to cause as little trouble as possible.'

A visit to my farmer friend, however, convinced me that my pamphlet had caused offence. My good intentions had backfired. Due, perhaps, to over-confidence I had been guilty of an error of judgement, with the not surprising result that certain people felt that it was time that I was taken down a peg. A little serious thought persuaded me that many of the criticisms were justifiable. There certainly was a tendency to overhunt the country. Busy with Pendley and television, I was not giving as much time to the Hunt as some would like, though I have to admit that I have always thought the value of a Master's summer hunting can be exaggerated, not every farmer wanting to see one in the middle of haymaking. In any case both Albert and the Hunt Secretary were constantly around the country, thus acting both as caretakers and ambassadors for the Hunt, while I personally never missed any social occasion or show or gymkhana. It was from September to April that I really concentrated on the Hunt, but my absence during the summer months, which everyone associated with television, made me an easy target for those who wished to find fault. While understanding these criticisms I nevertheless felt that mine was, on the whole, a successful régime. Only the Master himself knows the problems of Mastership. In particular I felt as I still do, that the problems of being Field-Master are seldom fully appreciated. The responsibility is enormous. Not only does one have to control a large field, to ensure that people do not ride too close to hounds; not only does one have to position oneself and the field in such a position as to ensure that they are not left; not only does one have to know those farms where the Hunt is not, for one reason or another, temporarily or permanently, welcome, but one also has to see that damage is kept to a minimum. As Field-Master one is sometimes accused of being unsociable, unapproachable but, of course, one's concentration has to be total. Not for a moment can one relax. If one does everyone might suffer by missing a hunt or by offending a farmer. A Field-Master needs eyes at the back of his head, so often the damage being done by people at the back. Nevertheless as hunting is supposed to be sport, and therefore fun, a Field-Master should be good humoured, only occasionally blowing his top in an effort to prevent members of the field doing something that might be to the detriment of the sport or the annoyance of the farmers. I was accused in the early days by a few of the real cognoscenti, of going too fast, between draws, or after a check. Knowing that all most people wanted was to gallop and jump I was trying to keep everybody happy, but after a few years I realized that if hounds are to hunt properly they need to be given time and space, however much this might slow things up from the field's point of view. Remembering that good sport is the priority I came to learn that only the hounds could provide the sport, and it was essential, therefore, to enable them to do so. Somehow one had to satisfy the field without ruining the hounds. It was not an easy problem for a young and inexperienced Master to solve.

I did my best, however, to heed the various criticisms. To begin with I tried to give more of my time to the Hunt. I refused all purely public address jobs at shows, as opposed to television. I cut down lecturing and public-speaking engagements. I tried to spend at least one day a fortnight visiting farmers. In an attempt to spare the vale I started meeting once a month north of the A5, in the wild, rough, unspoilt, generously wooded area that is now, alas, the new city of Milton Keynes. At first unfashionable it became our most popular Saturday country, providing us with some marvellous, natural, old-fashioned hunting. I suggested, too, that to reduce the size of the field we might limit the number of visitors, though the Secretary responsible for balancing the accounts did not regard the decrease in revenue too kindly, resulting, as is so often the case with hunting, in a conflict of interests, the Master invariably finding himself torn in opposing directions. The excellent sport that we were showing, however, the increasingly successful partnership between Albert and myself, the fact that Buzzie Judd, doyen of the Hunt, had invited us to hold the Opening Meet at his home at Stewkley – where it has been held ever since – the whole-hearted backing that we had from the farmers and the Whaddon Chasers, our Supporters' Club, all helped to damp down criticism. But there was still one aspect of my life that many found difficult to accept. This was the inevitable publicity that surrounded me, though compared with that suffered by film stars and footballers it was, in fact, insignificant.

Until recently publicity of any sort has been anathema to the so called upper classes, and to the old County families in particular. Other than in the society papers one's name should never appear in print, and one never allowed oneself to be interviewed or quoted. In contrast to the publicity surrounding entertainers and politicians, a certain anonymity as far as the media were concerned was considered essential for the country gentleman. In fact, most people in the public eye in no way seek publicity, though obviously there are plenty of exceptions – more often than not it is difficult to avoid. Journalists, naturally, are going to write about people who are 'news', and press photographers are going to take pictures of the people they recognize. It is easy in theory to put the telephone down on a journalist, but in practice it is a mistake. To co-operate with the press pays every time, for the press can be very unkind if thwarted, as many a celebrity has found to his or her cost. Constant attention from the press and regular appearances on television inevitably lead, unfortunately, to over-exposure. It certainly did with me, as it can with almost anyone from Angela Rippon to the Prince of Wales, but one is incapable of preventing it, however much one might wish to do so. One can only hope that it will gradually subside, that a new name will become the target of the press. The people with whom I associated as a Master of Hounds certainly found it hard to accept the publicity that at that time I was attracting, many even believing that I was deliberately courting it. Their reaction, for instance, to an article in a national daily by Kenneth Allsop was less than sympathetic. Described as the B.B.C.'s blue-eyed boy, I was quoted as saying: 'We must revive the spirit of the eighteenth century when culture and sport lived together in harmony: today, in the main, intellectual people are too intellectual, and horsey people too horsey': sentiments to which no one would now object and to which, in all probability, very few would really have objected then. But for a Master of Hounds to be quoted as saying such a thing, in a national daily, and, worse, described as tall and dark with a wide, white smile, was considered bad taste.

There was something else that, strange as it may seem now, militated against me. As recently as twenty-five years ago a respected Master of Hounds was hardly expected to have to have a job, other than as a landowner and a farmer, or, possibly, as something in the City. To be part of the media was totally alien, even a little common. My desire to popularize hunting, my enthusiasm for Supporters' Clubs, was definitely suspect. I was reported as riskily avant-garde. Nor were these junketings at Pendley with which I was involved wholly understood or appreciated, though Pendley proved to have its uses when it was considered by the M.F.H. Committee to be the ideal venue for their proposed weekend on the breeding of hounds.

This was in 1958. Attended by over sixty eminent Masters, with their huntsmen, it was a great success, but two of the sessions may have taught me more about Masters of Foxhounds than about the breeding of hounds. A demonstration on the judging of hounds having been arranged for the Sunday afternoon, Captain Ronnie Wallace, then Master of the Heythrop, brought over ten or a dozen hounds which his Kennel-Huntsman, Percy Durno, was to show before two or three of the senior Masters. They were invited to comment on both their good points and bad – some less good hounds deliberately being included – as if they were judging at a puppy show. For their benefit Durno had made a list of the hounds, with a brief note on each hound. I also had a copy. Unfortunately, in error, Durno produced one hound in the wrong order. It was, in fact, a recent Peterborough champion, but according to the list it was something quite different. The judges happily condemned it, therefore, for its curly stern, long back, being over at the knees; worse, when the moderate one came in next they praised it unreservedly. As far as I could see not many of the distinguished company had spotted the not-so-deliberate mistake, though a few were highly entertained at the pundits' fallibility.

I had been asked to speak myself at the final session, on Public Relations. I started by saying that these were just as important with foxhunting as with industry, entertainment, even Government. I continued by suggesting that relations with the local press could be helped by getting to know local reporters. I concluded by describing both the right way and the wrong way to deal with the press, with mildly amusing imitations of the blimpish Master – 'no comment, damn your eyes.' During the twenty minutes or so of my talk the faces of my audience seemed to be getting longer and longer. I was received in polite but stony silence. Only Ronnie Wallace, at the end, told me he had agreed with everything that I had said. A well-known titled Master kindly told me that he had been able to hear every word. At least my diction was appreciated, but I was left in no doubt that Masters of Foxhounds were not yet ready for Public Relations, and in the official report of the weekend issued later my paper was omitted. I was obviously regarded, too, as something of an *enfant terrible* – at the age of forty-five, *quel enfant!*

An incident the following season underlined the then establishment's attitude to publicity of any sort connected with foxhunting. In the William Hickey column of the *Daily Express* there appeared a story about the Whaddon Chase, mostly concerning Nubar Gulbenkian, at that time a regular follower, but also commenting upon the apparent enthusiasm for the Hunt to be found in the local pub. The style, as usual, was gossipy, slightly snide, but not, to my way of thinking, particularly offensive. I was surprised, therefore, to receive a letter from Sir Peter Farquhar, then Chairman of the M.F.H. Committee, in which he said that it was the unanimous opinion of the Committee that articles such as William Hickey's were not in the best interests of hunting. 'I have been asked to write and tell you so – not a very pleasant task, I am afraid, to a fellow M.F.H. – but attention to this unfortunate article has been brought to our notice from many sources.' He further suggested that I might care to contact the Secretary of the British Field Sports Society who, apparently, was shortly to investigate the whole matter of publicity. I replied, setting out the facts which were that a young lady had telephoned the Hunt Secretary asking if she could come out for a day's hunting. She was told that she would be welcome, but would have to pay a cap of £5. In the conversation she mentioned that she was a young journalist, though she did not give the impression that she was coming out professionally. Later she telephoned my wife to ask where she could hire clothes. My wife recommended the obvious outfitters, but also advised her to telephone me; this she never did. At the meet I was approached by a young lady who gave the impression of being fitted out by Nathans for a musical comedy which was the last I saw of her until at the end of the day when, riding back to my box, I met her coming down the road accompanied by a young man. Apparently she had fallen off in the first field and had spent the rest of the day, very happily, in the local pub. I explained all this in full.

Sir Peter replied, 'I am completely puzzled. Did Mr Hickey himself never come down at all? Was he not really out? Was it all made up? If so I must say the cheap press passes all understanding. If you can confirm all this then I will pass it on to the Committee.' I duly confirmed that William Hickey had not been out with us; indeed, did not exist: it was a syndicated column. Peter Farquhar, for a short time Joint-Master with Lord Rosebery of the Whaddon Chase, later a very distinguished Master of the Portman Hunt and pioneer in the introduction of Welsh blood into English Kennels, wrote me a charming letter, apologizing – and no doubt opened his Committee's eyes on certain aspects of publicity

In J. M. Barrie's enchanting play, *Dear Brutus* – surely one of the most beautifully constructed plays in the English language – there is a passage which has always impressed me: 'The laughter that children are born with', Dearth, the failed artist, tells his dream daughter, 'lasts just so long as they have perfect faith.' The smile had not exactly been wiped off my face by these deflating experiences, but my faith, or more accurately my self-confidence, had undoubtedly been shaken. Life had lost a little of its shine, and I was, if not a sadder man, certainly a wiser one. Everything in the garden was not always rosy, it seemed.

Even with television there was to be a jolt to my supremacy in my own particular field as the B.B.C.'s commentator on equestrian events. For twelve years as a commentator I had been very much the only pebble on the beach. Not only was I responsible for the public address commentary as well as the television commentary, but, show jumping being a new sport, as far as the public was concerned, I was also generally regarded as the 'expert', advising the producer on the most effective way to televise an event, even advising on the positioning of cameras. Hence the 'Mr Show Jumping' tag. In 1962 I.T.V. came into being, Raymond Brooks-Ward, who for some years had acted as my assistant and deputy in public address jobs, becoming their commentator. Compared with the B.B.C., I.T.V. did not do very much show jumping, but they did take over from the B.B.C. three important shows in the Royal Windsor, Richmond Royal and Hickstead. A few years later Hickstead came back to the B.B.C.

involving an extra thirty hours of television. As the B.B.C.'s coverage of show jumping was already heavy I was only too pleased when it was suggested that Raymond should join the B.B.C., enabling us over the years to build up a valuable partnership and friendship. First Lord Allenby, then Tom Hudson took over the I.T.V. commentaries. At various times Ann Moore, Michael Clayton, Richard Mead and Michael Tucker have been added to the B.B.C. team, while for a number of years David Vine has been involved in almost all transmissions as introducer and linkman. By the end of the sixties, therefore, I was far from being the only pebble on my beach. On the W. S. Gilbert principle that when everyone is somebody, then no one's anybody, I had obviously to look to my laurels. This did not prove easy as each year television was becoming more and more professional. It was very noticeable, for instance, that when I went to an occasion such as the Olympic Games, at which all the leading sports commentators were present, they were with few exceptions all full-timers, while I still had many other strings to my bow.

I have always thought it possible that the B.B.C., or its Sports Department, was seriously considering making a change when my contract expired after the Mexico Olympics. One day I was invited to lunch at Television Centre where I found all the heads of the various sports departments and the senior sports producer assembled with Kenneth Adam, then head of B.B.C.1, presiding. Having been treated to a first-class four-course lunch, washed down with excellent wines, followed by liqueurs and a cigar – this was before the days of economy – I was asked by Kenneth Adam if I had ever noticed that there was one way in which I differed from all their other sports commentators. I imagined that he was referring to the fact that I was less fully involved than the others, not so fully professional, and said so.

'No, not that,' he replied, and then, using a tone which could imply that he was joking, he said:

'You know, you are the only one of our commentators left still using impeccable King's English; who speaks with a public school accent. You must surely have some kind of accent or dialect that you could adopt. Why don't you try it?'

'Out of the question,' I replied quickly, also trying to make it sound as if I was regarding it all as a joke, while beginning to suspect that he was really implying that I did not quite fit in with the B.B.C. image: 'In the first place I know only one dialect, Hertfordshire, which having no consonants would never do for a commentator. Secondly, I can use only one accent and that is Welsh, but I am sure that, at the critical moment, I would forget to use it and lapse back into my usual bla-bla tones.'

Everyone laughed, so I told them of the time that I was commentating at a show in the north when a local told me that up in Yorkshire they all thought that I was 'nought but bloody la-di-da'.

No further mention was made of my accent, the lunch party broke up most amicably, and I was left wondering. A few weeks later my agent telephoned me to say that Bryan Cowgill, then Head of Sport, had been on to him saying that they would like my new contract to extend to four years, covering the next Olympics, instead of two. The following year a B.B.C. producer assured me that a research had been carried out to ascertain whether the British public liked or disliked my commentary. Apparently, according to him, a large majority liked it; hence the new contract. Whether or not all this is true I have no way of knowing. But it is not entirely impossible, Kenneth Adam always being quite open about his intense dislike of the Cavalcade at The Horse of the Year Show, the climax of which is my reading of the 'Tribute to the Horse' – hence its never being televised.

It was not only with the B.B.C. itself that during the sixties my relations subtly changed. Even more it was with the riders. When show jumping was first televised the leading riders were such as Harry Llewellyn, Ruby Holland-Martin, 'Monkey' Blacker, Pat Smythe, Jill and Dawn Palethorpe, Geoffrey Gibbon, Arthur Carr, Dougie Stewart, all personal friends of mine. Although I personally believe their basic ability to be the equal of today's riders, their approach to the sport was totally different, far less intense, far less professional; they still had time for a social life, even another occupation. Today show jumping is a way of life in itself. In 1958 Harvey Smith appeared on the scene for the first time, spearheading a complete change in attitudes. Though many were mildly amused at his somewhat rustic appearance, and the even more rustic appearance of his horse, appropriately named Farmer's Boy, it soon became obvious that Harvey and the other newcomer to the sport, David Broome, were adding a new dimension to show jumping. Their approach, especially the former's, was entirely professional. Appreciating that the old 'amateur' approach had gone for ever, I wrote an article at that time, in which I said that whether people liked it or not Harvey Smith was as inevitable to show jumping as Trueman was to cricket or George Best to football. I was to be proved correct, though for some years there lingered in certain areas a hankering after the old days, which deep down I may have shared. Instinctively, I accepted the inevitability of 'progress' while basically I regretted the loss of the old 'amateur' approach. I found myself, therefore, between two stools. In the introduction to his paperback *Harvey* (Arrow Books, 1976) Harvey, however, writes: 'Dorian Williams summed up the thinking of the establishment when he once wrote, "It may be that Harvey Smith is too ruthless, that he has got his values wrong, that he attaches too much importance to winning and too little to the sheer enjoyment of the sport." Later in the same piece he wrote: "There are people who consider his [Harvey's] influence in show jumping undesirable, even subversive: that his insistence on a rigorously professional approach to the sport has taken the fun out of it, has made it all too serious and commercial. Controversy has always surrounded me, he said, because I was a natural leader and had come to be regarded as the leader of the new set." '

Unfortunately he does not quote much else that I wrote of him in this particular book *Show Jumping, the Great Ones* (Pelham Books, 1970). For instance, I wrote 'Change, is inevitable and there must always be someone in the van. Harvey with his strong, dominant personality is a natural leader. Is there anything wrong in this? Is there anything wrong in his belief that show jumping is no longer a garden party, a sport exclusively for the enjoyment of "amateurs", people who can afford not to win? If he attaches too much importance to winning then it has to be accepted that it is only an exaggeration of the attitude towards the sport of a large number of other show jumpers.' I also wrote: 'He is first and foremost an individualist. He owes allegiance to no one but himself – and his horses, to which he is genuinely devoted. Each one is as individual as he himself: he knows each one intimately and treats it accordingly.' I then wrote in glowing terms of the condition of his horses, concluding the chapter as follows: 'There can be no doubt whatever that Harvey has injected something new into show jumping, something that in the present stage and standing of the sport was needed.'

I have quoted at length as it seems to me that this deliberate quoting out of context is evidence of Harvey's unfortunate determination from the very beginning to exaggerate the difference between 'them' and 'us'. 'Them', of course, being the 'establishment', those who have so frequently been referred to as 'the Colonels'; in others words, the ex-Cavalry officers, led by Mike Ansell, who built up the sport after the war. Inevitably, because of my close association with Mike Ansell, I was bracketed, in Harvey's eyes, with the Colonels, the 'establishment'. But this was only partly true. I was not wholly involved on either side, largely because both broadcasting and show jumping were part-time interests for me. I had my many other involvements.

Paradoxically, while the B.B.C. allegedly thought I was a bit of a 'toff ', as did the jumpers, the real 'toffs', the traditionalists, generally regarded in the world of show jumping as the 'establishment', thought that I was something of a non-conformist. There is an entirely apocryphal story sometimes told as a joke at the B.B.C. about my being measured for a blazer for the Mexico Olympics. When given the name of the popular outfitters – well-known in Oxford Street – I am alleged to have said: 'This is not a tailor with whose suits I am familiar.' I have often been told, too, that my voice was responsible for show jumping being considered an exclusive sport. One might just as well say that Peter O'Sullevan, who, oddly enough went to the same preparatory school as I did, turned racing into a snob sport, when the fact of the matter is that a commentator's one essential weapon is knowledge of the sport and, of course, an awareness of broadcasting technique. Though it is true that in such cases as Eddie Waring with Rugby League and John Arlott with cricket the voice has made a great contribution. It is probably true that I have never really been 'one of the boys', but this is, firstly, because I do not really like the matey type of commentary, and secondly, because I find that a certain detachment helps the integrity of one's commentary. Conversely, although involved with the administrative side of shows and show jumping, I have never regarded myself as part of the 'establishment', for the simple reason that I do not believe that there has ever been one, other than in Harvey's imagination. It is impossible to find more forward-looking, less hidebound people than Mike Ansell, Harry Llewellyn, Jack Webber, Jimmy Jack, John Blakeway, Duggie Bunn and others who, over the years, have been responsible for running show jumping in this country. They would be the first to agree with Harvey when he says in the introduction to his book: 'Our sport is only worth watching when it is truly competitive; the old-fashioned "Come on, boys, let's have a jolly good time" attitude is now strictly for the hunting field.' (A nice little crack there!) The remarkable reservoir of top-class young riders, devoting the whole of their lives to show jumping, is due equally to the influence and example of people like Harvey Smith and to the 'Colonels' who laid the original foundations.

Though it is a more complex operation, I have always enjoyed the televising of a three day event. For the most part I know the event riders no better than I know the show jumpers, but obviously I have a greater affinity with them. This is partly because many of them come from a hunting background, and partly because they are riding across country, something with which I am familiar; though when I walk a three-day-event course today there seldom seem to be more than one or two fences that I would ever be prepared to tackle out hunting myself. These young event riders are immensely talented as well as brave, none more so than Princess Anne, who unintentionally was once responsible for my missing what could well have been the biggest scoop of my television career.

In 1971 she won the European Three Day Event Championship at Burghley on the Queen's horse Doublet. When at the end of the Cross Country Phase she was in a commanding position, with victory the following day a real possibility, approaches were made by the B.B.C. to the Palace Press Secretary to see whether it would be possible to interview her at the end of the event; just as one would normally interview the winner and, as in fact, I had interviewed Mark Phillips a few months earlier when he had won at Badminton. The answer was a firm 'No'. Next afternoon Princess Anne duly won, most convincingly, both the Queen and Prince Philip being present. It was a moving and very exciting occasion. The television producer, Alan Mouncer, was obviously bitterly disappointed at getting no interview. His superiors back in London were more than disappointed – they were hysterical! More, they would not take 'No' for an answer. Through my earphones I could hear a violent argument going on between Burghley and London. Eventually to my horror I heard a voice say: 'Tell Dorian to bloody well go down to the collecting ring and ask her himself.' Despite my protests I was forthwith despatched, handing over my microphone to a colleague. With difficulty I forced my way into the collecting ring to which the prize winners were just returning. Fortunately John Miller, the Crown Equerry, was there. Seizing him, I begged him to let me have an interview with Princess Anne. He reminded me that the firm instructions were that there were to be no interviews, but he kindly agreed to approach her. In a few moments he came back with the great news that she had agreed to talk to me as 'we spoke in the same language'. The studio manager at the edge of the ring immediately informed the producer who then instructed him to tell me to pick up a microphone hanging hopefully over the rails separating the collecting ring from the arena. I hurried across, delighted at the opportunity for such a scoop. Princess Anne, still very young and a comparative beginner, which made her success all the more a triumph, had never previously been interviewed in connection with eventing. On the off-chance that she might, at the last minute, agree to be interviewed I had thought up an original, 'human', 'one horseman to another' line of approach. As I turned to walk across to her, having collected the microphone from the railings, I just could not believe my eyes. There was a reporter from the B.B.C. News Division, who had been lurking in the collecting ring, already interviewing her. He had nipped in while my back was turned, understanding, as he later lamely explained, that 'she had given permission'. I was not only furious, but embarrassed, believing that I had unwittingly deceived her. The most amusing part of the whole situation was that, so obvious and banal were the questions put to Princess Anne, so flat were her answers, that viewers were apparently far more intrigued by the livid, almost apoplectic face of the commentator in the background, deviously cheated of his scoop!

Often people assume that because I commentate on the sport with which Princess Anne is involved and, as Chairman of the British Horse Society, am concerned on the administrative side, that I know her intimately. This, of course, is not so. Because I have done a television programme with her and Mark Phillips from my home at Foscote, having been Master of the Worshipful Company of Farriers of which she is a Liveryman, and having been present and, therefore, inevitably met her at many major Three Day Events, I know her quite well. But the opinion that I have formed of her is as a detached observer with a closer personal knowledge of her than many, rather than as a close friend such as those who compete with her. It always annoys me when people suggest that she was only selected for the European Championships and Olympic Games because she is the daughter of the Queen. She is, in fact, an extremely talented rider. Few people realize that had it not been for what was genuinely an unlucky fall in Montreal she might very well have won an Olympic medal. She has been both winner and runner-up in the European Championships, on different horses. She is patient, dedicated and very courageous. She can laugh at herself, has a wit, obviously inherited from her father, which is sharp, penetrating and sometimes considered cynical. She also has great compassion, as is evidenced by her completely sincere interest in Riding for the Disabled and other charities connected with children. The strain that she experiences as a result from the determined sections of the press, especially when she is competing, has earned her a reputation for being moody, sometimes bad tempered; but while one can appreciate the press's close interest one can understand well enough how unwelcome this must be to her. Like her father, she is a real competitor, resenting anything, therefore, that interferes with her chances, not least any mistake or inadequacy of her own. Exposed to the glare of publicity to which she is subjected, it would be surprising if her image was perfect, but apart from her role as a Royal Princess she has made a tremendous contribution to her own sport and to riding generally for which the horse world should be grateful.

On the few occasions on which I have been privileged to interview her Princess Anne has been most friendly and co-operative, and easy to talk to, which is not always the case with those one is interviewing. I can only recall one experience more embarrassing than my lost interview at Burghley with Princess Anne. This was when, before its first ever coverage of the Grand National, the B.B.C. put out a programme from Fred Rimmell's in which well-known jockeys and trainers discussed the great race. At the conclusion of the programme I interviewed Mirabel Topham herself. Towards the end, knowing that she came from a theatrical background, I asked her if she had always been interested in National Hunt Racing.

'Oh, yes', she told me, 'for a very long time.'

'But even before the death of your husband?' I knew that it was her husband's family who owned the course.

'But my husband isn't dead', was her shattering reply.

I started to stammer an apology, but she laughed happily and told me not to worry, explaining that he took little interest in the business.

Next day out hunting, the programme having gone out live, everyone was pulling my leg about this appalling gaffe. On the way home, calling in for a cup of tea at a farm where I had left my horse-box, I had hardly entered the house before the farmer said:

'Well, you've really done it this time, Master.'

'Done what?' I asked.

'Killed off Mr Topham.'

'Killed off Mr Topham?'

'I'm afraid so,' and he showed me the stop-press announcement in the local evening paper. Mr Topham had died that morning. I was absolutely horrified. Such a coincidence was hardly credible. I immediately wrote a most apologetic letter to Mrs Topham, who replied, almost by return, setting my mind at rest by most charmingly inviting me to watch the race from her box and to put the sash of honour round the winner's neck – an honour that as a boy, so obsessed with the Grand National, I could not possibly have envisaged.

It was due to the B.B.C., or more accurately to Fred Viner, producer of the Grand National television, as well as all major show jumping, that I was able to fulfil another ambition: to watch the race from Becher's. In 1977 I was fortunate enough to enjoy the race – an historic race in that it was Red Rum's third, record-breaking, victory – from the B.B.C.'s Becher's camera position. It was an unforgettable experience, if nothing else convincing me that I was much better off as a show jumping commentator, with only one horse involved at a time, rather than as a race commentator with that great kaleidoscope of colours somehow to be identified as it flashes by. I was once referred to as show jumping's Peter O'Sullevan. Whoever wrote that did not know what he was talking about, even if our voices do suggest that we were educated at the same school. He is the complete professional, wholly absorbed in one sport. Show jumping is but a part of my life.

All his eggs are in the one basket: mine in many, which I like to think enables me to hedge if for any reason I am let down by any one of them, or bounce up again if I experience the sort of setbacks that I did in the late fifties and early sixties. There is, hopefully, always something else to turn to. If Pendley is a problem then there is the hunting; if hunting becomes a worry then there is television and so on. Such a way of life may prevent one reaching the pinnacle in any, let alone all of one's ambitions and objectives, but it is a way of life that I have chosen with my eyes open. I enjoy my involvement in a wide variety of activities. I have no wish to be a specialist, whatever it may deny me.

Chapter 13

From a find to a check

During the late sixties I became increasingly involved in the work of the British Horse Society due, of course, to my having been elected to the Council in 1952. Mike Ansell at that time was Director of the Society, shortly, in addition, to become Chairman. Largely through our close association in the running of the Royal International and Horse of the Year shows he came to regard me as his right-hand man. Over a drink as his office upstairs at No. 16 Bedford Square, or having dinner at the Cavalry Club, we would discuss plans and developments, problems and opportunities. My enthusiasm matching his, I was only too happy to play Sancho Panza to his Don Juan attempting to implement the flow of ideas that stemmed from his fertile mind. It was from his office in Bedford Square that everything emanated: the two Horse Shows, the British Horse Society, the British Show Jumping Association, of which he was also Chairman. He had as his devoted lieutenant David Satow, who occupied a series of jobs, each of which amounted to the same, general dogsbody to Mike Ansell – a position he both loved and enjoyed, even if at times he was sorely tried. There was also Jack Webber, the Secretary General of the B.S.J.A. and, for many years, his secretary, Biddy. Though there were on the General Purpose and Finance Committee and, indeed, on the Council, many able and dedicated people it is nevertheless true to say that in the sixties the horse world was run from that little office upstairs at No. 16 Bedford Square.

Mike, of course, being blind, would often use his colleagues as sounding boxes while he thought aloud. Being unable to read he was dependent on people reading to him, or on tapes used by various members of his staff to record matters of importance which he could then play on his own tape-recorder. He used a typewriter a great deal, sometimes bombarding one with notes and memos and, of course, he was well able to use the telephone. We would talk and plan, often long into the night: hours meant nothing to him. The two big shows and their organization were his life. 'It's all *such* fun', he would say, or 'We've damn well got to *win*!, discussing one of our teams chosen to represent Britain at the Royal International or at some show overseas which he knew was to be televised. 'Fun' and 'win' were the cornerstones of his vocabulary in those days. He was able to give far more of his time and of his mind to the two Societies and the two Shows than anyone else, yet his enthusiasm never waned. 'We're on to an absolute winner this time. Get me another gin and french.'

When I first started attending meetings and briefings at No. 16 Bedford Square I was not impressed. Indeed, it appeared to me as a somewhat uninspiring Victorian public convenience. The only room of any elegance was a large panelled room down a few steps from the lobby – one could hardly call it a hall. The conference room was bare and functional, facing on to the square; the office opened on to the lobby, and David Satow operated from the basement. Only Mike's room half-way up the stairs had any atmosphere – ironically it was lighter than the other rooms and the furniture was more comfortable. As is so often the way, though initially dismayed by its drabness I soon came to accept it, even became quite attached to it. On one or two occasions I did suggest, without any great conviction, that we ought to consider moving our offices out into the country: somewhere like Elstree or Stanmore, where we could also have a little land and our own riding school so that we need not always run our courses in other people's establishments. But the reply was always the same, and unanswerable: 'Where exactly? And how are we going to pay for it?'

Perhaps one might have accepted the situation permanently had not my father one day asked me what I thought of the idea of selling or letting Pendley to the Royal Agricultural Society, as a permanent site for the Royal Show. He had been told that they were looking for a suitable estate, and one of their Council had suggested Pendley. I was not in favour. In the first place I felt sure that they would require the house, which would mean closing down my now very successful Centre of Education. Secondly, I felt that despite the fact that we still owned all the farms it was not really large enough. The park itself sloped down sharply from the main road to the house, and the home farm was dissected by the canal and bounded by the railway. I doubted, too, whether the tenant farmers would favour such an idea. The suggestion was not, in fact, pursued, but as a result of it I found myself constantly thinking of Pendley as a possible home for the British Horse Society. Only thirty miles from London, on a main line and a main road, a mere twelve miles from the new motorway, the M1, Pendley was eminently accessible. There were stables and an indoor school, the park and the woodlands for cross-country riding and a grassed-down walled-in garden suitable for *manèges* and show jumping courses. Most useful of all there could always be accommodation available for the small courses for eight or ten people which the Society was running with increasing regularity. The necessary office accommodation could be provided in terrapin buildings or an annexe. The cost to the Society need be minimal: Pendley was a going concern; it would only mean shifting the emphasis towards equestrianism.

I put the idea to Mike Ansell, who was intrigued but uncertain whether it was either practical or timely. Without my being aware of it a small unofficial sub-committee, or more accurately, working party, was set up to consider the matter. The National Coach and one or two others came down to look at Pendley, but the general feeling was, apparently, against moving out of London. Naturally I was disappointed though, as usual, with my other interests and occupations I did not allow it to worry me unduly. The idea, however, of moving out of London, sometime continued to linger in the back of my mind. At the end of a meeting of the General Purposes and Finance Committee of the British Horse Society in December 1965, under 'any other business' the Chairman said that the Secretary Generals of the two Societies, Brigadier W. A. C. ('WAC') Anderson and Captain Jack Webber, had been approached by Lord Leigh with the suggestion that the two Societies might like to move their headquarters to Stoneleigh. Having heard that it would cost £20,000 to put the property in order and that three floors were available whereas only one would be needed, Mike Ansell, in the Chair, suggested that the offer should be declined. Ruby Holland-Martin, one of the Society's Treasurers, agreed, being of the opinion that the time was not ripe. It was the end of a long meeting and many members of the Committee had departed already, as was their wont. There was, in fact, hardly a quorum, but I felt that this was an opportunity that should not be allowed to slip by. I said, therefore, that I understood well the feeling of those opposed to leaving London, but I felt strongly that Bedford Square was the wrong image for the Society – a Society connected with outside activities should not be based in London. I appreciated that I was in a minority, but I would like it recorded in the minutes that I was in favour of investigating Lord Leigh's offer. To the Chairman's surprise there was a strong murmur of 'hear hear' from all round the table. What he did not realize, being blind, was that it was mostly members of the staff who were 'hear-hearing': they could not wait to get away from the dismal rabbit-warren of Bedford Square. However, hearing the approval for my proposal Mike Ansell asked if it was the wish of the Committee to look further into the matter. I urged that it should be and was supported by Bill Barton, a recent President of the Society and, surprisingly, by Leo Harris, the other Treasurer – two valuable and enlightened members of the Society. This was enough to sway Mike, who immediately suggested a working party consisting of Bill Barton, Jack Webber, Bob Hanson, a great patron of show jumping and enormously experienced, and myself. We arranged a visit to Stoneleigh as soon as possible after Christmas.

The abbey itself proved impractical. There was too much of it and the upkeep would have been prohibitive. However, Christopher Dadd, then Chief Executive of the Royal Agricultural Society, knew that we were paying this visit to Stoneleigh and invited us to meet him on the showground. He suggested that we should lease a site on their ground where we could build our own offices. The site he had in mind was right by the main ring, and there was also an adjacent site where we could build an indoor school. This seemed much more feasible, and the more we thought about it, the more it appealed to us, always assuming that we could raise the money, which was something in the nature of £100,000. It was my father who suggested the Founder Members' Scheme, whereby three hundred leading names in the horse world should each be invited to give 100 gns. David Satow ascertained that the Sports Council would be prepared to put up a 50 per cent grant. I was convinced that I could raise £10,000 by personal approach to Pony Clubs, Riding Clubs, even Hunts. A series of meetings took place, at which there seemed to be general enthusiasm for the idea, but at which money was invariably the stumbling block. Eventually it was suggested that the British Show Jumping Assocation should share the venture with the British Horse Society, each body loaning a certain sum of money. Bob Hanson's wife, Cis, most generously offered to loan the final amount required to make up the total necessary.

After almost a year of hectic to-ing and fro-ing, arguing and negotiating, it was agreed at the September meeting of the B.H.S. General Purposes and Finance Committee that the scheme was viable and should be recommended to the Council at their meeting at the end of November. A few weeks later Jennifer and I departed for Australia, where we had been invited to judge at Melbourne. Returning from a most enjoyable trip, which included a stay on the way there in Honolulu and a stay on the way back in California, we returned home just in time for the Horse of the Year Show. At the first performance Mike Ansell asked me if I had had time to open all my mail since returning two days earlier. A little tersely I told him that I had read what mattered.

'We must talk about it sometime,' he said.

'Why not tonight?' I asked. 'We are both staying in the same hotel.'

A letter in my post had informed me that a number of members of the General Purposes and Finance Committee had met and decided that in their opinion the financial climate was not right for a move from London, and had decided to call a special meeting to postpone the whole scheme – which inevitably, as I saw it, would mean to abandon it.

We argued into the night. I could see all the objections to moving to Stoneleigh, but was convinced that if we did not seize the opportunity of moving now, then we never would. I believed, too, that in his heart of hearts Mike, always forward looking, knew that this was the right moment, despite the inconvenience it would mean to him personally; though the R.A.S.E. (Royal Agricultural Society of England) had said that they could provide offices for the shows organization in the basement of their house in Belgrave Square. Thanks to David Satow, who by this time was living in one of our cottages at Foscote, and with whom I had spent hours discussing the whole matter, I had one trump card up my sleeve. The promised grant, now worth something between £25,000 and £30,000, thanks to the assistance of Sports Minister, Denis Howell, with whom I had become quite friendly, was available for only one financial year. In other words, if we postponed the scheme, even for one year, we would lose the money, and might not be so fortunate in a second application. It was obvious, too, that each year the project would become more costly. Before the night was out Mike agreed to have further talks with those opposed to the scheme. For a brief spell there was some furious lobbying which, in fact, proved unnecessary. Once it was known that Mike was in favour, everyone else fell in behind. A sub-committee to bring the scheme to fruition was appointed, but seldom met, the lion's share of all the work involved being undertaken by John Tilke, the proprietor of a neighbouring riding establishment at Stratford-upon-Avon. He not only had the knowledge and experience, but through his clients and contacts he knew most of the leading firms in Coventry. As a result he was able to acquire much not only at a handsome discount but also very promptly. He was also able to introduce us to people such as architects and designers who were prepared to give their services free. At the end of three or four feverish months of planning and meetings I had the honour of cutting the first turf on 22 January 1977. Unfortunately, I had broken my collar-bone in a fall out hunting earlier in the month, which made digging of any sort difficult. In addition the frost was so severe that it was impossible for anyone, let alone myself, to get a spade into the ground at all. At dawn, therefore, a few hours before the ceremony, David Satow went out with a knife and cut a turf which I would be able to lift. Almost unbelievably, thanks to the industry of John Tilke – my role for the most part being confined, as when I first became Joint-Master of the Grafton with Neil Foster, to public relations and fund raising – just five months later, in

May, the offices were opened. The daunting move from Bedford Square was achieved in four days under the supervision of 'WAC' Anderson and John Blackmore, the Secretary General of the B.H.S. respectively, and Jack Webber and Charles Stratton of the B.S.J.A. The National Equestrian Centre had come into being. A dream had come true.

The school, opened a year later, magnificently designed with most effective decor by Tibor Reich, boasted a unique roof of Filon plastic, a lounge bar generously provided by Whitbreads, a library, the gift of *Horse and Hound*, a lecture room and a first-aid room made possible by donations from Martini Rossi and Ronald Margolin. An arcade running the full length of the school with some thirty display cases made an imposing entrance, while the blue and white exterior was made impressive by Blue Circle's Sandtex. A gallery to seat some three hundred people occupied one side of the school, each seat being provided by a different Pony Club. Below the gallery ran a panel with a large blown-up picture of each of the different breeds of ponies which the various societies were responsible for, the Ponies of Britain having a special panel at the end. On the other side of the school was a full-length mirror provided by Spillers, allegedly the longest in the country. There was provision, too, for an extra bar at the end of the gallery and a spacious jumps store beneath it. Some sixty or seventy different Riding Clubs and Hunts also contributed in kind, as did many individuals. The school was ready just in time for the Royal Show at the beginning of July 1968, and proved to be one of the biggest attractions of the whole show, being visited by more than twenty thousand people.

Inevitably there were teething troubles. The great Filon roof resulted in the school being like a greenhouse in hot weather, an ice-box in winter. The radio microphone, which an instructor could use carrying only a battery in his pocket, proved temperamental in the extreme, and in wet weather the surrounds became a quagmire. On the other hand the first few months, building up the programme, selling the whole idea to the sceptics – and there were still plenty of them – were tremendously exciting, producing amongst the whole staff an atmosphere of dedication, enthusiasm and an absolute faith in the rightness of the venture, which proved marvellously infectious. Everyone was prepared to turn his or her hand to anything. That the scheme should succeed was absolutely imperative. We could not afford to fail. I was reminded of those early days at Pendley more than twenty years ago: exciting, exhausting, rewarding. A few mistakes were made, obviously: errors of judgement; there was the occasional row; we encountered criticism from the horse world as well as praise;

there were still pockets of undisguised hostility. But the National Equestrian Centre existed, was a tangible reality, a manifestation of the long-felt ambitions for a united, better integrated and more efficiently organized horse world, all, as it were, under one roof. Even more important, the whole complex, worth in excess of £120,000, had been produced at absolutely no cost to the membership of the two societies, other than three hundred Founder Members who between them had generously produced more than £30,000. In the first year some ten thousand people visited the school, in addition to the huge Royal Show crowds. Over fifteen hundred students attended courses. Most satisfactory of all, the school made a small profit: something unique for a national centre, the majority of which cost their individual sports anything up to £50,000 a year. Even more important, it was responsible for a steady increase in the membership of the British Horse Society. In 1967 it was barely ten thousand, and less than five years later it had reached over twenty thousand.

The management committee, with Colonel Bill Froud, the national instructor and Charles Stratton, the centre manager, met regularly, to plan and consolidate, always trying to think up new courses which would be of value to the membership of the societies, always trying to improve amenities. It was hard work, especially dashing all over the country 'selling' it, in addition to driving up to Stoneleigh two or three times a week and, of course, the numerous meetings in London. But as far as I was concerned, it was more than worthwhile. Is there anything more rewarding than seeing a dream come true? There were times when, almost Callaghan-like, I felt that I was leading the British Horse Society into the promised land which had at last been found. At the time I was probably carried away with the sense of achievement, the promise of El Dorado. I did not always appreciate the problems, realize what was practical and what was not, but at least the National Equestrian Centre was a reality. One could not help being smugly elated. Whatever obstacles might lie in the path ahead, at least we were on our way. The frustration of a few years earlier were forgotten, helped enormously by the move to our new home, conveniently nearer Stoneleigh, which had taken place a year or two earlier: another dream come true.

In the spring of 1963 I had heard that Foscote Manor, a beautiful Jacobean Manor near Buckingham, which I had known as a child, was up for sale following the death, in her nineties, of old Mrs Heyworth. Unfortunately, however, it was to be sold with five hundred acres, completely ruling out any thought of purchase, which was sad as we had both completely fallen for this lovely Cotswold-type house on the borders of Buckinghamshire and Northamptonshire, my childhood environment, with its miniature park and delightful little lake. We did not even attend the auction in July, but a week or so later at a local show an old farmer friend, considerably the worse for drink, insisted that I had made a deal with the purchaser to buy the house off him. I assured him that there had been no such arrangement, that I did not even know who had bought the property. But he was adamant.

'You're a naughty boy, Dorian,' he said, with uncharacteristic familiarity. 'I know exactly what you've been up to, but you've been trying to keep it quiet. You're a naughty boy.'

On the way home I told Jennifer of this conversation and suggested that we might find out if the house could be bought separately. At first the answer was in the negative, but twenty-four hours later the new owner's agent rang up, inviting an offer. Within less than a week it was all settled. We had become the owners of what we then believed to be the ideal home for us. Nor have we ever regretted our decision, hasty as it was – uncharacteristically hasty for Jennifer, but needs must!

The following Christmas I called on my old farmer friend to thank him for what, consciously or unconsciously, he had done, and gave him a bottle of whisky.

'I don't know what you're talking about,' he said. 'I had no idea you were interested in buying Foscote; what makes you think I had?'

It was too difficult to pursue the matter. Foscote was ours, which was all that mattered. I did not even regret the bottle of whisky.

There came to us, with Foscote, a delightful couple, Mr and Mrs Simmonds. I asked the husband to tell nobody that we were the new owners of Foscote until it was all signed and sealed. He agreed happily, adding, 'Of course, I've told the wife, because she already knew.'

'Knew?' I asked. 'But how?'

'Well, she's always had second sight. A year ago she was listening to you on television and suddenly she turned to me and said, "That gentleman's going to be our new boss", so it was no surprise to us when you bought it.'

'There are more things in heaven and earth—' I was reminded of Maurice and Capel Curig.

The move to Foscote was fortuitous in more ways than one. Not only was it closer to Stoneleigh, but there was considerably more land, which enabled Jennifer to develop her stud. Before we left Pendley she had taken up the breeding of ponies in a very small way, but with considerable success. She regarded it then merely as a hobby, but circumstances dictated that it was to become, over the years, very much a full-time occupation – fortunately, as it was to turn out.

Towards the end of the 1962–63 hunting season we had met one day at Woolston, close to the motorway. It was very cold, but when we found at Linford Wood in the morning scent was good and we enjoyed a typical Linford hunt over the wild, rough, well-fenced country, mostly grass, that the Milton Keynes area was in those days. There was only a small field out, and as usual I had held them at the end of the track on the south side of this big woodland, Thurston Knutsford going into the centre to act as liaison. Before very long he signalled a fox across the main ride. Within moments hounds were speaking and we could hear, down the far side, Albert's horn. The next moment, far away to our right, we could hear the whipper-in holloa-ing and away we went. By the time we reached the end of the track hounds were streaming away across the grass, Albert galloping alongside them blowing 'Gone-away', surely one of the most evocative sounds in the world. Swinging right towards the common we crossed the lane by Tinker's corner, down over a good line of fences to the canal, then right handed to Shirley's rough and up to the earths where for a moment we checked. Jennifer was riding a big bay five year old which we had bought in Cornwall, called Miguel. He was only a novice, but extremely bold, with a great jump in him. She told me, when we checked, that she had nearly been jumped off. I advised her to sit tight, as if we ran now in the usual direction there was a line of fences with some big drops behind them.

The earths had been stopped; hounds soon hit off the line, heading in the direction that I had anticipated. We had twenty glorious minutes before hounds marked at a drain by the river below Willen. Everyone was glowing, as indeed they needed to be as it had turned bitterly cold, so much so that when we found again at Shirley's rough there was no scent at all. For the best part of an hour hounds hunted very slowly back towards Linford, then left-handed in the direction of Woughton-on-the-Green. Being so cold, with hounds making little progress, I decided, as it was after three o'clock, that we might as well finish, but Albert suggested that as we were going towards the village, where our boxes were, we might as well let hounds hunt on slowly, then pick them up when we reached the lane. I agreed. A field ahead a hound spoke. Normally Albert would have opened the gate, an iron one, as we were not really running, but being so cold and as, for the last hour, we had not had much fun he popped over a set of rails. I followed. A moment later I heard a crack like a pistol shot, and then a crash. I looked round, just in time to see a horse turning a somersault over the gate. It was the saddle that I recognized. As Jennifer was about to jump the rails someone on her left broke them, the sharp report making Miguel swerve to his right and attempt to jump the gate. Jumping at an angle he got the top bar between his forelegs and over he turned. He rolled right across Jennifer, then, getting up, kicked her on the head. She lay there absolutely still, her hunting cap a few yards away – cut clean in half ! She was obviously very badly hurt. After a few moments, in her delirium, she started begging me not to leave her, insisting that she was dying. I covered her with my coat. Albert collected the hounds, and the few left out helped in any way they possibly could, catching her horse, galloping for assistance. But we were three fields from the lane, and each of those fields was ploughed. I could not imagine how we were going to move her.

For over half an hour we stayed there in the freezing cold, a bitter wind blowing across the plough, dusk creeping up. Suddenly I saw a little blue van coming steadily, jerkily, across the frozen plough. A young boy who followed regularly in his van had heard the news and come to the rescue. When he arrived I still had no idea how we were going to get Jennifer into the van but, unbelievably, in the back of the van was a large double mattress. The reason for its being there I did not inquire, nor did I care, but it probably saved Jennifer's life. By the time we reached the village there was not only an ambulance waiting, but a doctor standing by, and a stiff whisky for me, shivering with shock and cold. Within minutes we were on our way to the Royal Bucks Hospital, my great friends Thurston Knutsford and his daughter Diana Holland-Hibbert accompanying us. As it was Saturday, there was a delay before Jennifer could be X-rayed, while we removed her boots and breeches. She looked very poorly and was still unconscious.

It was suggested that I slipped back to Pendley to change; which I did, arranging to pick up Jennifer's great friend, Susan Sayer, on my return, asking her to bring some biscuits or sandwiches as I had not eaten since breakfast: it was now after seven o'clock. We were momentarily delayed getting into the hospital by a police car with its siren wailing and an ambulance with its lights flashing. The moment that I entered the hospital I realized that it was Jennifer in the ambulance. The matron confirmed it, informing me that she was being rushed to the Radcliffe at Oxford, with her skull fractured from front to back. I remembered her hunting cap. Dashing back to the car we set off in pursuit but did not catch them up until we reached Magdalen Bridge at Oxford where, to our fury, we were held up by a C.N.D. protest march. The procession took almost ten minutes to cross the road. At the hospital we were kept waiting nearly two hours in a bare, dingy waiting-room in the outpatients' department. Eventually a doctor entered the room and asked gravely if I were the husband. I feared the worst, but to my comparative relief he told me that he could give her no more than a fifty-fifty chance of surviving. It all depended on whether there was a haemorrhage, and it would be at least twenty-four hours, possibly forty-eight, before they could tell whether or not she had one. We drove anxiously home. At one o'clock I fell into bed exhausted. At about four o'clock I was awakened by that most eerie of sounds, the blood-curdling howl of a vixen, right underneath my bedroom window. I had never heard it so close. Remembering the superstitions associated with foxes and death I spent a restless, anxious few hours until I could telephone the hospital.

She was, I was told, holding her own, and had asked for her radio, which convinced me that the battle was won. As it was. Strong and wonderfully resilient, Jennifer was home within three weeks and made far better progress than anyone could ever have believed, even organizing the Point-to-Point Ball held at Pendley in the middle of April. Unfortunately, although unsuspected at the time, she had damaged her spine, which meant that riding for any length of time was both tiring and painful – with the result, of course, that she had to give up hunting. Her energies were devoted, therefore, to her stud, for which Foscote with its small paddocks as well as the park was far more suitable than Pendley. Over the years her stud has been an outstanding success, producing both the Champion Pony Stallion and the Champion Pony Mare of all Britain and, most interestingly, boasting one family of six generations, everyone of which has been a prize winner, all descending from a mare that Jennifer had bought originally for £40, her earnings from the *Daily Mail Ideal Home Exhibition*, and which she had eventually proved to be a thoroughbred by Fairway. All her progeny have been prizewinners, one of them, Enstone Artist, now being one of the most sought-after pony stallions, having produced many champions of his own. The stud, though virtually a full-time occupation, has brought her enormous satisfaction as, of course, has my own work at the National Equestrian Centre at Stoneleigh. Indeed, after three years as Honorary Director I was beginning to find it almost too absorbing; it was becoming a strain. The N.E.C. was getting busier each year, taking up more and more time. With the retirement of 'WAC' Anderson, who for many years had been Secretary General, I decided that the job was too much to be carried out in a part-time capacity. Dining with Mike Ansell in the Cavalry Club one evening I told him so. He entirely agreed and we decided that a full-time executive officer should be appointed – the expansion of the Society and the increasing activities of the Centre justified it in every way.

Mike then told me that, having given the matter much careful thought, he had become convinced that we should have in the horse world a proper Federation, as did other countries. At present, somewhat illogically, the British Horse Society acted as the Federation, though it was the British Show Jumping Association that was much more involved, our show jumpers frequently attending international shows overseas. To send a three-day-event team was rare in comparison. His suggestion was that the Federation should consist of three or four members from each Society, with a President or Chairman. This very much appealed to me, as I felt that it would do much to bring the two Societies closer together, something which I had for long set my heart on, even hoping that one day the two Societies, despite all their differences, might be completely united. Discussing it that evening, we agreed that the two Societies were likely to consider such a plan with a certain amount of suspicion. Each enjoyed its own autonomy, was proud of its independence, yet it seemed so right and logical that it was obviously worth attempting to achieve it.

Mike Ansell in his usual way set about the softening-up process, initially having more success with the B.H.S. than with the B.S.J.A. Possibly it was for this reason that he agreed to accept again the Chairmanship of the latter, at the expense of Douglas Bunn. This meant that he was again Chairman of both Societies, and therefore commanded great influence. There was no doubt after several months that he was bringing most people who mattered round to his way of thinking. Then, tragically, in August of that year, 1971, his wife Eileen was killed. He had lost his first wife, Victoria, to whom he was totally devoted, in October 1969, and a year later he had married Eileen, the widow of his great friend, Roger Evans, and also the mother of his daughter Sarah's husband, Sandy. The marriage had brought him great happiness and her death, therefore, was a terrible blow, understandably removing him totally from the centre of action for several months.

It was in these months that the idea of the Federation had to be piloted through the General Purposes and Finance Committee and the Council of the British Horse Society, a responsibility that had become mine as Vice Chairman of the Society. Not only did I know that Mike had set his heart on it, but I was convinced of its rightness. Before the final vital Council Meeting I briefed myself to the very best of my ability on the whole issue and its implications, being aware that during the last few weeks considerable opposition had built up. As the conference room in Belgrave Square was not available we met in what was for me strange territory, the Cadogan Hotel. The room was packed, with many standing, and it was hot and airless. Having outlined the many advantages I attempted to forestall the criticism by dealing frankly with the points which I knew worried those who had their doubts about the scheme. The advantages, I suggested, far outweighed the disadvantages, but there followed, nevertheless, a debate which was dominated by those against. I had, however, kept my trump card until the end. That morning the B.S.J.A. had agreed to the setting-up of the Federation. The B.H.S., when it was put to the vote, also came down quite heavily in favour. I arranged for Mike to be informed immediately as I knew that he would be delighted. It had been a difficult meeting and I was well pleased with the result, readily agreeing with Field Marshal Sir Gerald Templer when he said, as we left the hall, 'You'll never have a trickier meeting than that to handle when you are Chairman.'

It had been assumed from the start that if and when the Federation came to being – and it was obvious that it would sooner or later – Mike Ansell was the obvious, indeed the only person for the President-Chairman. This meant that he would have to resign from the Chairmanship of the two Societies. After my six or seven years as Vice Chairman it was assumed that I would become Chairman of the B.H.S. which I realized, despite the recent appointment of a full-time chief executive – and one so outstandingly able as General Jack Reynolds – would entail a great deal of work. At Mike's suggestion I had resigned as Chairman of the National Equestrian Centre as it seemed better that the Society's Chairman should not be too closely associated with any one Committee. I had also told my Hunt Chairman that I would inevitably have to curtail my work with the Hunt, and when the idea of the Federation had first been mooted I had, in fact, resigned as Master. I had been Master on my own for fifteen years, but in view of the fact that the future of the Whaddon Chase was uncertain, with talk of amalgamation, I had been persuaded to carry on, with Puggy Wyatt, who since 1961 had been such an exceptional Hunt Secretary, becoming Joint-Master. Peter Stoddart, who had hunted with the Whaddon Chase all his life and whose father as Hunt Chairman had originally invited me to be Master, also came in to make it a triumvirate that worked happily and in complete harmony until the sad and untimely death of Puggy in 1976.

With the Federation duly formed and Mike back in action he duly resigned as Chairman of the B.H.S., nominating me as his successor. That autumn, 1971, I was a little surprised to be told by John Blackmore, the B.H.S. Secretary, that someone else, in addition to myself, had been proposed and seconded as Chairman. There had never before been an election for Chairman, but apparently it was felt by some people that this was the time to emphasize the democratic aspects of the Society – sentiments with which I could not possibly disagree. This was because I had written to Mike Ansell when he had told me that I would be succeeding him, saying that I realized that I could never have the sort of stature that he had enjoyed as Chairman. I said that I would, in fact, attempt to operate on a more democratic basis, representing the whole body of the Society, rather than be the great figurehead that he had been, indeed had needed to be, to firmly establish the Society during the last quarter of a century. My opponent was Bill Barton, who had been President of the Society in 1964, was now one of the Treasurers, and a leading personality in the Hackney world. He had recently retired as a high-ranking executive of Rank's, having unfortunately suffered a slight stroke. He was able, kind and very popular, but I have to admit that when first I heard that he was standing I did not regard his opposition very seriously, having for so long taken it for granted that as Vice Chairman I would succeed to the Chairmanship on Mike Ansell's retirement. In the build-up to the election, however, despite the assurances of my most senior colleagues on the General Purposes and Finance Committee, and particularly of the officers of the Society, I was instinctively aware of the increasing support for Bill Barton.

The ballot, of course, was secret, the result in a sealed envelope being handed to the President, Lord Abergavenny that year, at the December Council meeting. Mike Ansell had discovered, fortuitously, that in the absence of the Chairman at a Council meeting the President should preside, as constitutionally there was no Vice Chairman. Opening the envelope John Abergavenny began 'William—' and then for a split second hesitated. I have always believed that he expected to read 'Williams, Dorian', for ever since he became President he had been one of my strongest supporters; instead it was 'William Barton'. There were one or two gasps, but for the most part members of the Council sat silent, stony-faced, showing no emotion. I had been defeated. During the last week or two I had begun to suspect it, but I cannot deny that when it happened it was a great shock.

Nor did it end there. As, officially, there was no such office as Vice Chairman I suddenly found myself, after more than twelve years, no longer a member of the General Purposes and Finance Committee. I was asked to stand for one of two existing vacancies, but as this meant that, if elected, I would oust one of the two senior members, both of whom had been on the Committee for many years – one even longer than I – and were eligible for re-election, I declined. There was also the chance, of course, that I might well be defeated and suffer another rebuff. I did agree to stand for one of the two B.H.S. nominations for the Federation, and I was defeated. Apparently, and this was understandable, the Committee preferred to be represented on the Federation by people who were on the Committee which, of course, I was not.

For all but twenty years I had been increasingly immersed in the affairs of the British Horse Society. Suddenly I found myself totally uninvolved, except for the Council, of which I had another two years to run as a member. The Council meets twice a year, which was something of a change from the minimum of two meetings a week to which I had been committed for so long. Whether it was the end of my career with the British Horse Society, a crashing set-back or just a check, I had no idea. I only knew that I had had an unexpected but a very considerable rebuff, and was hurt. It was enough to make me doubt whether my great theory about the advisability of not having having all one's eggs in one basket could be sustained. It could, but not before I had wallowed in a certain amount of self-pity, some of which was justified.

That a first I over-reacted to the situation cannot be doubted. I can appreciate now a number of very plausible reasons for my not being wanted as Chairman. In the first place it was understandable that after the long, inspired dominance of Mike Ansell, the Society preferred someone less active. There were, too, many people – people of influence – who were still not wholly reconciled to the move to Stoneleigh and the establishment of the National Equestrian Centre, with which I had been so closely involved. As I had for so long been Mike's No. 2 it is possible, too, that in the eyes of many I was a natural No. 2 rather than a No. 1. It is also conceivable, paradoxically, that I had retained something of my publicity-seeking image, so suspect with the establishment. I came gradually to accept all this. What I resented was that no one had told me. If I had been informed by people whose opinion I trusted that the Society did not at that time want me as Chairman I might easily have been persuaded to withthdraw my nomination. Or would I? Was I possibly too confident after so long as Vice Chairman and Honorary Director? It is hard to tell, but in retrospect I am inclined to believe that I would have been ready to avoid a situation which could only lead to humiliation.

Chapter 14

From a check to a view

Before long I found that being relieved of all my work with the British Horse Society had its compensations. To begin with, I could give more time to Pendley which was always rewarding. Because it was often much less of a rush my hunting became more enjoyable, and I spent much more time at Foscote, even moving my office there from Pendley. There was more time to read, and to write.

A year or two earlier when on holiday in Sicily with our great friends, Dick and Ann Hawkins, I had read a book on Napoleon by Gilbert Martineau, whose books I have always regarded as both authentic and authoritative in view of the fact that he has for many years lived as the French Consul, in Longwood House, on the island of St Helena. A few paragraphs had made a great impression on me, creating an entirely new picture of Napoleon after his defeat at Waterloo, at the end of the 'hundred days'. There emerged an aspect of his character which had never been evident in other books, the majority of which in any case tend to gloss over the end of his career, regarding Waterloo as the climax. I had for a long time been a student of Napoleon, and now I had the time to read more avidly. The more I researched the more I became convinced that those few days at the Elysée Palace and Malmaison had all the ingredients of a play. Through the spring and summer of 1972 I settled down with some ten or a dozen books, mostly contemporary memoirs and diaries, and co-ordinated all the facts that I could about those three intensely dramatic days: his arrival, exhausted, at the Elysée, his abdication, his removal to Malmaison, his attempt to re-instate himself, his departure for the *Bellerophon*. What particularly fascinated me was that so often the actual words used by Napoleon and others involved were available, and gradually one came to feel that one had been present oneself, so intensely vivid was the picture presented. But it turned out to be totally different from the picture that one had previously entertained. Here was no lion at bay: here was a sick, exhausted, vacillating human being; certainly he showed none of those qualities of tenacity and endurance that he had displayed prior to Elba. He was completely out-manoeuvred by Fouché and the Chamber of Representatives, and still found time, even at this moment of urgency, to wallow in hot baths, make a pass at his stepdaughter, philosophize with Benjamin Constant, the writer, and alternately posture and cringe. Ignoring the fact that three quarters of his army was intact south of the Loire, and dismissing the pleas of his brother, Lucien, that he should seize power and sack the Deputies, he feebly gave in. At Malmaison after twenty-four hours of self-pity and an attempt at suicide he suddenly, dramatically, appeared in his famous green uniform of the Chasseurs, demanding to be placed at the head of the army again. But on the arrival of an ultimatum from Fouché his sudden ardour fizzled out and sadly, in a most moving brief reunion with Marie Waleska, he spurned her offer to accompany him, and left on his own for the Isle d'Aix.

By the end of July I had amassed all the material that I needed. I retired to a villa in the Algarve with Wendy, my secretary, Piers, my son, and his great friend at that time, Danny Beckett, the son of Christopher Grimthorpe, who strangely enough was a great friend of my own at Hawtreys. In ten days I had written a play, in two acts, which I entitled *The Hundredth Day*. Almost 80 per cent of it consisted of authentic dialogue culled from the various memoirs, diaries and letters in which I had been absorbed during the previous six months.

I have never experienced such a feeling of achievement as I did when I had finished that play. So great was my sense of satisfaction that quite genuinely it was of no importance to me whether or not it was ever performed. Working on it and writing it had been all the reward that I required. I was in any event fully aware that a historical play with a large cast was not likely to appeal to any commercial West End management, although two well-known managements to whom a friend of mine had sent the manuscript had shown considerable interest – one particularly so. But both, in effect, took the same attitude. Apart from the usual how-on-earth-could-a-horsey-commentator-and-a-Master-of-Foxhounds-write-a-play? they wanted the play, or parts of the play, rewritten in such a way as to fictionalize it. This, of course, was out of the question for me: as immoral as rewriting *Macbeth*, omitting anything that suggested that he was cruel and evil. Napoleon, on his return from Waterloo, was weak, vacillating, at times despicable, certainly pathetic. Regrettably he was not noble, heroic, a lion at bay, which allegedly was what was wanted from a commercial point of view. *The Hundredth Day*, therefore, having served its purpose was quickly relegated to the background as I became involved in the twenty-fourth Pendley Festival for which I was producing *Love's Labour's Lost*. It is, in my opinion, one of Shakespeare's most delightful comedies though, interestingly, it always seems to be more popular with actors than audiences. No one, however, could resist the magical touch, only possible at Pendley, when the Princess of France and her ladies arrived in a delightful horsedrawn coach. At the end, with the sudden dramatic change of mood following the arrival of Mercade and news of the death of the King of France, the coach's departure up the glade, its little carriage lamps glimmering, was breathtakingly beautiful.

Before the end of the Festival I had to depart, reluctantly, for Munich and the Olympic Games. Although, obviously, it is always an experience to be at the Olympics I did not altogether enjoy those of 1972. The saving grace, of course, was our Three Day Event gold medal. The cross-country day of the Event was easily the most enjoyable of the whole Games, coming as it did immediately before the Israeli murders. Ann Moore's silver medal in the Individual jumping was exciting, too, though one could not help feeling that it really should have been a gold. There is an interesting link between the Mexico, Munich and Montreal Olympics. On each occasion a young girl riding for Britain was involved in an incident which was to cost us a medal. In each case the letter M plays a prominent part, not only in the venue – next time it is Moscow, another M! In Mexico Marion Mould won an Individual silver and then had that disaster at the treble in the team event. In Munich Ann Moore won a silver and then had trouble at the treble which contributed to our missing a medal. At Montreal Debbie Johnsey on Moxy should have won a silver medal in the Individual but her chances were ruined by the storm. In my opinion each of these young riders was deeply affected by her experience. Marion Mould stated categorically that she would never ride in another Olympics, and took several years to regain her form; might indeed never have done so had it not been for the sympathetic help she had from her husband, David, who gave up his own career to manage hers. Within two seasons Ann Moore had faded from the scene completely, though I believe she would like to have been involved from the sidelines; that is as a commentator. The B.B.C. tried her out for one season but then she was dropped – not entirely because she was not a success. She was, I believe, wrongly used. As an expert she had a great contribution to make, someone for the commentator to turn to for explanation of some interesting point or performance; but she was not so good at the straight commentary, which is perhaps more of an art than it is generally considered to be. She fell into the usual trap of talking too much, and her voice sounded monotonous in a commentary as opposed to a comment. This is nothing unusual: very few women have good voices for the microphone simply because it needs a voice with a low register, such as Isobel Barnet's. The ordinary range of a woman's voice is too limited compared with a man's. Most men can take their voice up almost to the falsetto; while few women can use the bass. I have always thought that the same mistake has been made in other sports, notably in tennis with Ann Jones.

To return to the Olympics and our young lady riders: the experience that the eighteen-year-old Debbie Johnsey had in Montreal must have been shattering. Not only did she have to suffer the appalling storm, even to the extent of having a tent-pole blow down on her horse; not only did she throw away, as she must have felt, a certain bronze medal, even a silver medal; but she then had that most humiliating of experiences, having the first fence down in both rounds of the team event. It is not surprising to me that she has, at least up to the time of writing, shown little form since Montreal. One can but hope that with the help of her wise and dedicated father she will return to form in the near future. David Broome once said that experience counted for 50 per cent of everything that mattered in the Olympics. He told me that in Munich, his third Olympics, the impact of riding into that arena was so great that he did not really come to until he was half-way round the course. For these young riders it must be an almost unbearable ordeal.

Munich was an ordeal for everyone. Once the terrible murders had been committed the atmosphere was tense and strained, and enjoyment of the Games became entirely artificial. I do not believe that they should have been abandoned, but I do believe that the victory ceremonies and the finale should have been cancelled. I know that I was glad to get home. I had not, in fact, felt at all well in myself. At first I thought it was just a case of feeling more tired the less one does. Compared with recent years, because I was no longer involved with the British Horse Society, I had had a very easy twelve months. I certainly did not associate feeling unwell with the lump that had been developing on my right breast. When I had had a medical for some B.B.C. insurance associated with the Olympics I had asked the doctor what he thought of this lump. After a cursory examination – as that was not the purpose of my visit – he suggested that it was mastitis, which caused us a good deal of amusement. I had always thought that mastitis was something experienced only by cows and pregnant women. He did suggest that I might like to consult my own doctor, but not taking it very seriously I did not bother, despite the fact that by the time I went to Munich I found that the movement of my right arm was becoming increasingly restricted.

It in no way affected my hunting, however, and within weeks of my return from Munich, and with the Horse of the Year Show safely behind me, I was enjoying my hunting as much as ever, more than ever perhaps, because of the lack of extraneous pressures. That December was one of the best months for hunting that I can remember. We had a four-mile point in ninety minutes from Wingrave. Three days later a Stewkley fox provided us with another four-mile point in seventy-five minutes, all over the best of our vale. Three days later, again, a Christmas Gorse fox was hunted for nearly two hours by Granborough, Maynes Hill and Hurdlesgrove, all good country to ride. Boxing Day itself was another first-class day, with, most aptly, Christmas Gorse yet again producing a good fox which was hunted at top speed by Swanbourne and Bluebell Wood to Salden; a five-mile point in seventy minutes. It was an exhilarating month, though, obviously one had to be more than usually fit to stand up to such consistent sport. That I was considerably more tired than usual at the end, occasionally even feeling ready to go home before getting on to my second horse, I put down to the fact that I was getting older and had missed several weeks of cubhunting in the autumn, because of the Olympic Games, resulting in my being less fit than usual. For my loss of weight I blamed all the hard days in the hunting field, and a recent loss of appetite. Jennifer, however, showed concern, eventually persuading me to see our doctor when he was visiting the house to see Carola, our daughter, who was suffering from an attack of 'flu. I knew that Dr Bostock, having been the Stowe School doctor for many years, would immediately recognize any malingering, any possibility that I was making a fuss about nothing. In fact, I realized at once, from the look in his eyes, that he considered it serious.

'I think this is something out of my field,' he said. 'I would like to arrange for you to see a very good man at Oxford, Mr Till – "Tim" Till: it looks much more in his line. I'll fix an appointment.'

It was 6.30 pm when he left Foscote. To my surprise he telephoned back at eight o'clock to say he had arranged for me to see Mr Till the following evening. I duly arrived at his consulting rooms in Banbury Road and was pleasurably surprised to find hunting prints on the walls as I went up the stairs. He greeted me in a most friendly way, explaining that he hunted regularly with the Heythrop, which, of course, relaxed me, making me feel that we understood one another. His examination was thorough but quite brief. When he had finished he said:

'I suppose you intend to go hunting tomorrow – it was a Friday evening – 'well, if I had my way you would come straight into the Acland Home for an operation: there's really no time to waste.'

I suggested that it would be preferable to wait a week as by then the children would be back at school, which would make it easier to play it down. To be rushed off at a moment's notice would need a lot of explaining all round. He saw my point, thought for a moment and then said that if that was the case he would very much like me to see Sir Hedley Atkins at Guy's. 'He is the top man in this field, and although I have no doubt that he will confirm my diagnosis I believe that it would be to your advantage to see him.'

Naturally, I agreed, Till getting on the telephone immediately to make an appointment for the following week. As I left, still very friendly and natural, he said, 'You do realize that there can be no thought of your hunting again this season?' Obviously I had no option but to accept the fact, though it seemed unthinkable. In nearly twenty years of Mastership I had never missed more than the odd day, two weeks at the most when I had broken my collar-bone. Now I would be missing the best part of three months.

The actual word 'cancer' had never at any time been mentioned, but it was clearly implied. Driving back to Foscote I decided to latch on to the omission of this fatal word, pretending that there was still some doubt as to what was causing the lump. But Jennifer was not fooled for a moment. She knew as well as I did what the trouble was: in fact, it confirmed her original suspicions. We just had to wait for Sir Hedley's official diagnosis in a few days' time. He was at that time President of the Royal College of Surgeons. Everything about him suggested his eminence, but he was charming, courteous and very friendly, putting me immediately at my ease by telling me that his brother-in-law had once been Master of the Essex Hunt. Strange, these hunting links, and helpful. His examination of me was similar to Till's, but more prolonged. When he had finished he invited me to sit down, but I preferred to remain standing. He explained that I had cancer of the breast, the size of the lump suggesting that it had been malignant for some time and the likelihood was that there were several secondaries. He would arrange for me to be X-rayed immediately.

Having there and then telephoned the X-ray department and learnt that I could not be fitted in until next day he explained that he had recently returned from America: it was now believed that the most successful way to treat cancer was not to operate until after the deep-ray treatment. In this way one was able to assess the reaction of the secondaries, usually the most malignant, by using the main, visible, lump as a barometer. If one just took out the lump one could lose sight of the secondaries. Sir Hedley's aspect is always a little grave. He now looked very serious indeed.

'I appreciate', he said, 'that this must be very worrying for you. I only regret that I have to confirm the news. But do try to remember that cancer is not automatically fatal.' He admitted that what I had was extremely rare: in nearly four thousand cases of breast cancer that he had treated at Guy's less than twenty had been with men. 'But I think that the majority recovered', he added – to encourage me?

'Is there anything you would like to ask me?' he inquired.

'Yes,' I replied quickly, spontaneously. 'Where can I spend a penny?'

If he was surprised at my answer he showed no sign of it, but conducted me down the passage, waiting for me at the top of the stairs. He arranged to meet me after I had been X-rayed the following day.

It was a Tuesday. Although my appointment was at 2.00 pm I decided to go out hunting for an hour or two. The meet was at Hulcott, probably the prettiest meet in the Whaddon Chase. I rode my spectacular grey, Monty. There was not a very big field, many people's horses being lame or exhausted after the wonderful month's sport that we had had over Christmas. We found in Hulcott covert and for twenty minutes hounds raced round the covert in a wonderful chorus. Finally the fox went away towards Bierton, hounds soon pouring out of the covert accompanied by the silver music from Albert's horn. They ran fast towards Aylesbury, taking us over a couple of really good fences and a nice set of rails before checking short of Plum Orchard. I looked at my watch and I knew that I must pull out. As I rode back to my box it flashed across my mind that this might be the last time I ever went hunting, but that strange protective reflex was already working and, unable adequately to consider the future, I quickly dismissed the thought from my mind. In any case I had to hurry if I was going to box up, drive home, change and get to Guy's in time for my appointment.

Sir Hedley himself accompanied me to the X-ray department. The whole process took half an hour or so. Later Sir Hedley confirmed that I would have to undergo immediate treatment. I had cancer in a fairly advanced state. He gripped my hand. 'I'm sorry,' he said, and it was obvious that he meant it. His quiet strength gave me confidence, but the inescapable, undeniable fact was that I had cancer. I cannot remember exactly what he said as he walked to the door of his consulting room, but I came away with the impression that one's chances were 50 per cent at best, and that much depended on me.

That circumstances now demanded a complete change in our life style hardly needs saying. To begin with, there was to be no hunting, something which had so dominated the winter months for well over twenty years. Puggy Wyatt had decided to make an announcement at the first meet which I did not attend. It was followed, apparently, by a very moderate day and, for me, some very helpful letters. One of our greatest friends, Diana Holland-Hibbert, a pillar of the Whaddon Chase, wrote: 'We do miss you so much: for so many years no hunting day has been without you, and the fun has mounted up to a large piece of one's life. I was glad that I was not out that first day. I should have felt disloyal to have been there. It must have been horrible. Everyone said so.' A farmer, George Simms, who lived for his hunting, wrote: 'To me these setbacks are like a big fence out hunting: when you once get to the other side fairly safely' – I loved the 'fairly' – 'you can look back and congratulate yourself that you have survived what could have been misfortune, and this gives you strength to face perhaps greater obstacles. I hope it gives you much pleasure to know that you have been our Master for nineteen years and that you have given us so much of your time and shown such good sport, which we all hope will continue. I say "we" because so many people keep asking about you.'

Bob Dixon, a subscriber, wrote from a bar in County Cavan telling me how many people over there inquired about me. Stanley White, in his eighties, but one of the staunchest supporters of the Whaddon Chase, wrote: 'I always remember thankfully your first season as Master and the really wonderful fun we had.'

Such letters meant a great deal to one in those early days, especially when one was adapting oneself to such a strange new routine. Sir Hedley had arranged for me to see Professor Bleehen at the Middlesex Hospital, with its excellent reputation in the field of cancer. Initially it was intended that I should have a fortnight, possibly three weeks, of intensive treatment daily, then have the operation. Somewhat to my surprise Professor Bleehen, having examined me and marked out the area for treatment – approximately a square foot – with an indelible pencil, arranged for me to have my first treatment, or more accurately my first two treatments, as I was put under two totally different machines, there and then. From beginning to end it all lasted only a few minutes, probably less than half an hour from the time I arrived at the X-ray department to the time I left. The treatment being daily, however, and, so I had been told, increasingly exhausting, it seemed logical that we, or at least I, should arrange to stay in London during the week. But the idea appealed to neither of us. In the end we decided to stay only the odd night in London, usually travelling up daily by train. At the end of a fortnight, having had my weekly examination, no mention was made of the operation. At the end of the following week, by which time I was in considerable discomfort and feeling very tired, I raised the matter with Professor Bleehen. He was of the opinion that I was not ready for the operation, but arranged for me to see Sir Hedley, who also advised further treatment. Knowing that the more treatment one could take the greater the hope of success, I was determined to go through with it: but after five weeks I was so burnt up, inside and out, that I could not, for the time being, take any more. I had a week in bed, resting, then Jennifer drove me up to the Middlesex again, but the Professor did not think I was yet fit to re-start the treatment. Nor did he a week later. After three weeks, however, and another visit to Sir Hedley it was decided that I should undergo a further fortnight's treatment. I rather dreaded it, but realized that it was essential. At the end of the fortnight I was examined again both by Sir Hedley and Professor Bleehen, had extensive X-rays and was finally informed, to my enormous relief, that there would be no more treatment. Unfortunately, however, Sir Hedley was adamant that I would not be fit enough for an operation for several weeks. It was now the beginning of April. He suggested operating in June, advising me to have a good holiday in the meantime. Accordingly, I arranged to rent a villa in the Algarve and do some writing. Frequently I have found in life that good can come from evil or, put another way, one can make a virtue out of a necessity. In bed after the first bout of treatment, I had been impressed by the loyalty and devotion of my little terrier, Coco, who would lie by my side on the bed hour after hour, reluctant to go down to spend a penny, or even have his dinner. I found this very moving, and thought, as every dog-owner does, how lost he would be without his master: more, how lost I would be without him. With so much time to think I found myself weaving a little story about a man and his dog.

This it was that I wrote in the Algarve that summer: little more than a *conte*, it was the story of a man, living along, losing his terrier, based on my own little terrier and, like him, called Coco, though fortunately the story was entirely fictitious. The book, called *Lost*, was published a year later by the Standfast Press, beautifully produced, with delightful illustrations in the text by Michael Lyne. It had a considerable success, being serialized somewhat unusually, in the *Sun*. It is doubtful if it would ever have been written had I not been laid up, but as it turned out the writing of it had an almost therapeutic value for me, coming between the exhausting treatment and a major operation, and following another sad experience which necessarily delayed for a few weeks my trip to the Algarve.

Shortly after I had finished the treatment my father, then in his eighty-eighth year, was taken seriously ill. I had not been to see him while I was having the treatment as I knew it would upset him: my illness had been a great shock to him. During the last few months, though still playing bridge regularly and enjoying the company of his friends, he had apparently aged considerably, except in his mind, which was as alert as ever. Once Sir Hedley had decided to operate I went over to East Burnham Park, told him the good news and assured him that it was now just a case of cutting out the offending lump, after which everything would be fine. He was in tremendous form, complaining bitterly that he had not been consulted before they produced the new Dressage test for Badminton, which (rightly as it turned out) he insisted would not be acceptable. He also went through various changes in the investment policy connected with the Estate, criticized in detail the recent budget and produced figures to show that his garden was making a profit. It was a shock, therefore, to hear that he was so ill. Apparently he had what can best be described as a stroke of the intestines (mesenteric thrombosis). Shortly after being taken ill he had slipped into a coma, from which his great friend and doctor, Maxwell Summers, said that he was unlikely to recover.

For more than twenty-four hours he remained in this state, until suddenly he was violently sick. For a few moments he was conscious and murmured 'Sorry': but it was the look of disappointment in his eyes that I remember. I am convinced that when Dr Max had initially given him a shot of morphia to relieve the intense pain he had hoped that he would never regain consciousness. Shortly afterwards he appeared to be sleeping, looking quite peaceful and relaxed. He remained like this all night. First thing in the morning, after Dr Max, who had kindly stayed the night, had seen him, I went in to his room to find him, to my amazement, sitting up in his chair, looking remarkably healthy.

'I've made medical history,' were the words with which he greeted me. 'Dr Max says so. Nobody else has ever survived – ' and then he got into a muddle with the difficult medical terms: he always enjoyed getting into a muddle with long words.

The following day, however, there was a relapse. When I went in he was in bed, frail, obviously exhausted. For a time he did not speak, then signalling to me with his now emaciated but still very expressive hand to come closer he said, slowly and deliberately: 'This is my statement. I do not on any account want a second opinion: I do not want an operation. I wish to be cremated. I would like my ashes scattered at Brooksby' (where his father was buried). He said no more, but smiled when I nodded, showing that I had understood. He then closed his eyes. Next morning he had another attack, again lapsed into a coma, lingering all through the following day. Barbara, my sister, and I, with Joan his devoted housekeeper and Varney his friend and gardener for twenty-five years took it in turn to sit by him. He died in the early hours of the following morning.

He was cremated as he wished, a memorial service being held for him at Tring three weeks later. The lovely old church was packed, the choir being provided by the girls' school which now occupied Tring Park where his father and grandfather had been born. Amongst their number was our daughter, Carola. It was just a hundred years since the family had left Tring Park to move to Pendley, so the wheel had come full circle. I gave the brief address myself, speaking first of his local associations, then of his career with horses – behind me hung a magnificent horseshoe made of crimson carnations – finally attempting to create a picture of his latter years at East Burnham Park: his wonderful sense of humour, his generosity, his love for the beauty of his garden, his courage; most of all his affection for his staff and his friends. Concluding I said, 'This I know, that those crinkles at the corner of his smiling eyes inspired only one thing, and that was love. Obviously it is not unique, but it must be comparatively rare for a son, or daughter, at the end of a relationship with their father lasting over fifty years to be able to say that they have never had a single quarrel, scarcely a cross word. But he was that sort of man. For him life was too short for pettiness: there was nothing mean or petty about him. He just wanted to give to life as much as he took from it. And when at the end he felt that he had no more to give he just wanted to leave it quietly and with no fuss. As he did.'

Naturally it was an ordeal; equally for my sister who had had a stroke in 1969 as a result of driving up and down to East Burnham Park from her home in Somerset, first during the long illness of Brenda, my stepmother, and then to look after my father. Both of us, however, found the service and the expression of devotion from so many friends inspiring. As slowly we left the church together, all that was now left of that wonderfully happy family of our childhood, it was as though we were engulfed in a great wave of sympathy, which was very moving. Once outside the church everyone was relaxed and cheerful, chatting in the sunshine, exchanging memories, reminiscing, all brought together in the memory of my father, just as he would have loved it. From the wonderful tributes, spoken and written, after his death it was obvious how greatly the horse world was indebted to him. But for me, as a son, it was the utter straightness of his character that had most influenced me. Shakespeare might well have had him in mind when he wrote: 'To thine own self be true, and it must follow, as the night the day, thou canst not then be false to any man'. His complete integrity, in whatever he did or said, did not always rebound to his own benefit, but he retained his self-respect to the day of his death.

I entered Guy's Hospital for my operation on 18 June. Sir Hedley called in to see me that evening with a Mr Broomhead, who was going to do the skin graft. He told me that the operation would take over three hours. I asked Mr Broomhead not to take any skin from the inside of my thigh as it would make riding difficult: which amused him; though in the end he did have to. Within twenty-four hours I was sitting up in bed, writing. (I had kept a detailed diary from the first day that I heard that I had cancer.) Reading my diary now it all seems very cheerful, with an endless stream of visitors, half-bottles of champagne, Ascot and Wimbledon on the television. Sir Hedley appeared delighted, equally Mr Broomhead. To my relief the Physio was prevented from making me do the exercises I had started as I was not allowed any movement in my legs. After a week or so I began to feel a little feverish, but was not really worried as I recalled from previous operations that after a few days one usually experiences a slight relapse. On this occasion, however, instead of soon feeling better I felt very much worse; increasingly so, until I was so weak as to be almost permanently asleep. This worried me. Suddenly in the middle of one night I was awakened to find a huge X-ray machine being moved into my room. I cannot remember any more of that night, but was alarmed to find Sir Hedley, who lives in Kent, standing by my bedside at eight o'clock the next morning.

Apparently one of my lungs was affected; it seemed that a clot had formed due to my lying absolutely still for ten days, without any exercise at all. An extremely nice Dr Robert Knight was called in at this stage. Both Jennifer and I immediately had complete confidence in him. Ironically it was he who put me on to Warfarin, sometimes used by keepers to destroy foxes, but occasionally responsible for poisoning hounds. The use of Warfarin had been discussed at length quite recently at a Master of Foxhounds Association Committee. Now the same poison was being used to save my life! The Warfarin and other treatment quickly took effect and I was soon making good progress, within a fortnight being given permission to leave hospital. We had decided that I should convalesce at East Burnham Park, partly because I would have the benefit of the attention of my father's devoted staff, who were staying on until the house was sold; partly because we felt that it would be quieter than being at home where, naturally, all our friends would visit us; which would be welcome, but not wholly in the interests of my recovery. It was less than three weeks to the European Show Jumping Championships at Hickstead. I had told the B.B.C. that I would be available to commentate – it was the first of the three targets I had set myself and naturally I did not want to let them down, or myself. East Burnham Park was the ideal environment in which to build up my strength, regain some of the two-and-a-half stone that I had lost and generally return to a normal existence. When I left hospital, a paragraph had somehow found its way into one or two papers telling the whole story of my illness. This produced many generous and moving letters, which I found extremely encouraging, especially as most of them came from complete strangers. Most moving of all was a paragraph that appeared in the Jack Logan column of *The Sporting Life*. He told how having read in William Hickey – no less! – of my recovery he passed on the good news to an old lady in the village, '. . . and she just stood and cried. Such is the devotion that Dorian inspires among the plain country people of England'. A most generous and gratifying comment, even if a little exaggerated. Most people who have been seriously ill have discovered that they can easily fall into bouts of depression, and a boost to one's morale is a great help.

I achieved the European Championships at Hickstead, on the whole managing quite well, much encouraged again by the warmth of my reception amongst the show jumping world. Hickstead was followed by the Royal International at Wembley which I took fairly easily, only attending the mid-day briefing, having lunch with Mike Ansell – a traditional working lunch – then resting all the afternoon before the evening performance. I took one evening off altogether, the first evening performance I had missed in twenty-six years. Jennifer drove me down to East Burnham Park where we had a most peaceful evening, watching the show jumping on television – an interesting experience!

My next target was the Pendley Shakespeare Festival at which, to celebrate the twenty-fifth anniversary, I had planned to produce *Hamlet* for the first time – my greatest challenge yet, but it turned out to be the most successful Festival so far. Immediately after the Festival I left for the European Three Day Event Championships at Kiev. This was very nearly more than I could manage. Indeed, I doubt if I would have survived had it not been for the care and kindness of Lilian Dean, Bob's wife, who was in the party of British supporters. In particular I had a nightmare experience on the cross-country day when, foolishly wearing leather-soled shoes, I slipped down a bank and no one would help me up. I had not the strength to get back up the bank by myself, but the surly, stone-faced Russians just 'passed by on the other side'. It was twenty minutes before I found help, in the shape of a sturdy Ukranian who pulled me up with a laugh which seemed to denote his opinion of the effete English. 'Spacebo,' I gasped, using the only Russian word I knew.

The third and final target that I had set myself at the very beginning of my illness was the opening meet. Ever since returning to Foscote after the Royal International Horse Show I had been swimming in our pool to get myself fit. I continued to do so until well into October. On 1 September I rode again for the first time, using a specially padded saddle. David Barker had bought a horse for me in Yorkshire – a size smaller than I normally ride, but narrow, good-mannered and, allegedly, a reliable hunter. Officially called Follyfoot, having appeared in a television series of that name, but known in the stables as Sammy, it proved the ideal vehicle. Riding and swimming, I was getting fitter every day, and by the middle of October I was out cubhunting. On 6 November we held our opening meet, as usual, at Stewkley Grange. With my right arm held to my side by a belt lest I should strain the wounds, I rode Sammy, thoroughly enjoyed a good hunt across Shorndown and the Swanbourne Vale, staying out until two o'clock, thus triumphantly achieving my third target. It was both physically and psychologically a tremendous boost to my morale. From then on I felt stronger each day, gradually staying out longer and longer, never missing a day, in fact, until 4 December, a Tuesday, normally a hunting day, but a day on which for three important reasons I had to be in London.

At 9.30 am I had an appointment at the X-ray department at Guy's. Half an hour later, armed with the plates, I presented myself at Keats House, an annexe of Guy's where Sir Hedley has his consulting rooms. I was shown in immediately, to be greeted by Sir Hedley and Dr Robert Knight. After a lengthy examination of myself they studied the X-rays. Sir Hedley then returned to his desk, for a few minutes studying my file. 'Well, it's all very satisfactory,' he said eventually, rising and shaking my hand. 'Congratulations. In our opinion, though obviously you will have to take it easy for some months yet, you are now 100 per cent. Your recovery is complete.' He added, smiling, that he thought he would advise some of his other patients to take up hunting as obviously I owed much to physical fitness: it had not only played a major part in my surviving the operation, but had enabled me to take the initial punishing treatment.

Delighted, I hurried across London Bridge and down Cannon Street to the Tallow Chandlers Hall for a meeting of the Court of the Worshipful Company of Farriers. I had become a Liveryman in 1962: in 1970 I had been elected to the Court. The Master, Brigadier John Clabby, a very distinguished veterinary surgeon, now head of the Animal Health Trust, in welcoming me back confirmed that I was the following year to become Renter Warden, one of the three Wardens, stepping-stones to becoming Master. In my case, in 1977, it was an honour which even then filled me with considerable apprehension.

Missing the lunch following the Court I made my way as quickly as I could to the Saddlers Hall where there was a meeting of the British

Horse Society Council. During the Horse of the Year Show two months earlier Mike Ansell had told me that he thought I would have to succeed Bill Barton as Chairman of the Society, as having had another stroke it was unlikely that he would stand for election again. I said that I would think about it, which I did, and Jennifer and I discussed it at great length before reaching the conclusion that I should accept the Chairmanship if invited. I no longer felt bitter about the previous election. I had enjoyed the freedom from total involvement with the Society, but realized that much of the Chairman's work having now been taken over by the chief executive, Jack Reynolds, the job should not be as exacting as four years earlier when first I was preparing myself for the post. I believed, too, that I still had something to offer. The interests of the British Horse Society had always been close to my heart, and in any case, as Mike Ansell had said, who else was there for the moment to do it?

As I entered the hall, Colonel Guy Cubitt, taking the chair for the sick Bill Barton, interrupted the meeting to greet me.

'I see we now have Dorian with us,' he said: 'I am quite sure that it would be your wish that I inform him immediately that, whether he likes it or not, he has this morning been unanimously elected as our Chairman, something that will, I know, give us all great pleasure.' There was generous and prolonged applause. Over the lunch that followed I was made to feel that I had well and truly been welcomed back into the fold. Again King Lear came into mind. 'The wheel has turned full circle. I am here.' But what a lot had happened in between. I only hoped that I could justify the confidence that was now reposed in me. It was a little daunting, but the view of all that lay ahead was both a challenge and encouraging.

Chapter 15

A handful of letters

In the five years since I became Chairman of the British Horse Society I have certainly been kept sufficiently busy. In recent years the Society has expanded enormously and continues to develop new activities, each of which demands a certain amount of attention. My own energy has been particularly directed in two directions: first the launching of the Riding Foundation which, hopefully, will bring in the funds necessary for a fully comprehensive training and instructional programme at all levels; secondly, the introduction of a revised constitution. With the membership of the Society increasing five-fold over the last twenty-five years the original constitution has become both irrelevant and unwieldly. The need for streamlining and rationalizing has been obvious for some time, but to introduce changes in a large and active society needs tact and patience. If at the end of my term of office I can see a society properly tuned to the equestrian needs of the times, vital and progressive, playing a necessary role in the horse world, then I will feel amply rewarded. Inevitably with the general public I am far better known as the show jumping commentator, but like the proverbial clown anxious to play Hamlet, I cannot help hoping that at the end of the day I will be remembered more for anything that I may have contributed towards an improvement in the lot of the horse through more enlightened horsemastership and more sympathetic horsemanship.

After twenty-five years with the B.B.C. I did, in fact, seriously consider retiring, but those in charge of outside broadcasts persuaded me to abandon the idea, at least for the time being. As Cliff Morgan kindly put it, if someone says bacon you think of eggs; if someone says show jumping you think of Dorian Williams. Having covered all the Olympic Games, except Helsinki, since 1948 I would like now to go to Moscow in 1980. I will then have been broadcasting for thirty years. Through television I have made many friends, not only amongst those with whom I have worked, but also with the viewing public. I do not often appear in front of the camera – it is difficult for commentators to do so, and as explained earlier I have only ever regarded myself as a commentator – but many people seem to find my voice friendly and familiar and are encouraged to write to me, by no means always about show jumping. Not everybody, of course, likes my voice, or my style. At the time of the Royal International in 1976 Dennis Potter, for whom I have considerable respect, wrote in the *Sunday Times* that he found both my voice and my enthusiasm obnoxious. When I said something like, 'All the country is behind you, David,' he felt obliged to shout back at his television set, 'Not me, mate!' A few days earlier Celia Brayfield wrote in the *Evening Standard* that Raymond Brooks-Ward and I 'managed to make an exciting sport dull and if they have any equestrian knowledge prefer to keep it to themselves'. One should never resent criticism, but one does have an urge, sometimes, to answer back. To do so would be a mistake as it should never be taken too seriously. Success on television is very ephemeral, only a handful of people in any one generation being remembered for their contribution once they have ceased to appear on the little box. Those who have added a new dimension to the average viewer's life are rare indeed: Kenneth Clarke with his *Civilisation* series, Alistair Cooke, Bronowski, Brian Horrocks, and, in his own inimitable way, Patrick Moore, an enthusiast if ever there was one and, therefore, someone for whom I have a profound respect, even if the only time we ever met was on opposite sides in a television debate on foxhunting.

In 1977 I was elected Master of the Worshipful Company of Farriers, one of the great City Livery Companies, an honour which as a simple country bumpkin I greatly appreciated. To be a part of something that goes back six hundred years is fascinating, and challenging. The Farriers only received their Charter from King Charles II in 1674 and is, therefore, a comparatively youthful company, though there is evidence of a Farriers Company as far back as 1356, their records sadly being destroyed in the fire of London in 1666. Having been an avid spectator at so many great ceremonial occasions, either watching on television, in the crowd outside the palace, as a special mounted police officer in the Mall, and greatly honoured as a guest at Princess Anne's wedding, it was a unique privilege for me to be a part of such ceremonial when Princess Anne was made a Freeman of the City. The Master and Wardens of the Farriers had the privilege of presenting Her Royal Highness, who, together with her husband, is a member of the Livery. I am not so naïve as to think that the world would come to an end if the City of London's famous Livery Companies were disbanded; nevertheless, convinced that they have a vital role to play, I believe passionately in their retention as something traditional, deep-rooted and of absorbing historical interest. The survival of so much that is worth while is frequently based on the illogical and anachronistic, but is nevertheless entirely justified. I cannot pretend that hidden away in one of my early photographic albums there is a picture of little Dorian standing on the steps of the Mansion House dreaming of the day when he would be Lord Mayor of London. But I cannot deny that to preside at the great Livery Banquet in the famous Egyptian Hall in the Mansion House, entertaining as my guest the Lord Mayor himself, made me feel very proud.

Hunting, too, is an anachronism, yet it gives pleasure to more people today than at any time in its history. In his book *Peculiar Privilege* (Harvester Press, 1976) Dr Itzkovitz, an American, suggests that in the eighteenth and nineteenth centuries hunting was looked upon 'as one of the chief promoters within a country district of unity, stability, harmony and devotion to traditional values'. I believe that a detached observer would agree that this is still so in the twentieth century, illogical as it may seem. The sport is necessarily controversial. It always has been. As I grow older I attempt never to get involved in an argument. Those who enjoy it will never change; nor, I fear, will those opposed to it. Paradoxically, after nearly thirty years' Mastership it seems to me that as hunting becomes more popular with a consistently widening basis of support so there develops a more active opposition. It is, I suppose, understandable, those against hunting inevitably becoming more determined to bring about the banning of a sport of which they disapprove the more widespread its support appears to be. It is, however, my opinion that the increased activity – particularly among the Hunt saboteurs – is symptomatic of the militant protesting minority so much in evidence today. Demonstrations are common enough at Hunt meets; but recently they have spread to point-to-points, and even to the harassing of personalities. Early in 1977 I had an embarrassing experience myself. I had been invited to talk on show jumping in a series of celebrity lectures held in a public library in south London. As soon as I mounted the platform I realized that a large number of saboteurs was present. They were not difficult to recognize. After twenty minutes they began interrupting my talk, shouting, and soon becoming quite violent and offensive, to the distress of those who had genuinely come to hear me on show jumping. Eventually an anxious chairman seized me by the collar, propelled me through a little door at the back of the stage and locked me in the ladies lavatory! What an indignity for a Master of Foxhounds! After half an hour or so I had to be rescued by the police, being driven at speed in a police car to the railway station. I cannot imagine anything so vicious happening in the early years of my Mastership. Nor, on the other hand, can I imagine in those days over three hundred and fifty people packing a hall in Bletchley, an industrial town, for a Hunt Supporters' Club dinner: the largest number, according to the manager, that had ever attended a dinner in that area. If opposition has grown, so has support.

Without doubt the biggest change that has occurred in foxhunting is the country itself. With intensive farming, electric and barbed-wire fences, electric railways, a criss-cross of roads filled with enthusiastic followers, it is, with rare exceptions, difficult for any hunt to experience the long straight runs of the past. Yet the chase can still give a thrill. Indeed, it could be that today we gallop further and faster than in the old days because to by-pass a field of seeds, or corn, or a new lay, or to avoid wire, or a now unjumpable brook, or even a farmer unsympathetic to hunting, we have to go round, covering two or three times as much ground as the hounds. If, for most, it is the pace that thrills, then there is still more than enough. Over the years, despite increasing difficulties, I have lost little of my own enthusiasm for hunting. To really have to ride to keep hounds in sight, watching hounds at work on a less good scenting day, the winter countryside with all its evocative sights and sounds – all these things still give me immense pleasure. I cannot pretend that I am any longer the fearless thruster I like to think that I once was. Today I prefer to return home in one piece, but I still enjoy enormously riding across country. In retrospect, however, looking back over the years I realize now that it is the pleasure derived from the unique community that comprises hunting that has meant most to me. Cyril Heber-Percy, for long Master of the Cottesmore, later a successful writer, summed it up in an article in *Horse and Hound*: 'What I loved as a Master was that you knew everyone; you could walk anywhere; you could knock at anyone's door in the country and ask "Can I come in?" – and always you were welcome.' This is something rare and warming. There are plenty of problems in being Master of a Hunt; there are long hours and hard work, but there are great rewards. Each year a particularly satisfying exercise for me has been visiting some eighty or a hundred farmers just before Christmas, taking round my Christmas card to those who in one way and another have contributed so much to our sport. The welcome that I receive is not only warm, it is often most moving, especially when, as is increasingly the case, either an old farmer friend or his wife has died since my last visit. The surviving partner always seems to particularly appreciate my visit, enjoying the opportunity to chat over old times. It is this sort of deep-rooted empathy existent in the countryside, so often connected with the local hunt, that those in no way involved might well find hard to understand. It could almost be described as a brotherhood. It is certainly genuine, and from a Master's point of view both encouraging and rewarding as, of course, is the huge turn-out that welcomes the local hunt on Boxing Day. Even after nearly thirty years I never fail to be moved when, on each Boxing Day as eleven o'clock approaches, we jog up the hill towards Winslow market square – in recent years fortified by the generous hospitality at Foxholes Farm. There is a joyous peal from the church bells; the town band is playing in the square, with a special version of 'John Peel' as we arrive (when Nubar Gulbenkian hunted with us they used to play 'Good King Wenceslas'!). Within minutes the square is a milling mass of horsemen and people on foot. One never ceases to marvel that no one is hurt. For half a mile down the road as we leave the town the pavements are thronged, as they might be for a royal procession – all for the local Hunt. One cannot fail to be both amazed and gratified at this remarkable manifestation of the countryside's affection for its oldest and most traditional pastime: an affection which, incredibly, seems stronger each year.

With such crowds good sport is unlikely on Boxing Day, yet one is unlucky if one does not, at some time during the day, experience that indefinable thrill that hunting can give one. Indefinable and for those who have never experienced it difficult, again, to understand. But so much in life is difficult to understand even if one is intimately involved. For one of my Christmas cards I composed a little verse, entitled 'The Huntsman's Thanksgiving'. It contained these lines:

> The huntsman knew that the Christmas bells
> Were calling people to celebrate
> A mystery that for a simple man
> Was never easy to contemplate.
> So the huntsman thought that today he should
> Thank God for the things he understood.

Like the huntsman I, too, find the mystery of the Immaculate Conception and much else to do with the Christian Church not easy to contemplate. As I grow older I increasingly envy those who believe, who have a simple faith, but while I accept that there is something greater than mere man, something beyond our brief span on this planet, I cannot accept unquestioningly the dogmas inherent in Christianity. Once again I am prepared to believe that 'there are more things in heaven and earth' than are dreamt of in Horatio's, let alone my own philosophy, but to attempt always to maintain an open mind is at present as far as I can go. It is elsewhere that I can often find spiritual inspiration, from great music, particularly the romantics, Brahms, Beethoven, Schubert; the exquisite piano music of Chopin, the grandeur of Sibelius, and, of course, many others; often, too, from something much simpler but no less effective, such as the sound of church bells floating across the fields on a Sunday evening, treble voices, even the sound of the sea and a moaning wind. These, on occasions, can have as great a spiritual effect on me as any sermon. Being fortunate enough to live in the country, each season, too, can, in its own beauty, bring me unending pleasure, even inspiration: the promise of spring, the sadness of autumn; winter with its black fences, bare trees silhouetted against a cold sky and its early dusk inevitably associated with hunting; summer and Foscote at its best with foals in the park, lillies – and the occasional mysterious heron – on the lake; a garden full of colour, fresh vegetables and mown lawns, thanks to Edward Booth who, with his wife Angela, joined us in 1976.

On the rare occasions when I feel tired, worried or over-burdened with problems and responsibilities I find that a walk by the lake or around the surrounding fields and woods soon revives me. Better still to drive over to the farm at Merrymead and go for a ride; especially if, fortunately, it should be one of those peerless early summer mornings unique in England: not a cloud in the sky, the air so still that one can hear clearly the sounds from the village a mile away, the shouts of children, a cock crowing, the whirr of a mowing machine. Riding down the lane one listens to the carefree cuckoo in the vale, the rooks cawing lazily in the branches above. The hedgerows are carpeted with primroses, the fields dotted with cowslips – all so reminiscent of childhood: picnics from Greens Norton: cuckoos and cowslips, dog-roses and new mown hay. Suddenly one is basking in something of the simplicity, the security of childhood when life was so enviably uncomplicated. An hour or two in the saddle, even if clouds are lowering and the wind blows cold, seldom fails to revive me, more, provides an opportunity to think, create, even disentangle problems. This for me is a kind of spiritual experience; one which is very important to me.

If it is Foscote, the surrounding countryside, and all that it encompasses, that can provide me with my relaxation, both physical and mental, it is still through Pendley, which is also beautiful, that in certain respects I can best express myself. After more than thirty years it is now firmly established, thanks to the devoted service over the years of the staff, led recently by Ronnie Evers, John Holifield and Bob Allsop. The annual Shakespeare Festival is now so popular that the majority of performances are fully booked weeks, even months in advance. The Sports Centre, too, is all the time a hive of activity. Founded in the mid-sixties on some twenty-eight acres of the park made available when Pendley Home Farm was sold, it now boasts two soccer pitches, three rugger grounds, a bowling green, four squash courts and a ladies' lacrosse pitch. With two club houses and a pavilion providing social amenities there is no doubt that it fulfils a need in the neighbourhood. With the opening of the Arts Centre in 1977 the whole complex was completed. Converted from the old stables and indoor riding-school – originally an indoor lawn-tennis court – it comprises a modern theatre, studios, craft rooms, workshops and dressing-rooms. It is this today that largely absorbs the cultural side of my life, giving me enormous satisfaction; not only because it provides an outlet for the same sort of creative energy that absorbed me thirty years ago in establishing Pendley, but even more because it seems to reflect something in which I have always so strongly believed, the wholeness of man. At Pendley there is now the Education Centre for the intellect, the Arts Centre for creativity and the Sports Centre for the body. While in no way a fanatic I believe implicitly in physical fitness. I have so often found that the fitter I am the more active is my mind. At the beginning of 1977 I had to have another operation. It was of an exploratory nature to investigate a second lump in the original area, mercifully proving negative. Thanks to the previous operation, however, there were difficulties in healing which resulted in my being out of action for six weeks or so. This should have provided the ideal opportunity for reading and writing, but in fact, due no doubt to my being unfit, I hardly read at all and found it an effort to write. Since then, fortunately, I have enjoyed excellent health and have more than made up for it – as, perhaps, this book suggests.

And that, one might say in the language of the serial, is the story so far. Once, lecturing at the Police College in 1947, I was asked which of five essential qualities in life – health, wealth, fame, friendship, mysticism – I considered the most important. I answered by a process of elimination. The first to be discarded would be fame because most who have it resent it; the second to go would be wealth because it distorts values, creating disproportionate problems; the third would be health because there is such ample evidence of people denied good health being cheerful and doing so much good; next mysticism, because life is complicated enough with what we do understand, let alone with what we do not; which leaves friendship, surely the most important, even the worst of experiences being eased if shared with a friend. No man is an island.

More than thirty years later I would give the same answer today. Personal relationships have meant a great deal to me. By nature shy, though this surprises some people, I do not find it easy to establish intimate relationships, and so have always had more acquaintances than friends, but such as I have had – such, indeed, as Jennifer and I have had together in our married life – have been of the kind who in times of trouble have more than demonstrated their constancy and reliability: 'beautiful friendship, tried by the sun and wind, durable in the daily dust of life'. Of all my friendships the greatest was, beyond doubt, with my brother Maurice, dead now for nearly forty years, yet still incredibly close. To think of him and of all that we shared and did together inevitably makes one nostalgic, long for a return to those laughing, carefree, hopeful days of our youth:

> Into my heart an air kills
> From yon far country blows:
> What are those blue remembered hills,
> What spires, what farms are those?
>
> That is the land of lost content,
> I see it shining plain,
> The happy highways where I went
> And cannot come again.

There is a sadness in A. E. Housman's lines, but it is, of course, a mistake to imagine that everything good belongs to the past, as it is to imagine that one could manage one's life better if one were given a second chance. Can anyone really control their own destiny? Looking back on my own life I realize that there have obviously been failures and frustrations, as this book has told, largely of my own making. But there has always been much happiness, modest success and plenty of variety, none of it really planned. It was more or less by chance that I became a schoolmaster, that I started Pendley, took on a pack of hounds, joined the B.B.C. Each development of my life has been fortuitous rather than premeditated. To reach the top today one has to be a specialist, but this was never my nature. I have never been sufficiently self-disciplined to limit myself wholly to any one activity. Rather I have attempted to co-ordinate that wide, sometimes disparate range of interests with which I have had the good fortune to be born, into a more or less ordered pattern.

The great composer Sibelius once wrote: 'A spiritual force – call it God – throws down a handful of letters, a message: and a voice says, "Make what you can of this".'

I have tried in this book to recount what I have made of my handful of letters.

Index